# A Room of Their Own

## Other Books by Marlene Wagman-Geller

*The Secret Lives of Royal Women: Fascinating Biographies of Queens, Princesses, Duchesses, and Other Regal Women*

*Unabashed Women: The Fascinating Biographies of Bad Girls, Seductresses, Rebels, and One-of-a-Kind Women*

*Fabulous Female Firsts: Because of Them We Can*

*Women of Means: Fascinating Biographies of Royals, Heiresses, Eccentrics, and Other Poor Little Rich Girls*

*Great Second Acts: In Praise of Older Women*

*Women Who Launch: Women Who Shattered Glass Ceilings*

*Still I Rise: The Persistence of Phenomenal Women*

*Behind Every Great Man: The Forgotten Women Behind the World's Famous and Infamous*

*And the Rest is History: The Famous (and Infamous) First Meetings of the World's Most Passionate Couples*

*Eureka! The Surprising Stories Behind the Ideas That Shaped the World*

*Once Again to Zelda: The Stories Behind Literature's Most Intriguing Dedications*

# A Room of Their Own

## Home Museums of Extraordinary Women Around the World

**MARLENE WAGMAN-GELLER**

CORAL GABLES, FL

For permission requests, please contact the publisher at:
Mango Publishing Group
2850 S Douglas Road, 2nd Floor
Coral Gables, FL 33134 USA
info@mango.bz

For special orders, quantity sales, course adoptions and corporate sales, please email
the publisher at sales@mango.bz. For trade and wholesale sales, please contact Ingram
Publisher Services at customer.service@ingramcontent.com or +1.800.509.4887.

A Room of Their Own: Home Museums of Extraordinary Women Around the World

Library of Congress Cataloging-in-Publication number: 2024935477
ISBN: (pb) 978-1-68481-522-7 (e) 978-1-68481-523-4
BISAC category code BIO022000 BIOGRAPHY & AUTOBIOGRAPHY / Women

To the women who mean home to me: my mother, Gilda Wagman, and my daughter, Jordanna Shyloh Geller; and to my Pythias, Jamie Lovett

—

"A woman must have money and a room of her own if she is to write fiction."

—Virginia Woolf, *A Room of Her Own (1929)*

# Table of Contents

# Foreword

**W**ith the exception of hours devoted to sleep, I've probably spent more time sitting at a desk, with my hands on a keyboard, than anyplace else. Kitchen, couch, hiking trails, library, lake, ocean, classroom, tub. I've put in my time in all of those spots, but if you tallied up where I've physically situated myself for the greatest amount of time over the past seven decades, it's my desk—some desk, someplace; I've known a few—that would win out.

As a person who's been engaged in the odd, deeply uncomfortable, not-always-remunerative, occasionally agonizing, periodically joyful, and sometimes downright thrilling occupation of writing, I've given more than an average amount of thought to the spaces in which I engage in my work. It's a source of undying interest to me, how other writers (good, bad, brilliant, terrible) have dealt with the problem of *where to put themselves* as they go about the business of trying to create a book, an essay, a poem, a play. For me, this is a crucial question. Before I set about the task of starting a new project—whether it's a five hundred page novel or (like what I'm writing now) a short meditation on some topic that interests me, the first thing I do is situate myself in a place conducive to thought, imagination, and flights of discovery.

I'm like a cat about to give birth, pacing around, looking for my quiet spot—a hidden one, maybe, or at least one in which I am least likely to be interrupted. A mother cat most definitely doesn't want some overly enthusiastic and very possibly drooling golden retriever barreling into the room just as her kittens are making their way in the world. I'm pretty much the same when it comes to birthing a book. Leave me alone in my space. As for the space: It matters. A lot.

I knew a man one time (OK, he was, briefly, a boyfriend, and maybe this story will tell you why he didn't hold that position very long) who wanted to be a writer. He was a lawyer, and he got paid a lot of money from clients who also made a lot of money, but he dreamed of writing a novel (for which he would possibly be paid a whole lot less money and possibly nothing at all). One day, he announced to me that in the effort to further this ambition, he'd bought a very beautiful antique desk. I still remember the price: $30,000, not counting shipping charges. This represented more money than I had earned that whole year, though there were also times—when things went well—that the figure might rise considerably above that one.

The success or failure of my work—or the monetary value assigned to it in the world of publishing, which is not the same thing at all—never had a thing to do with what desk I may have been seated at when I wrote. I remember thinking, when this soon-to-be-ex boyfriend of mine told me about this impressive and expensive desk, that if there was one sure sign his writing wouldn't go so well, this purchase might be it. The work is what you need to focus on, not the piece of furniture on which it's crafted.

This is not to say a writer's space (or by extension, the space occupied by anyone engaged in creative endeavor) doesn't make a difference. In the more than fifty years since I published my first book, I've worked in some great writing spaces and some impossible ones. Strangely enough, the ones I found least conducive to writing were never the shabby or low-rent places. On a few occasions, they were actually rather grand. Just not right for achieving what a writer most needs, which is to leave the world behind for a while and enter into the world of her characters and her story, with as little distraction as possible. And even less interior decoration.

The book you hold in your hands is about the places where women of accomplishment (mostly renown and in one or two instances, infamy) have not only lived but worked. This has to do not only with their desks and writing spaces of course (if they were writers; some whose spaces are explored here were not) but with the whole environment of the houses in which they carried on their lives. Here, once again, I will inject my own experience as a woman who has worked hard at what she does—writing—for more than half a century, virtually always alone in her home. If you ask me, that's pretty much a requirement—though motherhood offers significant challenges to attaining that goal.

Between the ages of twenty-two and twenty-three—before my first marriage—I had a job as a newspaper reporter in New York City. I went to an office then, sat at a metal desk in a giant room surrounded by other people at other metal desks, all of us clicking away on our typewriters. (This was the '70s.) Telephones rang nonstop. Editors paced up and down the aisles separating us. Now and then, a copy boy raced in with some breaking news torn from a machine whose name I can't remember (a machine that no longer exists). Sometime around dusk (not that there were any windows in that room, but I wore a watch) we could hear an interesting rumbling sound from several stories above. That meant the presses were running. The first edition went to press around six o'clock as I recall. Some days—most of them—the pressure was excruciating to get that story in on time.

I could never write in that room. I couldn't write the way I wanted to, anyway. For the entire time I held that job, reporting for the metro desk of the *New York Times*, I kept a well-guarded secret. Once I had the notes for my story and the reporting part of my work was done, I engaged in an act that felt as illicit as a love affair. I raced from my desk to the elevator, out the door onto West 43rd Street, and hailed a taxi. I gave the driver the address of my apartment.

Once there, I laid out my yellow legal pad and my reporter's notebook. Only there, in the small, unassuming space I'd made for myself—a space where I could be alone, but more than that, one in which I felt safe, and comfortable, and most importantly, undistracted by the world—I wrote my news story. In longhand.

When I was finished (and sometimes I only had half an hour, but I wrote fast in those days, as I do still) I reversed the route I'd travelled as recently as thirty minutes before. Got back in an elevator—the one in my apartment building this time. Hailed another taxi, back to the offices of the *New York Times*. Raced through the impressive doors, through the lobby, into the elevator, and back to my desk, where I could then type up what I'd composed on my couch at home.

I don't think I ever missed a deadline, and my editors generally seemed happy with what I delivered. Nobody ever learned my secret.

All my life, I've had to be in the right environment to do my work. I'll venture to say I'm not the only woman who feels that the room she inhabits has a big effect on her work. Particularly if the space she lives is also the space where she works. Particularly if the work involves her inner life and imagination, the sounds words make, and the rhythms of sentences. How do you hear those, when a printing press is grinding overhead, and those damn phones won't stop ringing?

No doubt it's my preoccupation with writing spaces, and the living spaces that contain them, that has fueled my intense lifelong interest in the places other writers and artists have created to do their work. In my years of making and working in a succession of such places myself (a dormitory room shared with a girl who loved playing recordings of her high school marching band; a farmhouse shared with a husband and three children and a dog, where it was not unheard of for me to escape to a closet or the car; a perfectly isolated treehouse in Guatemala in the middle of the pandemic; and so many more) I've visited the spaces of other creative types whenever the opportunity arose. I'm always looking for what it is that other people choose to surround themselves with, as they live and work.

Not everyone has a choice. I made a pilgrimage once to the place where one of my all-time favorite writers once lived when writing one of my favorite books—the one that influenced me first, and most, growing up. I'm speaking of the attic in which Anne Frank hid out for over two years, creating the diary that has moved millions of readers. All Anne Frank wanted, in the way of a space, was a place where she might succeed in eluding capture and murder at the hands of the SS. In the end, as we know, she didn't.

I visited Frida Kahlo's home in Mexico City, Casa Azul, where—severely injured and living in constant pain from an accident in her youth that left her impaled on a metal spike—she spent hours of her day painting in her bed, with a mirror on the ceiling overhead to assist her in making self-portraits. I visited Flannery O'Connor's childhood home in Savannah, where her earliest writings remain on display, along with the crib known as a kiddie coop, with a net over the top to keep out mosquitoes carrying dread disease, and the backyard where she once taught a chicken to walk backward.

What did that cold, forbidding structure with its stiff, formal settees and narrow little bed on 207 East Charlton Street reveal to me about the work of a writer whose dark, brilliant, painfully perceptive gothic short stories haunt me still? Maybe just this: A house can offer a rich palette. Or a blank slate. Who knows? Maybe the blank slate allows more room for imagination to expand and wander than the palette with its array of color does.

Unlike the homes considered in these pages—the spaces occupied by well-known women—the houses I've visited over my years of seeking out artists' spaces have belonged to men as well as women. I've visited the Ernest Hemingway home in Key West (ceiling fans, hunting gear, wide verandahs overlooking palms), the narrow rooms in which a penniless and tuberculosis-ridden John Keats spent his final days, alongside the Spanish Steps in Rome, the apartment where Berry Gordy presided over the Motown empire in its early years, above the studio where Diana Ross and the Supremes danced so hard, and so much, that in certain places, the floorboards remain rutted. Houses tell stories as much as writers and others do.

Possibly my favorite Famous Person Home of all was the home, in Santiago, Chile, of Pablo Neruda, which is also the place he died. The Neruda home, preserved as a museum, is filled not only with the poet's books and writings, but his vast and marvelously quirky collection of surprising, not necessarily valuable but beloved objects. Here stands evidence of a man who—had he lived in the days of eBay—might have found himself so buried in possessions his very desk would have left him no space to write. Or worse, no time. No concentration.

I loved the Neruda house in Santiago so much when I visited, that I convinced my husband to visit the two other homes Neruda had maintained in Chile—one of them in a remote seaside town reached only after a drive of many hours, the other in Valparaiso. What is a person to make of the fact that in all three homes, Neruda's collections were so vast that it left a person to wonder when he found time to write. Some people might be distracted, living in a space like those created by Neruda, but it would appear, based on his voluminous output, that if anything, his writing spaces had the opposite effect.

As for me, I move between three different living spaces, depending on the time of year and what I'm up to. One is a small house at the end of a long driveway in Northern California, where my desk is a big, simple table purchased at a consignment shop. More important than the table is the window above it that looks out over the trees. At night I hear owls.

Sometimes I write in Guatemala, where my desk (also simple) looks out over a lake and a volcano. Birdsong begins my day. Summertime finds me in a cottage in New Hampshire, where (like E.B. White, as good a role model as a writer could hope for) I work at a desk made from pine boards in a boat house, with the sound of loons out the perpetually open window when I'm lucky.

I love music, but never play any when I write. Silence is what I'm after. That, and birds. I have heard those stories about women who write their books at Starbucks. I can't imagine how that works. I'd be way too distracted by studying the characters around me to write about the characters in my books.

The proximity of endless amounts of coffee would be a plus, of course. But most important, in the end—for me, at least, and I suspect for most people who seek to explore what's going on in their imagination—is to keep one's external circumstances as peaceful, uneventful, and familiar as possible. The house, and the rooms it offers, are the container. But in the end, it's the person who inhabits the space who makes everything happen.

—Joyce Maynard, *New York Times* bestselling author of *Labor Day*, *At Home in the World*, *To Die For*, and others

# Women's Home Museums Revealed

*"Sing in me, Muse, and through me tell the story."*

## —HOMER

◇◇◇◇◇◇◇◇◇◇

The word museum originated from the ancient Greek word that denoted "place of the Muses." The nine Muses were the offspring of Zeus—who wasn't?—and Mnemosyne, the Goddess of Memory. Indeed, museums are the repositories of memories, of ancient civilization, of the apogee of artistry.

Everyone has heard of the major museums whose stories are as intriguing as the works they display: Paris's Louvre, London's National Gallery, New York's Metropolitan Museum of Art. Between these three iconic institutions, twenty million visitors walk their halls, approximately the same number as people living in Beijing. But what about the galleries that do not display canvases bearing the signatures of Old Masters such as Rembrandt, Rubens, or van Gogh?

Curiosity about the daily lives of the famous draws us to the places they called home. *A Room of Their Own* is an investigation into museums (sometimes referred to as memory museums) dedicated to fascinating women whose lives left indelible fingerprints on history. As these landmarks are situated in their subjects' homes, rather than passively gazing at paintings with accompanying brass plaques, visitors undergo a more intimate experience. Upon entering their thresholds, one encounters a three-dimensional diary with artifacts that comprised their everyday lives: furniture, photographs, and letters. Even the most mundane of objects takes on a magical realism, as they were the possessions of ladies of legend. The rooms where their residents lived serve as a confessional; here they laughed, mourned, and created. For those with a nod to the mystical, their ghostly chatelaines serve as guides. House museums are Pied Pipers to the curious. Walking where historic figures once trod presents the opportunity to hear the scratching of Emily Brontë's quill in her Haworth Parsonage, listen to an aria in Édith Piaf's Parisian apartment, or imagine the iridescent blue of the radium that doubled as Marie Curie's nightlight. Whether their homes be humble or *haute*, all double as biographer. Betsy Ross's miniscule dwelling in Philadelphia and Marjorie Merriweather Post's opulent estate, Hillwood in Washington, DC, are equally compelling. The closest we can come to time travel—or to a séance—is entering what were once the ladies' private places. Their spirits hover over the heads of their guests and whisper, "We were here. We mattered."

While working on A *Room of Their Own,* I chanced upon a delightful novel, *The Lost Bookshop,* by Evie Wood. Opaline, the protagonist, is a 1920s literary sleuth whose quest is to uncover a lost Emily Brontë book. As part of her research, Opaline journeys to the Haworth Parsonage. Evie wrote of her experience, "Merely to stand where the Brontë sisters had stood, to look out at the moors that inspired Emily's writing, was such a touching experience..." The passage encapsulates the mysticism that accompanies a visit to a storied address. In a subsequent chapter, Evie wrote words applicable to the women profiled in *A Room of Their Own*: "I was cursed with that most enduring of human desires—to make my mark."

Where one travels on vacation is as autobiographically revealing as home décor. Some ski the slopes of Switzerland; some lather suntan lotion on Hawaii beaches; those with an adventurous-slash-suicidal bent run with the bulls in Pamplona. But for those who enjoy communing with the ghosts of yesteryear, the best way to do so is head to the locales that helped define those who went before. The rarified atmosphere of such places retains the memory of the writers who arm-wrestled their muses as they searched for the *mot juste*. In Florence, we can enter the bedchamber where Elizabeth Barrett Browning penned her poems; in Nairobi, we can visit the farm and country that inspired Karen Blixen's *Out of Africa*; in Wellington, we can scrutinize Katherine Mansfield's belongings.

Although most women's home museums are situated in the United States, other countries also have shrines to the ladies who left legacies, including England, Canada, Mexico, Holland, Poland, Germany, Switzerland, New Zealand,

France, the Dominican Republic, and Kenya. When visiting these locales, these are must-see landmarks.

One method of obtaining a peephole into the past is by gazing out the windows of historic homes; each chapter ends with a few lines on what may be **Seen from Her Window**. Geographical locale and gardens play an integral part in the makeup of one's psychological DNA. When Isabella Stewart Gardner looked out her window, her view was of the courtyard that housed gems of civilization such as a Renaissance Venetian canal-scape, an ancient Roman sculpture garden, and a medieval European cloister. Surrounding these treasures are rotating flower displays depending on the month—orchids in the winter and hanging nasturtiums in the spring. Isabella's mantra comes as no surprise in light of these surroundings: "the best of everything."

Artist Frida Kahlo lived in the Casa Azul in Coyoacán, a suburb of Mexico City. Her collection of animal companions in the course of her life, who often served to inspire her paintings, included indigenous hairless dogs, a black cat, a couple of turkeys, an eagle, two spider monkeys, and a fawn. From the courtyard, her tequila-imbibing parrot squawked, "No me pasa la cruda." "I can't get over this hangover." Visits to the Kahlo home invariably proved a boredom-buster.

By touring storied addresses, tourists experience off-the-beaten-path destinations that double as magical mystery tours. Whether we love or loathe these women, walking in their shoes makes for a better understanding of their legacy. While traditional galleries allow us to gaze upon well-known canvases, the thrill is nevertheless a passive experience. In contrast, stepping over the threshold of a famed long-ago resident allows for an up close and personal encounter.

While some view museums as repositories for the dustbins of the past, watched over by guards who prefer patrons keep solemn silence, galleries can provide high drama. One of the greatest whodunnits occurred in Boston's Isabella Stewart Gardner Museum. In 1990, two thieves dressed as police officers tied up the guards and made off with Rembrandt, Vermeer, and Manet masterpieces. The stolen items represented a $500 million loss, and despite a ten-million-dollar reward, the theft remains the greatest unsolved mystery of the art world. When gazing at the empty frames that once held storied canvases, one can hear Isabella's cries emanating from the Mount Auburn Cemetery at the desecration of her former home.

Historical homes oftentimes serve as an essential backdrop to their owners' accomplishments. After Jane Austen left the rectory in Hampshire that was her childhood home, she did not write again until she secured a permanent address in Chawton House. Weary of her nomadic existence, when her brother offered her the use of one of his residences, a delighted Jane wrote, "Our Chawton home, when complete, will all other houses beat." Leonard Woolf philosophized, "What cuts the deepest channels in our lives are the different houses in which we live." His wife Virginia concurred: "A woman must have money and a room of her own if she is to write fiction."

# PART I

# The Writers

# CHAPTER 1

# Quiet Earth

*"My home is humble and unattractive to strangers,
but to me it contains what I shall find nowhere else in
the world—the affection which brothers and sisters
feel for each other."*

**—CHARLOTTE BRONTË**

◇◇◇◇◇◇◇◇◇◇

## Brontë Parsonage Museum
### opened 1928 | Yorkshire, England

Historic houses reverberate with secrets, and one is how an isolated parsonage on a windswept moor produced the passionate natures that birthed two immortal love stories. To enter the confessional of the original weird sisters—Emily Jane, Charlotte, and Anne Brontë—one can journey to the Brontë Parsonage Museum, a British literary shrine second only to Stratford-on-Avon.

Environment shapes destiny, a theory made manifest by visiting Haworth in Yorkshire, a village encased in amber. The timeless landscape fertilized the imagination of the Brontë sisters, who were as linked to one another as paper-doll cutouts. Charlotte described her hometown to her publisher, George Smith, as "a strange, uncivilized little place." Walking the cobbled streets, one can visualize the sisters standing at the original wooden post office counter to send out their manuscripts—though their gender made their aspirations far-fetched at the time. In the Black Bull Inn, their brother Patrick, who went by his middle name Branwell (since Patrick was also their father's given name), downed endless bottles of stout. In a far different local establishment, the Reverend Patrick Brontë, father

to the literary siblings, preached from his pulpit at the church of St. Michael's and All Angels.

The patriarch of the parsonage had moved from Ireland to attend Cambridge, where he changed his surname from Brunty to Brontë, Greek for thunder. He fell in love with Cornish-born Maria Branwell, who teasingly called him, "My dear saucy Pat." Their hope was for lives of "eternal felicity." However, two factors marred their courtship: he proposed in a crumbling abbey and her bridal veil disappeared in a shipwreck. Seven years after they married, Patrick declared, "Providence has called me to labour in His vineyard at Haworth." In 1820, the Brontës moved to their new residence, where Gothic gloom emanated from the ancient tombstones in the neighboring church. A year and a half later, the cemetery had another headstone upon the untimely passing of Maria. On her deathbed, she cried out, "Oh God! My poor children!" Four years later, the family's two oldest children, Maria and Elizabeth, aged ten and eleven, died from the Dickensian conditions at the Cowan Bridge School in Lancashire—the very place that served as a model for *Jane Eyre*'s hated Lowood.

Isolated in a parsonage bookmarked by a cemetery and the moors, the children turned to the world of imagination. Their foray into make-believe had begun when Patrick gave his son toy soldiers. The playthings have long disappeared; what remains is the prose and poems they composed, written in miniscule letters in tiny booklets that related adventures in the fantasy lands of Angria and Gondal. The Brontë Parsonage later offered $610,000 for one of these juvenilia but was outbid by the French. Cut from a different cloth than his free-spirited offspring, each evening at nine Patrick retired from his study. After knocking on his children's doors to tell them to mind the time, he climbed the stairs and wound his grandfather clock.

The siblings understood that upon their father's passing they would lose their home and financial support. Branwell tried his hand as a portrait painter and as a railroad employee, though both endeavors proved unsuccessful. He lost his job as a tutor when he had an affair with his student's mother. His sisters became governesses, one of the few options available to a clergyman's daughters. Charlotte confided the following description of her youthful charges, whom she viewed as semi-feral, to her diary: "The apathy and the hyperbolic & most asinine stupidity of these fat-headed oafs."

As much as life at Haworth alienated the women, Charlotte recalled of their return to its moors, "The highest stimulus, as well as the liveliest pleasure we had known from childhood upwards, lay in attempts at literary composition. We had very early cherished the dream of one day becoming authors. This dream, never relinquished even when distance divided and absorbing tasks occupied us, now suddenly acquired strength and consistency; it took the character of a resolve." A letter Charlotte sent to poet laureate Robert Southey, asking consideration of her poems, received the response that while she demonstrated that she had the faculty of verse, "Literature cannot be the business of a woman's life, and it ought not to be."

In 1846, the sisters published their poems under the pseudonyms Currer (Charlotte), Ellis (Emily), and Acton (Anne) Bell. As only two copies sold, Charlotte convinced her sisters to turn to fiction. Emily's literary creation Heathcliff was the archetypal bad boy, though his consuming devotion to his Catherine in some way redeemed his sins. Charlotte's Bertha Rochester proved unforgettable as the mad woman in the attic. In her poem "Wuthering Heights," Sylvia Plath later stated they "wrote...in a house redolent with ghosts."

As the only son, the family's hopes had been focused on Branwell, whose fragile self-esteem further eroded in the face of his sisters' success. At age thirty-one, ill from gin and opium, he succumbed to tuberculosis. Of her brother's passing, Charlotte wrote, "I do not weep from a sense of bereavement—there is no prop withdrawn, no consolation torn away, no dear companion lost—but for the wreck of talent, the ruin of promise, the untimely, dreary extinction of what might have been a burning and a shining light." A short time later, after refusing all medical treatment, Emily perished from the same disease. Gravely ill with the affliction that had carried off her brother and sister, Anne left for Scarborough to end her days by the sea. Anne is the only Brontë not interred in Haworth. In a

*Brontë Parsonage in Haworth* | *Wikimedia Commons, De Facto*

letter, Charlotte poured out her grief, "I let Anne go to God, and felt He had a right to her. I could hardly let Emily go. I wanted to hold her back then, and I want her back now. Anne, from her childhood, seemed preparing for an early death. They are both gone, and so is poor Branwell, and Papa has now me only—the weakest, puniest, least promising of his six children. Why life is so blank, brief, and bitter I do not know."

Upon occasion, Charlotte ventured to London, where she socialized with famous authors. William Makepeace Thackeray called her "a very austere little person," and one evening took pains to avoid "the She Author." He assumed what troubled Charlotte was she did not feel attractive enough to catch a man. She stood four feet ten inches tall with unsightly teeth, many of which were missing.

And then, dear reader, Charlotte wed her father's curate—whom she had previously rejected—the Irish-born Arthur Bell Nicholls. Nine months later, during her pregnancy, she passed away, likely due to hyperemesis gravidarum. The museum has a white baby bonnet that Charlotte's friend, a Miss Wooler, had made for the impending birth. In his old age, Patrick Brontë, by then almost blind, had outlived his wife and six children. He remained in Haworth, cared for by his son-in-law.

**The Brontë Parsonage:** The entrance hall opens to the stairway, where, on the first landing, the Barraclough grandfather clock ticks away the hours. The kitchen conjures a yesteryear when the Brontë brood gathered around the fire, entranced by their housekeeper Tabby Aykroyd's tales of the Yorkshire moors.

When Emily took over housekeeping duties, the aroma of fresh baked bread filled the air. The furniture and utensils that belonged to the family remain, as if awaiting their return.

Ghosts hover in Charlotte's bedroom. Maria Brontë passed away there at thirty-eight years old, likely from uterine cancer, in 1821. After his wife's passing, Patrick moved across the hall. The room's last occupant was Charlotte, who died in 1855. The Reverend had lived through Luddite and Chartist violence; as a result, every morning he fired a bullet across the graveyard. Branwell, after allegedly setting fire to his bed in an alcoholic stupor, took to sharing his father's bedroom. Branwell died there ruing he had "done nothing either great or good." The Brontë family lost its last member when Patrick took his final breath at age eighty-four.

The dining room was where the sisters wrote on their mahogany table, sharing inkwells and tea. When tired of sitting, their ritual was to walk around the table, discussing their ideas for Charlotte's *Jane Eyre*, Emily's *Wuthering Heights*, and Anne's *Agnes Grey*. In the back of the room is the couch on which Emily died. After losing her sisters, Charlotte walked alone. A servant, Martha Brown, recalled, "My heart aches to hear Miss Brontë walking, walking on alone."

In 2022, a book made by thirteen-year-old Charlotte entitled *A Book of Rhymes* returned to the parsonage after a century. On the reverse of the title page, Charlotte offered a modest disclaimer: "The following are attempts at rhyming of an inferior nature it must be acknowledged, but they are nevertheless my best." The price for the miniature book was hefty: $1.25 million.

Upon exiting the Brontë Parsonage Museum, visitors can look to the back of the house and imagine Anne, Charlotte, Emily, and Branwell wandering the moors. Those who gaze upon the cemetery can recall the final words of *Wuthering Heights*: "I listened to the soft wind breathing through the grass; and wondered how any one could ever imagine unquiet slumbers for the sleepers in that quiet earth."

**Seen from Her Window:** The moors reminded Charlotte of Anne and Emily. After their passing, the purple heather was no longer a source of comfort or escape.

# CHAPTER 2

# Coded Diary

*"The more spontaneous the pleasure,*
*the more happy the result."*

**—BEATRIX POTTER**

◇◇◇◇◇◇◇◇◇◇

## Hill Top

### opened 1946 | Near Sawrey, Lake District, England

For over a century, children have delighted in the adventures of Peter Rabbit, the bunny who dressed in a blue coat with brass buttons. To enter the whimsical world of his creator, Beatrix Potter, hop on over to the Lake District's Hill Top.

Helen Beatrix Potter never forgot what it was like to be young—the hallmark of all great children's authors. She recalled, "I have just made stories to please myself because I never grew up." Ironically, the woman who captured the magic of childhood was deprived of a happy one herself. She was born in 1866 to Rupert Potter, an attorney, and mother Helen; the family residence was at Two Boulton Garden in Kensington, an upscale London enclave. Her parents abided by the Victorian adage asserting children should be seen and not heard, and Beatrix spent her childhood with her nanny in the third-floor nursery. Fearful of their daughter contracting germs, Beatrix had no friends and did not attend school. Of her lack of formal education, Beatrix stated, "Thank goodness I was never sent to school, it would have rubbed off some of the originality." At age five, she was thrilled by the birth of her brother, Bertram. Unhappy in her home, she described it as her "unloved birthplace."

*Beatrix Potter* |
*Wikimedia Commons,*
*Charles G. Y. King*

The siblings, with the complicity of Mr. Cox, their butler, snuck a rotating cast of pets into their nursery. Brother and sister amassed a curious collection such as Punch, a frog, Toby and Judy, two lizards, Xarifa, a dormouse, and Tiggy, a hedgehog. The pet menagerie also included mice, snails, salamanders and a tortoise. The budding artist sketched her four-footed companions in exacting anatomical detail, except that they walked upright and wore bonnets and vests. Impressed with her drawings, Rupert took his daughter to visit John Everett, renowned for his painting *Ophelia*. Her father enrolled her in classes at the South Kensington Museum (now the Victoria and Albert Museum), which currently owns the largest collection of Beatrix Potter's drawings, manuscripts, and photographs in the world.

As a teenager, Beatrix vacationed with her family in a Georgian style house, now the Ees Wyke Country House Hotel, so named from Norse and Old English words that translate to "the house on the shore," overlooking Esthwaite Water. She remarked the house was "as nearly perfect a little place as I ever lived." At age fifteen, with Bertram at boarding school—which she could not attend due to her sex—Beatrix had only her diary in which to confide. An intensely private person, she wrote in miniscule letters and in a complex code. She continued this activity till age thirty.

When Beatrix was sixteen, Helen hired Annie Carver as her daughter's governess. Annie was only three years older than her student, and they developed a deep friendship. After two years, Annie announced she was leaving to wed Edwin Moore. Distraught at her departure, Beatrix purchased a Belgium rabbit she named Benjamin Bouncer that she sneaked up to the third floor in a paper bag. "Bounce" was partial to hot buttered toast and gooseberries, and she walked him using a leather dog leash. He kept her company through a bout of rheumatic fever that caused most of her hair to fall out; she was left with a lifelong bald spot. Sidelined once more by a second illness, she was bedridden for almost

**Home of Beatrix Potter** | *National Trust Images/Pete Tasker*

eight months. During that time, she sketched pets such as Bertram's bat. For verisimilitude, she measured the bat's wings. Upon her recovery, Beatrix's parents allowed her to visit Annie in South London, where she delighted in the young Moore children, Noel and Eric. The brothers were thrilled she had brought along Benjamin Bouncer. Bounce expired "through persistent devotion to peppermints."

In 1893, when Noel was ill, Beatrix decided to cheer him up with a letter that related the tale of four rabbits—Peter, Flopsy, Mopsy, and Cottontail—and the carnivorous Mr. McGregor. Peter, along with fellow Victorian the White Rabbit, became the most famous hare in history.

In addition to her furry literary creations, Beatrix was fascinated by mycology, the study of mushrooms; Two Boulton Garden became home to many samples of fungi that ended up under Beatrix's microscope. She wrote a report, "On the Germination of Spores and the Agaricineae," that earned a presentation at the Linnean Society of London. Her female sex, however, precluded the aspiring scientist's attendance.

Eight years later, Beatrix wrote Annie—who was now the mother of eight— requesting to borrow the letters she had written to Noel as she hoped to turn the characters into a storybook. In 1902, *The Tale of Peter Rabbit* proved wildly popular; to date, it has sold 250 million copies and has appeared in thirty translations, including Braille. Twenty-six more books followed. Letters from fans flooded the Potter mailbox; one wrote, "May your bunnies and squirrels live forever!" British author C. S. Lewis later shared that when he was young, he loved *The Tale of Peter Rabbit*: "The idea of humanized animals fascinated me perhaps even more than it fascinates most children." Her book inspired the young Lewis to write about his own anthropomorphic creatures in a story that he called, "Animal-Land." He entertained his brother, Warnie, with his story on rainy days in Belfast, Ireland, where they holed up in their father's old wardrobe.

In a brilliant marketing move, Beatrix patented her characters and produced the first Peter Rabbit doll, making him the world's oldest licensed literary character. The savvy businesswoman also created a Jemima Puddle-Duck doll with a fabric bonnet and shawl, a Peter Rabbit teapot, and a board game. When people remarked that her paintings were art, her customary response was, "Great rubbish, absolute bosh!"

The three sons of the founder of Frederick Warne & Co. published the Potter books. The youngest, Norman, fell in love with Beatrix and proposed. At almost forty years old and still unmarried, Beatrix was thrilled; her parents, however, were not pleased as the Warnes were from a lower social class. Helen and Rupert insisted Beatrix accompany them on a trip to Wales to ponder her decision. A few weeks later, her fiancé passed away from lymphatic leukemia. A barometer of the level of dysfunction at Two Boulton Gardens is that Beatrix's brother Bertram was married for eleven years before he shared with his family the existence of his wife, Mary Welsh Scott.

A few months after Norman's passing, in 1905, with an inheritance from her Aunt Harriet and the proceeds from her books, Beatrix purchased the seventeenth century Hill Top Farm. This was a bold move for a woman of her era. Hill Top Farm is a thirty-four-acre, two-story farmhouse in England's Lake District. The wisteria-draped house has a pitched roof constructed from local gray stone as well as a green wrought-iron gate. At age forty-seven, she married William Heelis, a local lawyer with whom she lived in a nearby secondary residence, Castle Cottage. Of her happy marriage, Beatrix quoted from *The Tempest*, "Spring came to you at the farthest, at the latter end of harvest." Beatrix's mother Helen, by then a widow, lived with them until her passing at age ninety-three. The reason Beatrix bought a nearby home was she desired Hill Top to be hers alone. Even when married, she walked across the field, through Tom Kitten's Gate, and into her the place she felt most comfortable. Before leaving Castle Cottage for Hill Top, Beatrix would tell William, "I'm going to keep the old house company." Hill Top remained Beatrix's private domain, where she wrote, tended her garden, and sought tranquility. At her farm, her constant companion was her beloved sheepdog, Kep, with whom she roamed in her magnificent country garden. In 1925, in an article in the American magazine, *The Horn*, Beatrix provided her encapsulated biography, "Beatrix Potter is Mrs. William Heelis. She lives in the north of England, her home is amongst the mountains and lakes that she has drawn in her picture books. Her husband is a lawyer. They have no family. Mrs. Heelis is in her 60th year. She leads a very contented life, living always in the country and managing a large sheep farm on her own land... I don't think anybody requires to know more about me."

**Hill Top:** For Beatrix, Hill Top was more than a farm; her "room of her own" represented independence. She filled her country retreat with sentimental objects such as antiques, locally made furniture, and paintings that made Hill Top resemble a personal museum. In keeping with the Lake District rural life, simplicity ruled Hill Top as evidenced by a spinning wheel and rag-rugs made from scraps of waste fabric. Beatrix's beloved home retains her belongings, such as metal-tipped clogs and a broad-brimmed straw hat. In the entrance hall is a cast-iron stove, a flagstone floor, and a nineteenth-century wooden dresser. A corner cupboard holds a teapot commemorating the coronation of King Edward VII. In an example of art imitating life, the teapot belonged to Ribby, the pussycat in *The Pie and the Patty-Pan*. A series of plates above the cupboard display designs of birds and other animals painted by Beatrix's father that had originally hung in the nursery at Boulton Place. A bookcase displays a sepia-toned photograph of the later-in-life gentlewoman farmer attending an agricultural show, dressed in a no-nonsense tweed suit, a far cry from the lacy white frocks of her youth. French dolls are on view, likely the models for Lucinda and Jane in *The Tale of Two Bad Mice*. Beatrix's writing room is the home's largest; its walls showcase landscape paintings by Bertram Potter. One of his works is entitled *Geese at Sunset*; his works reflect his inner torment partially borne from his affliction of alcoholism. Other canvasses were by children's book illustrator, Randolph Caldecott—the namesake of the Caldecott Medal. The eighteenth-century grandfather clock depicted in Tabitha Twitchit continues to tick the hours. Beatrix described the ticking as "the heartbeat" of the house. A large window of glazed crown glass distorts the light, thereby creating patterns on the oak floorboards. On a stand is an alabaster figurine of *The Reading Girl*, a copy of a work by the nineteenth century Italian sculptor Pietro Magni. Two oversized paintings hang on the staircase wall. One is by the seventeenth century Genoese painter Giovanni Castiglione entitled *Thanksgiving after the Flood*. The other is a copy of the *The Hon Mrs. Graham* by the acclaimed

Thomas Gainsborough. Both paintings came from Boulton. In contrast to the rustic charm of the entrance, the parlor, where she entertained, is far more formal. The wood-paneled room holds a rosewood writing box, a mahogany card table, and framed outlines of silhouettes. The corner cabinet displays Chinese and English porcelain. On the mantlepiece are two Staffordshire pottery greyhounds, each with a hare in its mouth. A shelf above the fireplace in Beatrix's bedroom, inscribed with the letters WHB, was William's handiwork that he added to celebrate the couple's twenty-first wedding anniversary. The Treasure Room holds a nineteenth century cabinet that houses miniature bronze creations of characters based on Beatrix's books, pieces from the Potter's dinner service showcasing the family crest, and some silverware. A fully furnished dollhouse contains items that appeared in *The Tale of Two Bad Mice*, as well as miniature food, such as the ham that Hunca Munca and Tom Thumb stole. Above the dolls' house is Peter Rabbit's red and white spotted handkerchief. Hill Top outdraws William Wordsworth's nearby Dove Cottage and runs neck-and-neck with the Brontë Parsonage as England's second most visited literary site (next to Shakespeare's Stratford-Upon-Avon).

As she aged, the real animals on her farm took precedence over her artistic ones, and Beatrix was delighted when her sheep won competitions. Beatrix, at last married, became Mrs. Heelis, who often wore wool skirts, men's boots, and a burlap sack-shawl. Although her bunnies and squirrels would live forever, in 1943, Beatrix died from bronchitis. As her final illness coincided with the Blitz, she wrote regarding the war, "The sheep and cattle take no notice." The Potter bequest left more than four thousand acres, including many farms, to the National Trust, which now maintains Hill Top and its grounds. Her will specified, "Hill Top is to be presented to my visitors as if I had just gone out and they had just missed me." Her shepherd, Tom Storey, scattered Beatrix's ashes above Hill Top. In her will, Beatrix left everything to William; after his death, the royalties and rights to her books went to Norman Warne's nephew, Frederick Warne Stephens.

As it transpired, the female St. Francis of the Lake District possessed a less than sentimental side. Firstly, there was that disturbing chapter where Mrs. McGregor turned Peter Rabbit's father into a stew. Next was a letter Bertram wrote to his sister from his boarding school in which he provided instructions about his bat: "If he cannot be kept alive...you had better kill him, + stuff him as well as you can." As Farmer Heelis, she sent pigs off to market to be transformed to bacon. Then, in 1997, *The Times* of London charged Ms. Potter with bunnicide; it claimed she occasionally dispatched her furry friends to gain a greater understanding of anatomy. The newspaper contended Miss Potter boiled Peter Rabbit, an image that rivals the horror of the boiled bunny in *Fatal Attraction*. A display case at a Victoria and Albert Museum exhibit showed a flattened hare's hide with the sign: "Rabbit pelt, thought to be that of Benjamin Bouncer." What a way to treat one's muse. A 'hare-raising' joke announced a recently found Potter manuscript: *The Beatrix Potter Cookbook*.

An accurate understanding of to what extent Beatrix was the Victorian Dr. Jekyll or Mr. Hyde would be revealed if one could decipher Miss Potter's coded diary.

**Seen from Her Window:** From her cherished Hill Top, gazing out on her garden, filled with flowers, herbs, and vegetables, with the backdrop of her beloved Lake District environs, Beatrix wrote, "It is here I go to be quiet and still with myself. This is me, the deepest me, the part one has to be alone with."

# CHAPTER 3

# *Mr. Darcy*

*"It is a truth universally acknowledged,
that a single man in possession of a good fortune
must be in want of a wife."*

## —JANE AUSTEN

◇◇◇◇◇◇◇◇◇

## Jane Austen's House

### opened in 1949 | Chawton, United Kingdom

Jane Austen's nephew observed concerning his aunt, "Of events her life was singularly barren; few changes and no great crisis ever broke the smooth current of its course." Although Jane may have had a seemingly placid existence as she never left England, she nevertheless had her share of both sunshine and storm.

In the blink-and-you-miss-it Hampshire hamlet of Steventon, Jane was born in 1775. Her father, the Reverend George Austen, and his wife, Cassandra, had six sons and two daughters. The full house was further crowded as the rectory doubled as a boys' boarding school. In 1779, Thomas Knight, a wealthy relative, along with his wife, Catherine, taken by Jane's twelve-year-old brother Edward Austen, became his adoptive parents; the childless couple went on to make Edward their legal heir. Another sibling absent from the parsonage was Jane's second-born brother George, who was disabled and boarded with a foster family. Cassandra and Jane studied at a school in Oxford that subsequently relocated to Southampton where they contracted typhus and returned home in 1783. Two years later, the siblings started boarding at the Abbey School in Reading. For

*Portrait of Jane Austen |*
*Wikimedia Commons,*
*National Portrait Gallery*

unknown reasons—perhaps financial—
the Austens withdrew Jane and Austen,
thus ending their formal education.

Lore holds that Cassandra and
Jane embarked on their quest for the
Holy Grail: landing suitable husbands.
Enamored with matrimony, a youthful
Jane had penned imaginary wedding
entries in the parish register. A
contemporary (though one who had only known Jane as a child) described her
as "a husband-hunting butterfly." At a 1796 ball, Jane met Thomas Lefroy, usually
referred to as Tom; of the meeting, she wrote in a letter, "I am almost afraid to tell
you how my Irish friend [Lefroy] and I behaved. Imagine to yourself...everything
most shocking." To her disappointment, Tom married an heiress and became
Chief Justice of Ireland. He named his daughter Jane.

At age twenty-six, Jane Austen stayed at Manydown Park, the 1,500-acre
estate of Hampshire heir Harris Bigg-Wither. He popped The Question and,
initially, Jane agreed. However, twenty-four hours later, her heart trumped
expediency. Some potential reasons for not grasping this marital life preserver:
Bigg-Wither had a stutter, Jane did not want to take on his surname, and she
preferred to produce offspring of pen and paper. Thomas Fowle, Cassandra's
fiancé, a ship's chaplain and a former student of her father, died from yellow fever.

A wrecking ball to Jane's soul occurred when Reverend George Austen, at
age seventy, announced his retirement, one that entailed leaving Steventon.
Along with his wife and daughters, the Reverend relocated to Bath. After his death,
his family drifted to various addresses. They spent three years living with John
Austen, along with his wife Mary and their children. The years without a room of
her own proved artistically fallow. Serendipity stepped in when Edward, heir to
his adoptive parents' fortune, offered his mother and sisters the use of Chawton
Cottage, located near his Elizabethan manor in Hampshire. A delighted Jane
wrote, "Our Chawton home, when complete, will all other houses beat." Through
another brother's intercession, a London publisher bought Jane's novels *Sense*

*and Sensibility* and *Pride and Prejudice.* By 1816, John Murray, Lord Byron's publisher, had taken her on as an author. Although her books did not mention her name (authorship was "By a Lady"), her identity leaked. Proof positive of her success was the fact that the Prince Regent (the future King George IV) kept all her novels in each of his residences. When he "requested" she dedicate *Emma* to him, she complied—albeit under pressure, as she disliked the profligate royal.

Wrapped in the cocoon of her home and her literary success, illness intruded. Some theories are that Jane suffered from Addison's Disease or Hodgkin's Lymphoma. Cassandra took her sister to Winchester for medical treatment. With her head in her sister's lap, at age forty-one, Jane passed away. Cassandra lamented, "She was the sun...the gilder of every pleasure, the soother of every sorrow...and it was if I had lost a part of myself."

Jane Austen died in 1817, and her family arranged her interment in Winchester Cathedral. The girl from a rural parsonage achieved posthumous immortality: Sir Walter Scott praised her mastery, Winston Churchill brought her novel along on a White House visit. In his short story, "The Janeites," Rudyard Kipling described how World War I soldiers, serving in the Front, enjoyed her writing, a reprieve from the horror. Helen Fielding, in *Bridget Jones's Diary*, christened her character Mark Darcy. The novelist's face stared back from the ten-pound note, along with a quotation from *Pride and Prejudice*, "I declare after all there is no enjoyment like reading!"

**Jane Austen's House:** The Mecca for Jane Austen adherents is Chawton Cottage where Jane lived for the last eight years of her life, a residence she shared with her mother, sister, and friend, Martha Lloyd. The literary landmark is a sixteenth century red brick structure originally built as a farmhouse. In the late eighteenth century, the farm became the home of the Knight family's bailiff. A plaque on an exterior wall explains the site is where the novelist "sent all her works out into the world;" it is the birthplace of *Mansfield Park, Emma, Persuasion,* and the fragment of *Sandition* and is also where she revised *Pride and Prejudice, Sense and Sensibility*, and *Northanger Abbey.* London lawyer T. Edward Carpenter purchased the property in 1948 and donated it to the public trust in memory of his son who died in World War II.

***Jane Austen's House*** | *Permission of Jane Austen's House*

Only two known portraits of Jane Austen exist, both drawn by her sister Cassandra. One, owned by the Austen family, portrays Jane from behind, sitting outdoors dressed in a blue bonnet and gown. The other, circa 1810, is a frontal view of the author sitting on a chair, her arms folded. Upon Cassandra's passing, she left her possessions to various relatives. In the 1920s, two of his granddaughters, Jane and Emma Florence Austen, pressed for money, sold the painting to Austen collector Frederick Lovering. Following his death, Sotheby's auctioned off his Austen memorabilia, including the painting of the author; it currently resides in the National Portrait Gallery in London.

In the drawing room is a piano from Jane's era, which is very similar to the one on which she played. Jane wrote of the instrument, "Yes, yes we will have a Pianoforte, as good a one as can be got for 30 guineas." Music books bearing her signature rest on the instrument. Visitors can hear recordings of pianoforte pieces that once echoed throughout the house.

One emotionally laden spot is the dining room where the author penned the pages that transformed her from merely another single woman—a cause of shame in eighteenth-century England—into the Regency chronicler who so vividly explored the eternal dance between the sexes. What sets pulses racing is a twelve-sided table of walnut wood barely wide enough to hold an inkwell, a quill, and a few sheaves of paper, on whose scuffed surface the author's quill conferred immortality on Emma Woodhouse and

Mr. Knightly, Elizabeth Bennett and Mr. Darcy. As museum director Lizzie Dunford explains, "People will cry in front of it because it is so significant." The dark-green wallpaper with a leaf pattern is based on an original scrap unearthed in 2017.

The Jane Austen House has a collection of first editions, including Lady Caroline Lamb's copy of *Pride and Prejudice*, and the Godmersham set of first editions. The museum routinely rotates their exhibits.

The museum is the repository of sixteen Austen letters as well as a signed extract from Prime Minister Winston Churchill's memoir in which he describes how *Pride and Prejudice* brought him solace during a period of illness in the middle of World War II.

Jewelry lends autobiographical insights into its owners, and Jane's conjures her spirit. Two topaz crosses were presents from Charles, whom his sisters referred to as "our own particular brother." The crosses carried great emotional significance; Jane mentioned them in her letters, and they were an influence on *Mansfield Park*. Jane reserved her blue bead bracelet with a gold clasp for special occasions. In 2012, an Austen descendent put Jane's gold ring with an oval turquoise stone up for auction at Sotheby's. The winning bid of $230,000 came from *American Idol* alumna turned talk show host Kelly Clarkson. Alarmed at losing Austen memorabilia, Britain declared the ring a national treasure and placed a ban on its export. The museum raised the money for its purchase.

The museum has one particular display that represents more than the writer's possessions. When Jane passed away in Winchester, in keeping with a ritual of the times, Cassandra cut off several locks of her sister's hair to give to her family as mementoes of their lost loved one. Cassandra set one lock in her pearl ring; her niece, Fanny, used hers in a brooch. The strands of hair in the museum, encased in a brass locket with a ribbon crest, were originally the possession of Harriet Palmer, Charles Austen's second wife. Charles' granddaughters sold the heirloom. A Mrs. Alberta Burke, an American, ended up with the chestnut-colored strands and donated them to the museum. In stark juxtaposition to the Regency mementoes is a 1990s *Clueless* doll replete with accessories (including a feather pen) in the original box. The inclusion is a nod to the film director Amy Heckerling, who based the hit movie on Jane's 1815 classic, *Emma*.

Popularization of *Pride and Prejudice* reignited because of Colin Firth's portrayal as Mr. Darcy in the 1995 BBC TV adaption, which portrayed him emerging from a lake, his shirt clinging to his muscled torso. Giddy after viewing the garment, museum visitor Queen Camilla lamented, "But he's not in it, that's a bit sad." Cheeky Camilla is not alone in her reverence for the celluloid incarnation of Mr. Darcy.

**Seen from Her Window:** In 1811, Jane wrote to her absent sister Cassandra about Chawton Cottage's gardens, "The Shrubbery Border will soon be very gay with Pinks & Sweet Williams, in addition to the Columbines already in bloom."

# CHAPTER 4

# *I Still Believe*

*"I want to go on living after my death."*

## —ANNE FRANK

◇◇◇◇◇◇◇◇◇◇

## The Anne Frank House

opened in 1960 | Amsterdam, Holland

William Shakespeare's Romeo observed, as he walked the streets of Verona, "Here is much to do with hate but more with love." The self-same words apply to an Amsterdam building that receives over a million visits each year. The hate emanated from the moustached madman of Berlin, while the love stemmed from the shared devotion of the Frank family.

The world's most famous diarist, Annelies Marie Frank, was born in 1929 in Frankfurt, Germany. Her father, Otto, worked in the family bank while his wife, Edith, raised daughters Margot and Anne. The girls affectionately called him Pim. Otto had received the Iron Cross during World War I, but the fact that Otto had fought heroically for the Fatherland held no clout in the Third Reich.

In the 1930s, twin shadows permeated the family's' home life; the Depression shuttered Otto's bank, and Chancellor Adolf Hitler blamed Germany's economic ills on the Jews. With mounting dread, Edith and Otto watched the Nazis parade through Frankfurt. To escape the descending noose, the family sought sanctuary in the Netherlands.

In their adopted homeland, Otto's business, Opekta Works (which produced pectin used in the production of jam), was initially located at the Singel and later on Prinsengracht, in an eighteenth-century canal building near the famous Westerkerk Church. Pectin production proved lucrative, and his

**Anne in her
Montessori school |**
*Wikimedia Commons,
Unknown photographer;
Collection Anne Frank
Stichting Amsterdam*

**Site where Anne wrote her diary |**
*Wikimedia Commons,
Massimo Catarinella*

daughters adapted to life in Amsterdam. Margot was shy, unlike her extroverted sibling, who craved attention. The mother of Anne's friend Hanneli Goslar pronounced, "God knows everything, but Anne knows everything better." While Anne loved books, she also enjoyed figure skating. Because she had heart trouble, instead of taking physical education classes, she participated in Heilgymnastiek, a program that consisted of exercise therapy. Her math teacher nicknamed the loquacious Anne "Miss Quack Quack." In a letter to her paternal grandmother in Switzerland, Anne wrote, "Yesterday I went out with Sanne, Hanneli, and a boy. It was lots of fun. I have no lack of companionship as far as boys are concerned."

In 1940, Germany launched *Fall Gelb* (Case Yellow), the codename for an attack on the Netherlands that caused the Queen Wilhelmina of the Netherlands to flee to London along with her cabinet. She requested her subjects "to think of our Jewish compatriots." Anti-Semitic ordinances began; "*Voor Joden Verboden*" ("Jews Prohibited") signs proliferated. The celebration of Anne's thirteenth birthday was a ray of light in the darkness. Since Otto had a projector from the time Opeka had toured the country, during which they played a promotional film, for his daughter's party he showed a reel of *Rin Tin Tin*. Anne gave her friend

Hannah Goslar and probably also her friend Jacqueline van Maarsen an invitation in the form of a cinema-style ticket. Another present was a red plaid diary with a metal clasp that led her to declare it "one of my nicest presents." In her first entry, she wrote, "I hope I will be able to confide everything to you as I have never been able to confide in anyone. And I hope you will be a great source of comfort and support." She addressed her diary as "Kitty" after Kitty Francken, a fictional character in Cissy van Marxveldt's series, *Joop ter Heul*.

Further horrors followed: Jews had to wear a yellow Star of David marked *Jood*, and Dutch police smashed doors and windows of Jewish residences and arrested those who attempted to flee. Due to Aryanization, Otto transferred assets to his Gentile colleagues, Johannes Kleiman, Victor Kugler, and Jan Gies. In vain, the desperate Otto sought visas for his family to travel to the United States. In 1942, when the sixteen-year-old Margot received a notice from the Zentralstelle für Judische Auswanderung with a summons for deportation, the Franks went into hiding. In a coded postcard to his sister Helene Elias in Basel, Switzerland, Otto informed her they were going underground. Not yet aware of the enormity of the looming horror, Anne confided to Kitty of hurrying into hiding, "I began to pack some of our most vital belongings into a school satchel...this diary, then hair curlers, handkerchiefs, schoolbooks, a comb, old letters." So as to avoid suspicion, the Franks did not carry luggage to their hiding place, and Anne had to relinquish treasured toys.

The family's refuge was in the *achterhuis* ("backhouse") of Ottos's former office, its entrance later obscured by a moveable bookcase built by employee and helper Johannes Voskuijl. Other residents were Hermann van Pels—who had been part of arranging the hiding place—along with his wife, Auguste, and their son, Peter. In her diary, Anne called them by the pseudonym "the van Daans." Anne explained why they invited Fritz Pfeffer, a dentist, to join them: "Daddy says we must save another person if we can." Fritz took over Anne's bed, meaning that she had to sleep on a settee lengthened by chairs. Anne's entries related the overwhelming boredom of life in seclusion, as well as the ever-constant fear of detection. She also shared with Kitty her feelings for the sixteen-year-old Peter, noting that when they were alone together, "It's as if a light goes on inside me." She described the blossoming of romance to Kitty: "Oh, it was so wonderful. I could hardly talk, my pleasure was too intense; he caressed my cheek and arm, a bit clumsily." What spoiled her romance was her concern that her sister Margot would feel jealous and therefore even more isolated. The diary also reveals the teenager's mature insights, "It's really a wonder that I haven't dropped all my ideals, because they seem so absurd and impossible to carry out." Upon learning that a Radio Oranje broadcast from the Dutch government in exile in London had appealed to citizens to retain records of life under siege, Anne commenced writing in a more serious vein. Her personal notebook became a message in a bottle to posterity. She gave her narrative the title *Het Achterhuis* (*The Secret Annex*).

After two years, the refugees' spirits soared with news of the Allied invasion—a hope that died with the Nazi raid of their hiding place. The accepted story behind the arrests was an anonymous call had arrived at the *Sicherheitsdienst* (German Security Service) revealing the whereabouts of Jews in hiding. (The going rate for informing on Jews in hiding was $1.50 per person.) The Anne Frank website, however, postulates another theory. The Sicherheitsdienst may have stormed 263 Prinsengracht because they suspected fraudulent use of ration coupons, and in the process stumbled upon the secret annex. The prisoners ended up on the last train from Westerbork to Auschwitz. Authorities later transferred the sisters to Bergen-Belsen, where Anne's friend Hannah was also held captive behind the barbed wire. The Frank sisters perished from typhus in the camp, probably at the beginning of February 1945. The family's sole survivor, Otto, returned to Amsterdam, vainly praying for a reunion with his loved ones. Miep Gies, who along with other helpers had been instrumental in keeping the factory's occupants alive, presented him with his daughter's journal. Reading his deceased daughter's words proved so painful it took Anne's father three weeks to finish. After the diary's revelations of Anne's intimate thoughts, Otto said, "I didn't really know my own child." He recalled that on the day of his arrest, soldiers had ransacked the annex, taking currency, silverware, and jewelry. They did not bother with a small journal bound in plaid cloth. In a nod to Anne's aspiration of becoming a writer, he arranged the 1947 publication of her diary under the title *Het Achterhuis*. Under the staggering statistic of six million Holocaust victims, the diary, as an eyewitness to the heart of darkness, vividly illustrated that each victim's life held heartbreaking stories. Publishers have translated Anne's account into more than seventy languages, and the book has sold more than thirty million copies, a figure close behind that of sales of the Bible.

**The Anne Frank House:** The museum that bears her name and keeps Anne's legacy alive is on the site where she spent her final years. Climbing the steep stairs of the brick house presents a chilling reminder of a painful past. Eight decades ago, Dutch officers, headed by SS-Hauptscharführer Karl Josef Silberbauer, forced their victims, into a black van at gunpoint, the first time the prisoners had been outside in twenty-five months. Entering the building is extremely emotional as the experience confronts visitors with the horror that human beings can perpetrate. The building also serves as a grim reminder of the potential and promise extinguished by genocide.

Due to the advanced age of the moveable bookcase, the museum encased it in glass. What in ordinary circumstances would be inconsequential takes on tragic overtones: Otto had charted Anne's growth with pencil marks on a wall, knowing his child might never obtain her adult height. A seemingly innocuous object—a metal tin filled with colorful marbles—also carries grim overtones: before she went into hiding, Anne had entrusted her toys to her next-door neighbor, Toosje Kupers. Toosje never parted with this keepsake of her friend, and her children later played with them. Seventy-five years later, Toosje donated the marbles to the museum.

In Anne's room (shared with Fritz, the dentist, to their mutual irritation) are faded pictures of Greta Garbo, Deanna Durbin, Norma Shearer, Ginger Rogers, the young British princesses Elizabeth and Margaret, Rembrandt's self-portrait, and the Pieta. The hiding place also held a map of Normandy and Brittany on which Otto placed pins to trace the advances of Allied troops.

The Anne Frank House is comprised of two museums. One is the secret annex, a structure which remains as it was on the day of the arrests, caught in a 1940s time capsule. Rather than refurnish it with authentic period pieces, Otto directed that the rooms were to remain bare. In 1962, he explained his reason: "When the Anne Frank House was restored, they asked me if the rooms should be refurbished. But I replied, 'No. During the war everything was taken out, and I want to keep it that way.'" Another reason for wanting to keep the sacred space barren is its echoed emptiness, a nod to seven of its former inhabitants who never returned. However, in response to visitors' questions regarding how the rooms looked when he lived there, Otto agreed to the installation of replicas. The main part of the building is the enclave that once served as Otto's company, which now displays exhibits of the Frank family, the Nazi Occupation, and Bergen-Belsen.

The Anne Frank House website lists items in its collection, including a silver cup with Hebrew lettering, the Olympia typewriter that belonged to Miep Gies, a

1942 cloth Star of David, a plate manufactured by Rosenthal Bavaria, the bobbin that opened and closed the bookcase, and a fragment of the wallpaper from Anne's room.

The holy relic is seen in the display case that holds the red plaid diary—the Holocaust's foremost symbol of slaughtered innocence. The diary bears witness to an unspeakable evil and stands as a rebuttal of the erasure of the memory of Europe's Jews. Anne had shared with Kitty, "I want to go on living even after my death." Through her diary, through her museum, her wish has come true. The gift shop offers Anne's book in a variety of languages, including Hindi, Korean, and Persian. The English version came out in 1952 as *Anne Frank: The Diary of a Young Girl*. Anne's words offer a beam of light in the darkness of the Holocaust: "In spite of everything, I still believe that people are really good at heart."

**Seen from Her Window:** In 1944, Anne Frank wrote to Kitty in the pages of her diary, "I feel as if I were about to explode...I walk from one room to another, breathe through the crack in the window frame...I think spring is inside me."

# CHAPTER 5

# *God's in His Heaven*

*"I like imagining better than remembering."*

**—L. M. MONTGOMERY**

◇◇◇◇◇◇◇◇◇◇

## The Anne of Green Gables Museum

opened 1972 | Prince Edward Island, Canada

There must be something about a gabled house that sets the literary juices flowing. Nathaniel Hawthorne, inspired by a dwelling in Salem, Massachusetts, wrote *The House of the Seven Gables*, in which he portrayed a residence haunted by the injustice of the Salem witch trials. Lucy Maud Montgomery's cherished home in Maritime Canada gave birth to *Anne of Green Gables*, a tale of the triumphs and tribulations of an orphaned girl. For the legions who love the Montgomery series, the Anne of Green Gables Museum is irresistible.

In the summer of 2008, thousands of visitors descended on Prince Edward Island to attend the one hundredth birthday of the country's most famous fictional redhead. Youthful fans wore straw hats with long, flame-colored pigtails—their own or synthetic braids. Anne, who insisted on spelling her name with an E at the end as it "looks so much nicer," is the precocious protagonist of the classic that—along with the Mounties and hockey—is Canada's most famous export.

The woman who put the province on the international literary map was Lucy Maud Montgomery: Lucy (named after her grandmother) and Maud without an E (named after Queen Victoria's daughter, Princess Alice Maud Mary). She hailed

from the rural community of Cavendish, transformed in her writings into the fictional Anne's Avonlea. Lucy was born in 1874 in a modest residence, now one of several of the author's home museums. Highlights of the house include the room where she was born, a display case that holds a reproduction of her wedding gown and her bridal shoes, as well as the pair she wore on her England and Scotland honeymoon. Scrapbooks reveal memories of her years at the Prince of Wales College. Period pieces transport the visitor into the Victorian era, with items such as a Franklin stove, an organ that displays a copy of the sheet music for "Island Hymn" (composed by Lucy in 1908), and her handwritten letters. The walls display framed photographs of family members such as her mother, Clara, who died from tuberculosis when her daughter was only twenty-one months old. Not relishing the role of single father, Hugh took off for Saskatchewan; distance did not make the heart grow fonder. Her maternal grandparents, Lucy and Alexander MacNeil, who lived several miles away, became her de facto parents. Already in their fifties and the parents of six, they had little patience with Lucy's wild imaginings, which clashed with their Presbyterian conservatism. Lucy sought beauty in her island home and in her books, such as *Little Women*. Based on her dual reflection in the glass plate of a cabinet, Lucy named her imaginary friends Katie Maurice and Lucy Gray.

When Lucy turned fifteen, she left for Saskatchewan to reconnect with her father, who had married Mary Anne McRae, with whom he had children Kate and Donald. Stepmother Mary disliked Lucy and used her as a nanny and maid. A year later, Lucy returned to Prince Edward Island. Anne's words echoed her author's own thoughts, "My life is a graveyard of buried hopes."

Lucy worked at several schools until she resigned to care for her widowed grandmother. During that time, she contributed short stories to *Ladies Journal*, *McClure's*, and other magazines. In her journal, she wrote that her freelancing had earned five hundred dollars, the equivalent of a male stenographer's annual New York income and a very considerable sum at the time. Of those who had doubted she would succeed, she gloated, "The dollars have silenced them. But I have not forgotten their sneers. My own perseverance has won the fight for me in the face of all discouragements."

In 1905, Lucy began a novel about an orphan who finds the poetic in the prosaic. She typed up her manuscript on an old typewriter with a broken W key that necessitated writing in each missing letter in ink. After five publisher rejections, she relegated the pages to a hatbox. During spring cleaning, she chanced upon the abandoned manuscript and sent it to the Boston based L.C. Page & Company; they went on to publish *Anne of Green Gables* in 1908. In five months, the book sold 19,000 copies; the current number is over fifty million copies, and it has appeared in twenty translations. Fan letters arrived from all over the world, including one from Mark Twain with high praise: "Anne of Green Gables is the dearest and most moving and delightful child since the immortal Alice." King George V appointed Lucy to the Order of the British Empire in a ceremony presided over by Canada's Governor-General Lord Bessborough in Rideau Hall, Ottawa. Lucy became the first Canadian woman member of the British Royal Society of Arts.

In the novel, Gilbert Blythe, a fellow student in Anne's one-room schoolhouse, pulled her braid and called her Carrots—fighting words, as she despised her flaming locks. Her knee-jerk reaction was to smash a chalk slate over his head. As punishment, the teacher made her write on the blackboard, "Ann Shirley has a very bad temper." A further humiliation was she had to write "Ann"—without an E. In the fifth book of the series, *Anne's House of Dreams*, the adult Gilbert reconnected with Anne and told her, "You've thwarted destiny long enough." Succumbing to Gilbert's "roguish hazel eyes" and realizing he was her "kindred spirit," they married and raised six children in an Avonlea fairy tale.

Art did not imitate life. The writer fell in love with a farmer, whom she eventually rejected as she could not commit herself to an uneducated husband. In her thirties, she wed the Reverend Ewen MacDonald, whom she felt would provide her with a comfortable lifestyle and social prestige. But when Ewen received a position in Ontario, Lucy left her heart in Prince Edward Island. She referred to 1919 as "a hellish year": Her cousin Frederica Campbell died from influenza. Four months later, her husband suffered from what was referred to as "religious mania,"

*The home where Maud spent the happiest times of her childhood |*
*Courtesy of The Anne of Green Gables Museum*

a condition that would currently be classified as bipolar disorder. Ewen endlessly feared eternal damnation.

Mischief and Anne always went hand in hand: She dyed her hair green, accidentally intoxicated her best friend, Diana Barry, on currant wine, and almost drowned while enacting Alfred, Lord Tennyson's poem, "The Lady of Shalott." The MacDonalds' oldest child, Chester Cameron, had more serious scrapes. Unable to hold jobs, he badgered his mother for money, abandoned his wife and two children for another woman, and had a propensity for indecent exposure. Police arrested him for embezzlement. Her second baby, Hugh, was stillborn. She called her youngest, Stuart, her "one good son." He became a respected Ontario obstetrician. When Ewen's mental illness forced him from his pulpit in 1935, the couple bought a house in Toronto. Lucy christened her new residence "Journey's End." It could also have been known as Lucy's House of Nightmares. To treat both Ewen's disorder and Lucy's depression, doctors prescribed barbiturates, leading to the hell of husband-and-wife addiction.

While the author arm-wrestled her demons, *Anne of Green Gables* became a beloved classic. Polish resistance fighters took the novel to the Front; in Sri Lanka, it aired as a television series; Canada featured her famed opus on a postage stamp, with its title both in English and translated to French, "*Anne...La Maison aux pignons verts.*" In the 1950s, the book—with the title *Akage no An Red-Haired Anne*—became part of the Japanese school curriculum due to the number of post-war orphans who related to the protagonist. In Japan, Anne mania was so intense that a Japanese businessman signed a contract to import more than $1.4 million worth of potatoes from Prince Edward Island.

**The Anne of Green Gables Museum**: As William Shakespeare dominates Stratford-Upon-Avon, Anne is the princess of Prince Edward Island. Lucy's orphan fuels the province's multi-million-dollar tourist industry with offerings that include theatrical performances, horse-drawn carriage rides, and a mock Anne of Green Gables village.

The 1872 white, green-trimmed House of Green Gables Museum is in the former two-story farmhouse where Lucy experienced her happiest memories, which belonged to her Aunt Annie and Uncle John Campbell. Lucy named the house Silver Bush and referred to it as "the Wonder Castle of My Childhood." Visitors enter through the kitchen, whose black wood-fired stove still heats the rooms. The parlor remains the same as when Lucy was wed in front of its fireplace; the organ played the "Wedding March." A plaque on the wall reads, "Room where I was married, standing before the mantle"—the French translation: "La salle où j' étais mariée." The artifacts include the enchanted bookcase that inspired Anne's imaginary friends, and under glass is the Crazy Patchwork Quilt the author worked on from ages twelve to sixteen. Also on display is the weathered Blue Chest described in "The Story Girl;" its contents once belonged to a bride jilted at the altar. An upstairs bedroom has copies of the literary series with the sign, "First Edition Books Autographed by L. M. Montgomery to members of the Campbell family." Another bookcase holds the novel in its various translations. Throughout are mounted prints bearing quotations from Lucy's journals, the place where she truly entered the confessional. The sign on the lawn bears the words from the author's 1917 journal, "I only wish that I could have a house of my own like it and I would be satisfied." The author's tragedy is she never obtained a room of her own.

Lucy Maud Montgomery passed away from a drug overdose in 1942 at Journey's End. She left a note ripped from her journal, "My position is too awful to endure and nobody realizes it." How different from the last line of *Anne of Green Gables*, where Anne whispers a line from Pippa, the Italian orphan in Robert Browning's poem: "God's in his heaven, all's right with the world."

**Seen from Her Window:** The nearby lake inspired the setting for Anne's Lake of Shining Waters; beside it is a carriage such as the one in which Matthew Cuthbert first brought Anne to Green Gables from Bright River station.

# CHAPTER 6

# *Edankraal*

*"No dream can live unless somebody lets it live or die
unless somebody kills it."*

## —ANNE SPENCER

◇◇◇◇◇◇◇◇◇◇

## The Anne Spencer House & Garden Museum

opened 1977 | Lynchburg, Virginia

The Harlem Renaissance of the 1920s was so named because the Manhattan neighborhood was the epicenter of Black artists, writers, and entertainers. Virginia-based poet Anne Spencer proved that such a flowering of culture was not dependent on a particular geographical locale. To experience her whimsical home, take the midnight train to the Anne Spencer House & Garden Museum.

Despite an inauspicious beginning, Anne left an indelible imprint on both literature and a historical movement. Born in 1882 on Rock Spring Plantation, a farm in Henry County, Virginia, Anne was the only child of Joel Cephus Banister, who was born into slavery. His wife, Sarah, was the child of a union between her father, a member of the slaveholder family who owned the Reynolds Tobacco Company, and his slave. As Joel was determined to be his own boss, the family moved to Martinsville, where he bought a saloon. If life was not already difficult enough for a Black girl in the South in the wake of the Civil War, the Bannisters separated when Anne was five. Reverting to her maiden name of Scales, Sarah moved with her daughter to Bramwell, West Virginia, where her brothers worked as coal miners. Because of her grueling schedule as a cook at the Bluestone Inn, Sarah arranged for Anne to board with

*Anne Spencer on her wedding day* |
*Wikimedia Commons,*
*Photographer: Unknown*

William T. Dixie, the proprietor of a barbershop. Since Sarah did not wish her daughter to associate with the children of coal miners, Anne did not attend the local school. To find a quiet spot away from the five Dixie siblings, Anne would retreat to the outhouse, where she brought a Sears, Roebuck & Company catalogue in the hope she could learn to read. When Joel discovered Anne was not attending school, he gave his ex-wife an ultimatum: Put their daughter in a classroom or he would take her to the Midwest, where he had started a job at the Stony Island Railroad Company. Together they came up with the considerable eight-dollar-a-month tuition for the Virginia Theological Seminary & College, then the most prestigious Black secondary school and currently the Virginia University of Lynchburg. Although eleven years old and illiterate when she began her studies, a few years later Anne delivered the valedictorian address entitled "Through Sacrifice to Victory," which highlighted the struggles of the Black community.

The Virginia Seminary introduced Anne to poetry and also to fellow student Edward Alexander Spencer; he tutored her in math and science, while she helped him with languages. When Anne was seventeen, the relationship turned romantic. Despite the yoke of Jim Crow, Edward wore many hats as Lynchburg's first Black postman, real estate developer, and landlord. But the role he prioritized was that of Anne's husband.

The British poet Matthew Arnold wrote, "It is of advantage to a poet to deal with a beautiful world," and Edward did his utmost to make his wife's as perfect as possible. He built her a Queen Anne style house at 1313 Pierce Street where they raised daughters Bethel Calloway, Alroy Sarah and son Chauncey Edward, all of whom attended college. Chauncey also left an imprint on history. Charles Lindbergh's flight from New York to Paris inspired many men to become pilots, but the famed aviator had expressed skepticism over the ability of Black people

*The Harlem Renaissance of the South* | Wikimedia Commons, Pubdog

to operate a plane. Both in rebuttal and due to his love of the freedom of flight, Chauncey became a pilot and the founder of the National Airmen's Association of America. In 1939, he persuaded Harry S. Truman, then a senator, to integrate the armed forces.

Aware his wife found tranquility in nature, Edward acquired a rear vacant lot so that her garden could double in length, and he built her a backyard cottage (or in the current colloquial phrasing, a she-shed). Her retreat furnished her with a room of her own in which to pen her poetry. In tribute to her husband, Anne wrote, "Twenty-five years ago, I drew from the lottery of matrimony its greatest prize, an understanding heart." After Anne's mother moved in with the Spencers, she assumed the lion's share of childcare and chores, freeing Anne to garden and to write. The extra time also allowed Anne to work outside the house. On the strength of her credentials as a published poet, she obtained a position in Lynchburg's first Black library, located in the segregated Dunbar High School.

In 1913, the Spencers founded the Lynchburg chapter of the NAACP, whose members created its charter in their living room at 1313 Pierce Street. Through her activism, the Southern Mrs. Spencer became part of the Harlem Renaissance due to the presence of writer James Weldon Johnson, who was in Lynchburg to help establish the new Lynchburg branch. Because of segregation, Black visitors to the South could not stay at hotels, so the Spencers offered Johnson their home for the duration of his stay. As the house had Anne's poems written on playbills and grocery lists, on a recipe for peach pie, on the inside of a pantyhose box, and even on the walls, Johnson was moved to share his hostess's writing with New York publishers and the Harlem poets. Subsequently, Anne became the first African American woman featured in the acclaimed *Norton Anthology of Modern Poetry*. 1313 Pierce Street transformed into a salon for eminent visitors such as Langston Hughes, Zora Neale Hurston, Thurgood Marshall, and Dr. Martin Luther King Jr. The walls echoed with Marian Anderson's baritone, Paul Robeson's poetry.

Although most guests were eminent trailblazers, one represented a forgotten and painful chapter of American history. The missionary and scientist Samuel Phillips Verner had kidnapped Ota Benga, a Congolese Pygmy, and exhibited him at the 1904 St. Louis World Fair and the Bronx Zoo. Thousands gawked at his 103-pound frame and his teeth, which his tribe had ritualistically sharpened to points. The Black community was enraged, and the Reverend James H. Gordon rescued Ota and enrolled him at the Virginia Seminary. Distraught over his tragic life, Anne invited him to her home, where he met Booker T. Washington. She tried to teach him to read and to regain his humanity. Unable to shake his torment, Ota later shot himself in the heart.

Although Anne was an integral member of the Harlem Renaissance, her subject matter differed from that of her fellow poets who portrayed the horrors of racism. Instead, her pen depicted nature, love, the passage of time, and death. As to what drove her pen, she explained, "I write about some of the things I love. But I have no articulation for the things I hate." However, on a nonliterary plane, she took several stabs at racial injustice. One day, Anne and her sister-in-law were in the whites-only section on public transportation when a conductor ordered them to move. When he called them "n***** washerwomen," they remained where they were. In protest, following the incident, Anne travelled through Lynchburg on foot or rode in an ice wagon. She also organized a successful campaign to replace the White teachers at the all-Black Jefferson Street High School. Her argument was that as Black instructors could not work at White schools, White teachers should not have jobs at Black ones. Another source of tongue wagging was her wearing custom-made pants; she reveled in the shocked stares the masculine attire elicited.

Anne passed away at age ninety-three; her grave is alongside that of Edward, who predeceased her by eleven years. Had the Spencers lived till 2020, they would have marveled at an irony: The United States Postal Service honored the wife of a mail carrier with her own stamp.

**The Anne Spencer House & Garden Museum:** Initially, Anne's son Chauncey maintained the home museum; currently, Anne's granddaughter Shaun Spencer-Hester—who lives across the street—serves as its docent. The green, purple, and yellow walls and boldly patterned wallpaper hold photographs of famous visitors. When Maya Angelou stepped into the parlor in the 1980s, she stated, "I feel the spirit of Anne Spencer." Not a fan of the adage "everything in its place," newspaper clippings, political flyers, and pages of her poetry are visible in notebooks and on walls. Inexplicably, gas cards—stamped with "Esso Happy Motoring"—hang over the Spencers' twin beds. A purple sink, salvaged from a local hotel, still works. Another unique decorating touch is provided by the bright red, leatherette-padded doors to the kitchen that Edward salvaged from the all-Black Harris Movie Theater. Running vertically down a filing cabinet is a painted verse of Anne's poem, "A Lover Muses." On the dresser in Anne's bedroom the visitor finds her perfume, hairbrush, and lipstick.

The garden is awash with flowers and adorned with birdhouses. The backyard holds a pond fashioned by Edward; NAACP cofounder W. E. B. DuBois added a fountain in the form of a mask of an African prince. The stone cottage, Anne's sacred space, has a note from Langston Hughes thanking her for her hospitality. A shawl is draped over a chair by her desk. A metal-painted sign displayed on the roof bears the name she gave her retreat: "Ed" for Edward, "an" for Anne, and *kraal*, the word in Afrikaans for enclosure: Edankraal.

**Seen from Her Window:** Looking from her second-floor window onto her stone cottage, Anne must have marveled that her Edankraal garden was more Bloomsbury than Old Virginia.

# CHAPTER 7

# *Bid Time Return*

*"Let us enjoy the beautiful things we can see, my dear,
and not think about those we cannot."*

**—JOHANNA SPYRI**

◇◇◇◇◇◇◇◇◇◇

## The Johanna Spyri Museum

opened in 1981 | Hirzel, Switzerland

L iterary orphans are associated with their respective locales: Jane Eyre with England, Dorothy with Kansas, Anne of Green Gables with Prince Edward Island. The paradigm holds true for Heidi and her Swiss homeland. The Johanna Spyri Museum affords visitors a glimpse into the author's life, while its environs provide a postcard of pastoral perfection.

Die-hard devotees of the 1880 classic can make a pilgrimage to the setting of *Heidi*, located near the Liechtenstein border. Visitors may explore the Alpine meadows and climb the steep trail that leads to Heididorf, the village modeled on the book, as well as the stone and wood house of Heidi's fictional childhood. The tour includes the experience of resting in straw to emulate Heidi's sleeping in a hay-filled loft. Although there may be those who complain of hiking rough terrain at a high altitude, Heidi did it daily...and barefoot.

Children love the classic, and so they long for Adelheid's (Heidi's) carefree existence: cavorting in the meadows, sharing adventures with Peter the Goatherd, drinking milk fresh and warm from her cow. The appeal to adults is the story's theme that aligns with the parable of the prodigal son and the Christian message of redemption.

*Author of Heidi* |
*Wikimedia Commons*

*The museum dedicated to Switzerland's beloved fictional orphan* |
*Wikimedia Commons, Roland Zumbuehl*

The endearing and enduring classic makes the world associate Switzerland with the pure of heart Heidi, an image that endures even in the face of Swiss financial scandals such as hoarded Jewish Holocaust bank accounts and Nazi gold. The Pollyanna of the Alps moved in with her grandfather, who, embittered by his past, shunned religion and humanity. Despite his gruff personality, his granddaughter loved her home above the village of Dorfli, from whose windows she gazed upon a valley of white crocuses. The conflict arose when Heidi's aunt Dete arranged for her to serve as a companion to the wheelchair-bound Clara Sesemann in Frankfurt. Although the two girls became firm friends, Heidi hated city life. In a nod to the adage that all's well that ends well, Heidi ends up united with her grandfather, who has made peace with the villagers and returned to their church. When Clara visits, she is able to cast away her wheelchair as she has regained the use of her legs.

Although the book has sold millions of copies, the author's life, due to her dislike of attention, remains murky. Johanna Louise Heusser was born in 1827 in the picturesque village of Hirzel. Her white, three-story house afforded a vista of the green of fir trees, the blue of Lake Zurich, the white of the snow-capped Alps. Other residents were Dr. Johann Jakob and Frau Meta Heusser, their six children (Johanna was the fourth), a maternal grandmother, and two maternal aunts. The doctor's patients also resided in the home while convalescing. In addition to his medical practice, Dr. Heusser acted as the pastor of the hamlet's Protestant church.

Down the path from the family home is the grammar school founded in 1660 that Johanna attended until age fourteen. Hating the confines of a desk, she was an apathetic student whom a teacher pronounced "a dunce." Afterwards, Johanna attended the *höhere Töchternschule* in Zurich, followed by a lengthier educational experience in the French-speaking city of Yverson. In 1852, Johanna married her older brother's friend Johann Bernhard Spyri. The couple settled in Zurich, where Johann became a respected lawyer; three years later, their only child, Bernhard Diethelm, arrived. It was a double blow when her son passed away at age twenty-nine, likely from tuberculosis, and her husband died a few months later. Johanna ended up an invalid who pursued writing until her passing in 1901.

One difficulty in the Spyris' marriage had been Johanna's distaste for city life; to escape into nature, she often visited her childhood friend, Anna Elisa von Salis-Hössli, who lived in Jenins, in the Bünder Herrschaft (Canton of Grisons). The village seems lifted from a picture postcard: its homes have shutters decorated with heart shapes, and the window planter boxes are awash with geraniums. On one of her Alpine walks, Johanna met Heidi Schwaller, who lived in Chur in the Swiss Alps with her grandfather. As he was strapped for cash, Johanna paid for the child's schoolbooks. From the picturesque setting and her enchantment with Heidi—the daughter she never had—Johanna gleaned the inspiration and setting for the books that would put Switzerland on the literary map.

Heidi acted as a muse for Johanna and was thrilled when her name and story appeared in a novel, especially one that became an instant bestseller. As Johanna was reclusive, the press subsequently beat a path to Heidi's mountain home. She recalled that "Grosspapi" tried to shield her from the press and turned down requests for interviews. Unlike the author, the adult *Heidi* gravitated to the spotlight, and she became the 1930s darling of high society. Contributing to her international fame was the 1937 film version of *Heidi* starring America's sweetheart, Shirley Temple, in which she sang, "In Our Little Wooden Shoes." In 1968, during the Super Bowl championship game between the Jets and the Raiders, television executives curtailed the game to air the seven o'clock showing of a new production of *Heidi*.

Her manager, Jürg Boschung, arranged for Heidi to make guest appearances on a world tour. Under Jürg's influence, Heidi broke off her engagement to Peter, who she had been close to since childhood. She married Jürg, a relationship that came with an expiration date. Peter, who still held the torch for his youthful crush, became her second husband. They took their vows in Maienfeld and bought a lovely home where they raised their four children. The relationship disintegrated when Peter became as dedicated to the bottle as he had been to his goats. Although they did not divorce, the couple ended up living apart. After Peter's 1981 death, Heidi reverted to her maiden name.

In 2008, journalist Clare O'Dea tracked down the ninety-two-year-old Heidi, a resident of a luxurious retirement facility in Ruhetal. While sipping champagne, Heidi reminisced about her bygone glory days. She recalled, "Bob Hope was such a charming and amusing gentleman, and he was very interested in Switzerland because his grandmother was Swiss. We stayed in touch for a long time." The former mountain dweller owned an extensive collection of photographs that showcased her with famous international stars, including one of her dressed in traditional costume in the company of the sultan of Brunei. In the 1950s, Heidi worked as a court storyteller for the Brunei royal family. She recalled of her singular experience, "I used to go there for a fortnight every year to entertain the children. We communicated in French, but I used to teach them funny phrases in Swiss German." In her later years, Heidi spent time with her grandchildren and great-grandchildren, answering fan mail, and walking in the Ruhetal gardens.

**The Johanna Spyri Museum:** While Wilhelm Tell remains Switzerland's most famous male folk hero, Heidi is the country's most enduring literary heroine. In a 1968 marketing campaign, Swiss Air portrayed an Alpine paradise with the slogan, "Heidi wouldn't lie." Two years later, the message had changed to "Heidi lied" as a blonde-tressed hippie cavorted in the mountain meadows. The updated version's intent was to modernize the country's image, showing it as more than the land of chocolate and cuckoo clocks.

By the hundredth anniversary of Johanna's passing (when *Heidi* turned 120), the book had appeared in fifty languages and sold fifty million copies. To mark the milestone, Zurich arranged for a *Heidi* exhibition at its Strauhof museum, and Hirzel experienced an upsurge in tourism.

On the eightieth anniversary of the writer's death, teacher Jürg Winkler converted Johanna's old grammar school, which had fallen into disuse after

World War II, into a museum to honor Switzerland's foremost author. From the window, guests are greeted with the spectacular views of the snow-capped peaks of the mountain ranges of Rigi and Pilatus and the slopes above the Canton of Zug. Guests can immerse themselves in an 1840s Hirzler primer and look upon the desk that holds original objects such as letters and manuscripts. The first floor has white-washed walls displaying photographs; among them, one may behold Johanna on her wedding day in her bridal finery, consisting of a black velvet dress and a red print Indian shawl draped across her arm, as well as images of the Heusser family. In one corner, set against a backdrop of majestic Alpine mountains, is a lifelike tableau. In front of a cabin reclines the papier-mâché figure of an old man with a gray wool beard smoking a long-stemmed pipe. Off to the side, Heidi, dressed in a dirndl skirt, pets her goat. A barefoot Peter, crook in hand, sits cross-legged amid wildflowers.

In terms of authentic artifacts, the museum has the Spyri family's wheelchair, as well as a large copper kettle. The upstairs floor houses Johanna's childhood dollhouse; a glass-fronted bookcase holds twenty-two first editions of *Heidi* as well as translations in Arabic and Japanese. The German publisher F. A. Perthes released the first book of the series in 1889 under the title, *Heidi...Mountains and Marvels*. A video plays the 1952 *Heidi* film classic that starred Heinrich Gretler and Elsbeth Sigmund. Immersed in the world of childhood innocence, visitors might long for the sentiment expressed in Shakespeare's *Richard II*, "O call back yesterday, bid time return."

**Seen from Her Window:** Johanna, in her first book, *A Leaf on Vrony's Grave*, employed the landscape of her childhood when she wrote, "There is an old house next to the small white church in the mountain village where I lived for a good twenty years. I enjoyed, with open eyes, the glory that God poured out on this little spot of earth."

# CHAPTER 8

# A Room of One's Own

*"For most of history,*
*Anonymous was a woman."*

## —VIRGINIA WOOLF

✧✧✧✧✧✧✧✧

## Monk's House

### opened 1981 | East Sussex, England

Leonard Woolf observed, "What cuts the deepest channels in our lives are the different houses in which we live." His words apply to Monk's House, a setting that served as a lighthouse for him and his writer-wife, Virginia.

Adeline Virginia Stephens (known as Virginia), born in 1882 as the third of the four children of Julia and Sir Leslie Stephens, would go on to leave an immortal literary imprint. Both her parents had lost their spouses from their first marriages. Her father, Sir Leslie Stephens, had been the husband of Harriet Marian (Minny) Thackeray, the daughter of the acclaimed author of *Vanity Fair*. Their only offspring, Laura, was deranged and died in an insane asylum. Virginia's mother, Julia, was the widow of Herbert Duckworth, with whom she had a daughter and two sons.

The times were such that Virginia was not permitted the educational opportunities of her brothers, but she did have access to Sir Stephen's vast library. She devoured George Eliot's *Silas Marner*, Charles Dickens' *A Tale of Two Cities*, and Samuel Taylor Coleridge's *The Rime of the Ancient Mariner*.

*Author of famous essay, "A Room of One's Own" |*
*Wikimedia Commons,*
*George Charles Beresford*

Visits from guests such as Henry James, Thomas Hardy, and George Eliot helped broaden her horizons. Her youthful endeavor was penning weekly essays under the title, "The Hyde Park Gate News," so called after the name of the Stephens' London address. If her work failed to elicit parental praise, Virginia wallowed in depression.

While child labor was an open shame in nineteenth-century England, Hyde Park Gate had a hidden one. In her 1939 memoir, Virginia recalled how her fourteen-year-old stepbrother, Gerald Duckworth, started inappropriately touching her when she was four years old. Following the death of her father, her other half-brother, George Duckworth, participated in the abuse. In 1841, she wrote her friend, Ethel Smyth, "I still shiver with shame at the memory of my half-brother, standing me on a ledge, aged about six or so, exploring my private parts." Her youthful sexual experience left her fearful of heterosexual intimacy. Her literary protagonist, Clarissa Dalloway, slept in her own room rather than share her husband's bed.

Julia Stephens passed away from rheumatic fever when Virginia was thirteen, an event that triggered her daughter's first nervous breakdown, one that led to anorexia, depression, and hallucinations. Another symptom of her psychological disorder: the birds sang to her in Greek. The following decade brought the deaths of her beloved brother Thoby, her half-sister Stella, and her father. To cope with Thoby's passing, her sister Vanessa married Clive Bell. Virginia initially accepted a proposal from writer Lytton Strachey; he had made the offer in empathy, and since he was homosexual, he was relieved when she turned him down.

What helped Virginia elude her ever-present demons was writing, a compulsion she likened to "being harnessed to a shark." In a letter she confided,

**Home of Virginia Woolf** | *Wikimedia Commons, Elisa.rolle*

"I am ashamed, or perhaps proud, to say how much of my time is spent in thinking, thinking, thinking about literature."

Virginia's first meeting with Leonard Woolf was not one associated with the phrase "made in heaven." His family referred to her as "the haughty Goy," while she referred to him as "the penniless Jew." However, they shared common interests, and he promised to respect her sexual boundaries. She informed him, "As I told you brutally the other day, I feel no physical attraction in you. There are moments—when you kissed me the other day was one—when I feel no more than a rock."

Woolf's frigidity did not extend to women, and she had a pivotal relationship with Vita Sackville-West. Their affair was the talk of the town as Vita was British aristocracy—she could trace her lineage to William the Conqueror. Virginia's novel *Orlando* had been inspired by Vita and bore the dedication: *To V. Sackville-West*. Vita told Virginia that she fell in love with herself after reading the novel. Nigel Nicolson, Vita's son, approved of both his mother's relationship with Virginia and the novel. He wrote that the book was "the longest and most charming love letter in literature." The fact that both women were married did not pose a problem: Vita's husband was homosexual, and Leonard was content if his wife was able to experience fleeting joy. In contrast, Vita's mother was humiliated that her cross-dressing daughter and Vita's lesbian paramour blighted an ancient lineage. She wrote to the editor of *The Observer* begging him not to carry a review of the book, since she felt it to be "all that is so coarse and will be so shocking to the middle classes." She aimed her fury at Virginia, whom she referred to as "the Virgin Wolf." Early in their affair, Vita had declared, "I am reduced to a thing that wants Virginia." However, her ardor waned, and she left Virginia for Mary Campbell. The rejection further bruised Virginia's tortured psyche.

When Virginia was thirty-three, the Woolfs had three aspirations: to buy a bulldog, lease a house, and establish a printing press. They never bought the dog, but they established Hogarth House. Their publications—including Virginia's—altered the fabric of twentieth-century literature. Some of Hogarth Press' authors were Katherine Mansfield, T. S. Eliot, and Sigmund Freud. Free of censorship, Virginia tackled taboo subjects such as gender inequity and same-sex relationships. She pioneered the stream of consciousness technique that provided readers with insight into the thoughts, not just the actions, of her characters.

With the publication of acclaimed novels such as *To the Lighthouse*, Virginia was the high priestess of the Bloomsbury Group, which consisted of London's leading artists, writers, and intellectuals, including Vanessa and Clive Bell, E. M. Forster, and John Maynard Keynes. The members of the bohemian Bloomsbury Group were serial bed-hoppers of whom Dorothy Parker wrote that they "lived in squares, painted in circles, and loved in triangles."

In 1919, the Woolfs bought Monk's House, a seventeenth century cottage in the village of Rodmell. One attraction was its country charm, and another was that it was a four-mile walk from Charleston Farm, the home of Vanessa and Clive Bell, which is also currently a home museum. Upon occasion, Vanessa's lover Duncan Grant visited; in contrast with his homosexual identity, he fathered Vanessa's daughter, Angelica Bell. Virginia doted on her nieces and nephew as her surrogate children; Leonard vetoed having any of their own as he felt they would prove detrimental to his wife's emotional fragility. At Monk's House, the devoted Leonard created a routine to stabilize his wife's moods. Leonard worked in his upstairs study that had a view of the Ouse River and the Sussex Downs. Virginia wrote in an additional room they built at the foot of their garden. She thought of scenarios for her novels while soaking in her large, claw-footed bathtub.

Despite her long-desired literary success—with Virginia appearing on the 1937 cover of *Time* magazine—she continued to wrestle with the "hairy black devils" of her mental illness. Calamity plunged Virginia into a downward spiral. Vanessa's son, Julian, died fighting in the Spanish War, her beloved friend Lytton Strachey passed away, and the Blitz destroyed both sisters' London homes. Virginia feared a Nazi invasion of England would signify the death knell for her Jewish husband.

The birds once again sang in Greek. For the last time, Virginia sat at her desk, where she wrote to Leonard, "Dearest, I feel certain that I am going mad again. I feel we can't go through another of those terrible times. And I shan't recover this time. I begin to hear voices, and I can't concentrate...I don't think two people could have been happier till this terrible disease came. I can't fight any longer..."

Virginia left Monk's House wearing an overcoat whose pockets she loaded with rocks. Her obituary reported that before wading into the Ouse River, on its bank she deposited her hat and walking stick. She also left her three-dimensional diary in the form of Monk's House.

**Monk's House:** Virginia Woolf penned an explanation of the fascination people take in visiting authors' homes, "It would seem to be a fact that writers stamp themselves upon their possessions more indelibly than other people." Myriad tourists continue to descend on Monk's House to view the remnants of this literary light and to resurrect the voices of the bohemian Bloomsburys.

Along with a preponderance of books (with which even the stairway is lined), art held a pride of place. The walls and furnishings bear the imprint of Vanessa Bell and Duncan Grant. Later touches came from South African-born Marjorie Tulip Ritchie, nicknamed Trekkie. After Virginia's death, Leonard fell in love with Trekkie, who spent time with both her husband and Leonard. In the sitting room are matching tables and chairs that Vanessa painted, bearing the initials V.W. A sculpture of Virginia rests on the windowsill. The dining room sports the best-known portrait of Virginia, painted by her sister; Trekkie painted another canvass of Leonard. To commemorate the release of *To the Lighthouse,* Vanessa created a cobalt-blue ceramic-tile border around a fireplace in Virginia's bedroom that depicted a lighthouse with waves breaking on the rocks. She based the scene on Cornwall, a magical place where the sisters had vacationed as children.

The home has an English garden of which Leonard was the landscape architect. There is also an Italian garden patterned after places the Woolfs visited in their travels that holds a pond, stone figurines, and a peacock topiary. Bordered by mulberry trees, a vegetable garden offers a view of the kirkyard of St. Peter's Church. In a nod to the fact that her garden shared a wall with the church's cemetery, Virginia wrote to her friend, "When we are looking at our beehives, they are often burying someone on the other side of the wall." Two intertwined elm trees, which the couple named Virginia and Leonard, once stood on the grounds; one perished from a storm, the other from disease. Under the elm, a grieving husband scattered his wife's ashes. Two linden trees now stand in the same spot alongside bronze busts of Virginia and Leonard. The grounds are the final resting places of the Woolfs.

The most emotional corner of Monk's House is Virginia's writing room. In a letter to Vita, Virginia wrote that they had built the one-room gabled lodge to "harbour the sun." In one corner is the trunk that Leonard took on his 1904 journey to Ceylon. The desk radiates poignancy; it holds Virginia's glasses, a kerosene lamp, and a plant. In an essay, Virginia had written about Judith Shakespeare, the playwright's sister, who never achieved the success of the Bard because of her gender. The ghosts of gifted women, likewise silenced, hover. The essay's most heartfelt sentence reads: "A woman must have money and a room of one's own if she is to write fiction."

**Seen from Her Window:** From her garden room, Virginia looked out upon her garden with its view of Mount Caburn, a stone sentry who protected her privacy.

# CHAPTER 9

# Ready to Depart

*"God made the world round so we would never*
*be able to see too far down the road."*

## —ISAK DINESEN (BARONESS BLIXEN)

◇◇◇◇◇◇◇◇◇◇

### The Karen Blixen Museum
#### opened in 1986 | Nairobi, Kenya

66 I had a farm in Africa, at the foot of the Ngong Hills..." are the opening words of Karen Blixen's memoir of her seventeen-year sojourn in Nairobi. To visit her former home, now the Karen Blixen Museum, is to return to a yesterday where the "Dark Continent," then defined as the domain of British East Africa, was the paradise-playground of rich Europeans.

Author Karen Christentze Dinesen, later known as Isak Dinesen, was born in Denmark in 1885 at Rungsted, a nineteenth-century family estate on the seaside fifteen miles north of Copenhagen. Her mother, Ingeborg, who was descended from the conservative Westenholz clan, married the footloose Wilhelm Dinesen, a naval captain in the Franco-Prussian War. After Wilhelm's proposal, Karen's maternal grandmother asked, "How shall we reckon with an erotic element among us?"

Wilhelm Dinesen later lived among the Pawnee people as a hunter and trapper in Minnesota, before coming to an unfortunate end. Daughter Karen, then ten years old, was devastated when he hung himself, due to shame brought on either from then-incurable syphilis, which often exacerbated mental problems, or siring another child out of wedlock.

Karen rejected her mother's and country's "homeliness" (her word for *bourgeois*) and attempted to escape a Prufrockian existence through writing, painting, and travel. Later, she sought an exit through marriage to a wealthy man. She admitted to being "God's chosen snob." She first fell for her Swedish second cousin, Baron Hans von Blixen-Finecke, a distant cousin of King Christian of Denmark. But when Hans slipped through her net, she settled on Bror, his twin, who offered her a title and a ticket to a storybook land.

The couple were wed in 1914 in Mombasa, with Prince Wilhelm of Sweden as a witness. With Westenholz family backing, they purchased a six-thousand-acre coffee plantation in the Great Lakes area of Africa. They filled the estate with trappings from Denmark: Limoges china dishes, silverware, and an Irish wolfhound. She christened her home "Mbogani," which means "a house in the woods." One unique decorating touch was a millstone she acquired after its former owner's murder that she fashioned into a table where she sipped tea, smoked, and wrote.

Karen and Bror hunted big game; afterwards, she gushed over the "ecstasy" of the kill. Ernest Hemingway, also smitten with Kenya, used Bror as his model for the character of hunter Robert Wilson in his short story "The Short Happy Life of Francis Macomber." Her husband's fondest memory of her was the time she used a whip on two lions that had attacked an ox, lashing them back into the jungle. The act earned her the title of "the Honorable Lioness." Despite the disapproval of fellow expatriates, Karen established a school and provided medical care for her workers. When one of them named Kamante, from the Kikuyu tribe, who later worked as her chef, refused treatment, she bandaged his running sores herself. Karen Dinesen's love affair with Africa is embodied in her words, "Here I am, where I ought to be."

Growing coffee proved unprofitable due to the soil as well as Bror's laissez-faire attitude regarding money. While he was often away on big game hunts, Karen

*"Mbogani" "A House in the Woods" Karen's Kenyan home |*
*Wikimedia Commons, Ruslik0*

came to realize animals were not all he hunted, especially when he infected her with syphilis. Doctors treated her with arsenic, further compromising her health, since antibiotic treatment had not yet been discovered. She ended up paying a staggering price for the title of baroness. The couple separated and eventually divorced in 1925.

As determined to save Mbogani in Kenya as Scarlett O'Hara was to save Tara in Atlanta, Baroness Blixen persevered. On one occasion, the Prince of Wales—the future Edward VIII—was her guest. Not only did she struggle financially, but life was also disheartening socially for a strong-willed woman in a patriarchal society.

Romance arrived with an English safari hunter, Denys Finch Hatton, a younger son of the Earl of Winchilsea. He literally swept her off her feet when he took her for a flight in his *Gypsy Moth* over the Serengeti. She wrote to her brother: "I believe that for all time and eternity I am bound to Denys, to love the ground he walks upon, to be happy beyond words when he is here, and to suffer worse than death many times when he leaves." On a New Year's evening, Denys and Karen sat at the millstone table watching Venus and Jupiter "all close together, in a group on the sky; it was such a radiant sight that you could hardly believe it to be real, and I have never seen it again." However, her bedroom was often bereft of both husband and lover. The problem was that the baroness wanted to trade in the name Karen von Blixen-Finecke for Karen Finch Hatton, a level of commitment that her free-spirited lover refused.

A few days before an expected reunion, Denys perished while piloting his plane. The devastated Baroness Blixen arranged for his burial in the Ngong Hills, where the summit of Mount Kilimanjaro and Mount Kenya can be seen in the distance on cloudless days. She marked his burial site with an obelisk that hold a brass plaque, subsequently stolen, inscribed with the words from Coleridge's *Rime of the Ancient Mariner*: "He prayeth well, who loveth well / Both man and bird and beast." She hoisted a cloth banner high enough over the grave so that she could view it from Mbogani.

The Depression spelled the end for the Karen Coffee Company's plantation. Crushed by the loss of her livelihood, health, marriage, and lover, Kenya was no longer "where she ought to be." Her story could have ended with the return of the prodigal daughter to Rungsted, but instead it was the start of a new chapter. She took up the pen name Isak Dinesen—"Isaac" translated from the Hebrew as "he who laughs;" in her case, her subject was the human comedy—and wrote her memoir on her father's slanted desk overlooking the harbor. As she observed, "All sorrows can be borne if you put them into a story." With the publication of *Out of Africa* and her noted short story "Babette's Feast," she garnered a Nobel Prize nomination. After Ernest Hemingway received the honor for *The Old Man and the Sea*, he declared the award should have gone to "that beautiful writer Isak Dinesen." Several gin and tonics later, he added that he was still happy that he had won, as he needed the dough. On a final trip to America, the former lion-hunter was herself lionized, and she dined on oysters with Arthur Miller and Marilyn Monroe. She visited with Southern writers Truman Capote and Carson McCullers. Carson claimed the elderly baroness danced atop a marble table along with her and Ms. Monroe. Her memory might have been fanciful, but it was one that would have delighted Dinesen.

Although she did not have hundreds of workers as she did in Mbogani, in Rungsted she employed a housekeeper, two maids, a private secretary, and a coachman. The author wore turbans and exotic clothing; makeup consisted of a heavily powdered face and kohl-rimmed eyes. A diet of fruit, oysters, and champagne resulted in her seventy-pound frame. She became a compulsive talker, perhaps an effect of use of amphetamines. One scandalizing comment was that despite her venereal disease, her marriage had been worth it as it had gifted her the title of baroness.

The great Dane passed away in 1962 from extreme emaciation. The woman of two continents ended up with a museum dedicated to her in each. As set forth in her will, Rungstedlund became the Karen Blixen Museum, inaugurated by Queen Margrethe of Denmark. The home in which she was born, wrote, and died commemorates and gives vivid insights into her life in Denmark. The house museum holds her old windup gramophone, a gift from her beloved Denys, as well as a screen she painted with scenes from the stories she told him in the evenings. Every day the docents fill its rooms with the fresh flowers Karen adored. The lace window curtains in the living room trail seven feet across the wooden floor. Behind the house is a bird sanctuary, with a chart showing their migratory flight paths from Denmark to Africa. In front of a beech tree lies Karen's grave, where the restless woman is at last at rest.

**The Karen Blixen Museum:** Dinesen wrote, "If I know a song of Africa...of the giraffe and the African new moon lying on her back, of the ploughs in the fields and the sweaty faces of the coffee-pickers, does Africa know a song of me?" The answer lies in Mbogani, a three-dimensional diary of the colonial era and the life of one of the most fascinating women ever to choose to live in Africa. From the home museum's columned veranda, visitors can envision white-suited colonials sipping their tea, maintaining the customs of Britain in this far-flung outpost of the Empire.

In 1964, the Danish government purchased her former African home—a remnant of a colonial bungalow—and gifted it to Kenya as a token of the country's newly won independence from Britain. The director of *Out of Africa*, Sydney Pollack, donated eight thousand dollars and many of the film's props toward the establishment of the center. Her home retains her possessions; Louis Vuitton suitcases and black-and-white photographs of her guests, including one of Marilyn Monroe. The green walls display her paintings; the shelves hold Denys' monogrammed books. In one corner is a lantern that the baroness hung on her veranda to let her lover know she was home, waiting.

While the name Karen currently carries pejorative connotations in the Western world, in Nairobi this is not the case. The answer to the baroness' question, "Does Africa know a song about me?" is a resounding "yes." In memory of the Dane who loved their land like her own, the Kenyan government named the area of her former plantation "Karen." Down the road from her museum is the Karen Blixen Coffee Garden, a restaurant with an adjoining shop. The store offers bronzes, paintings, jewelry, and assorted crafts. One unique offering was a six-inch-high crested crane, an East African bird, made of sisal. The items are on display in an old home; lunch is also available. Dinesen quoted the poet Walter Savage Landor to express her own feeling: "Nature I loved, and next to Nature, Art; I warmed both hands before the Fire of Life; It sinks, and I am ready to depart."

**Seen from Her Window:** From the window of Mbogani, Isak Dinesen gazed upon the view of the Ngong Mountains; she wrote that they were "crowned with four noble peaks like immoveable darker blue waves against the sky."

# CHAPTER 10

## *The Past*

*"Never relight a dead cigarette or an old passion."*

**—KATHERINE MANSFIELD**

◇◇◇◇◇◇◇◇◇◇

## Katherine Mansfield House & Garden

### opened 1988 | Wellington, New Zealand

Those who possess sphinxlike personalities prove challenging subjects for their biographers, who must strip off various masks. In her journal, Katherine Mansfield paraphrased Polonius' words from Shakespeare's play *The Tragedy of Hamlet*, "True to oneself! Which self?" To best understand the enigmatic New Zealander, journey to the landscape of her childhood: the Katherine Mansfield House and Garden.

The woman who put this land down under on the international literary map was born Kathleen (Katherine) Mansfield Beauchamp in Wellington, New Zealand, in 1888. She had four sisters: Charlotte, Vera, Jeanne, and, until she passed away at age four months, Gwendoline. Leslie was the youngest child and the only boy. Her mother, Annie, worshipped at the altar of propriety; her father, Harold, was the chairman of the Bank of New Zealand. Annie and Harold Beauchamp were conscientious but cold; fortunately, Margaret Dyer, the children's maternal grandmother, proved nurturing. In tribute, Katherine used her middle name—her grandmother's maiden name—as her surname.

Katherine was the black sheep of the family; as future frenemy Virginia Woolf described her in Bloomsbury-speak, she had "gone every sort of hog since she was 17." In her teens, Katherine had simultaneous affairs with a Māori woman, Maata Mahupuku, and Edith Kathleen Bendall, an artist. Katherine reveled in

sensuality. "O Oscar!" she wrote in her diary, invoking her muse, Oscar Wilde, "Am I peculiarly susceptible to sexual impulse? I must be I suppose, but I rejoice."

Along with two of her sisters, Katherine attended Queen's College boarding school in Britain where she met Ida Baker. The women became lovers, and Ida served as Katherine's on-again, off-again Alice B. Toklas. Her time abroad left her dissatisfied with provincial Wellington, especially when her parents squashed her dream of becoming a professional cellist. Three years later, with a hundred-pound annual stipend from her father, Katherine set sail for England. A few months later, Katherine was pregnant; her relationship with musician Garnet Trowell ended due to his parents' disapproval. A panicked Katherine married the older George Bowden, a singer she had known for three weeks. On their wedding night, she bolted. Katherine found herself alone in "cheap and horrible digs."

News of her pregnant, runaway bride daughter brought her mother to England. She took Katherine to *Bad Wörishofen Therme* (spa) in Bavaria, where the waters were purported to cure sexual deviancy. Annie returned to Wellington and cut Katherine out of the Beauchamp will. In Bavaria, Katherine miscarried and embarked on an affair with the Polish writer Floryan Sobieniowski. He gave her gonorrhea, a then-incurable condition that plagued her for the remainder of her life and left her infertile. When she made money from her books, her East European lover resorted to blackmail.

Katherine led a nomadic existence and in eight years had twenty-nine postal addresses. She moved in with John Middleton Murry, the editor of the magazines *Rhythm* and *Athenaeum*. He was an aspiring writer who lacked the requisite talent. They began as roommates, and each evening, before retiring to their respective rooms, they would shake hands and say, "Good night, Middleton. Goodnight, Murry." Katherine changed their platonic relationship when she

***Katherine Mansfield's Childhood Home*** *| Jason Mann Photography*
*Permission of Katherine Mansfield Museum*

asked, "Why don't you make me your mistress?" He hesitated, voicing his concern, "I feel it would spoil everything." John did become her lover (although an inept one). He nicknamed her Tig, and in a letter to her, he wrote, "Oh, Tiggle, we are the lovers of the world. We are the lovers that were dreamed by God." Their landlord, upon discovering they were living together in sin, evicted them. They moved from one squalid flat to another, even leaving for Paris to escape their creditors.

Secretiveness was Katherine's trademark; Virginia Woolf described her as "inscrutable." Over the years, Katherine tried on various names: Kass, Katiuska, Kissuenka. When she achieved acclaim as an author, she lunched with James Joyce and crossed paths with literary lions such as T. S. Eliot and Rupert Brooke. In awe of Virginia Woolf, the Bloomsbury bluestocking, Katherine was thrilled to be part of her charmed circle, though its members treated her as "the little Colonial walking in the London garden patch—allowed to look, perhaps, but not to linger." Rupert Brooke mocked her accent. Virginia and her husband, Leonard, published "Prelude," Katherine's longest short story, at their Hogarth Press in 1918. Later, Virginia confided to her diary, "I was jealous of her writing—the only writing I have ever been jealous of."

Another relationship was with D. H. Lawrence and his girlfriend (later his wife), the German-born Frieda. In a letter to John and Katherine, Lawrence wrote, "We count on you as our only two tried friends, real and permanent and truly blood kin." Mansfield and Murry were witnesses at the Lawrences' 1914 wedding. The two couples rented neighboring homes in a remote part of Cornwall; Katherine suggested that Lawrence call his cottage The Phallus. Lawrence used Katherine as a model for Gudrun in his novel *Women in Love*; his comment on his neighbor was that she possessed "a desire to run away from herself." Lawrence later turned on Katherine, and in a letter wrote, "You are a loathsome reptile—I hope you will die."

In 1915, Katherine took a break from John to join a new lover, her husband's friend Francis Carco, a poet from New Caledonia who was fighting on the Western Front. John accompanied her to the edge of the combat zone. World War I claimed her brother Leslie's life when a grenade exploded in his hand. Fellow soldiers said his dying words were, "Lift my head, I can't breathe." Later, Katherine claimed that her brother's final words were addressed to her.

In 1917, a doctor discovered a spot on Katherine's lungs. On the chance a spiritual change would prompt a physical one, she dabbled in Roman Catholicism. Of her treatment at the hands of physicians, her serrated tongue pronounced, "Saw two of the doctors—an ass and an ass." Desperate for a cure, she followed medical advice to go abroad for a warmer climate. Accompanied by the ever-faithful Ida, she left for Italy. John's letters enraged her by their utter self-absorption; when she wrote of spitting up blood, he responded by complaining of his constipation. To emphasize his narcissism, she underlined all the times his letters mentioned "I."

When she returned to London to marry John, he was shocked by her change in appearance as she had lost a drastic amount of weight and was clearly deathly ill. Nevertheless, when she headed to France in a bid to stave off her sickness, John remained in England to flirt with the former prime minister's daughter.

A desperate Katherine had turned to the Armenian-Russian cult leader George Ivanovitch Gurdjieff, who ran the Prieure Institute, located in an old château in Fontainebleau, France. Her husband was aghast at her choice of cure, and almost all communication between them ceased. Treatments practiced in Fontainebleau included dancing to any of the five thousand tunes that Gurdjieff had composed. The guru's prescription for Katherine was to stay in a barn to inhale the air the cows exhaled. Months later, Katherine broke the marital silence, imploring that John join her, and he arrived four days later. That evening, while they were climbing the stairs to her room, the thirty-four-year-old Katherine suffered from a massive hemorrhage and died.

When John failed to pay for the funeral expenses, Katherine's remains ended up in a pauper's grave. Six years later, after a family member visited the cemetery, she contacted Harold Beauchamp who arranged for a more fitting final resting place. John had his Tig's tombstone inscribed with one of her favorite quotations from Shakespeare's *Henry IV*, "But I tell you, my lord fool, out of this nettle, danger, we pluck. This flower, safety."

After Katherine's passing, John published every scrap of his late wife's writing—partially to enshrine her in a literary stained glass window, but also partially for financial reasons. A critic claimed he was "boiling Katherine's bones to make soup." For his perceived exploitation of his wife, her fans bared their teeth. Bertrand Russell pronounced him "beastly." D. H. Lawrence, seemingly oblivious of his earlier attacks on Katherine, called Murry a coward, an obscene bug, and a mud-worm. Virginia Woolf's take was that John was a "posturing Byronic little man."

**Katherine Mansfield House and Garden:** The writer's life proved that you could take the girl out of Wellington, but you could not take Wellington out of the girl. In "The Garden Party" and "The Doll's House," Katherine skewered the pretensions and cruelty of New Zealand's gentry. The author recalled the house as "that awful cubbyhole" and "that horrid little piggy house which was really dreadful."

In 1888, Harold Beauchamp built the home that housed his family, including his mother-in-law, Margaret, and his sisters-in-law, Kitty and Belle. The Katherine Mansfield Birthplace Society arranged for a restoration of the property on Tinakori Road. The organization acquired original furnishings and possessions and retained authentic features such as the bamboo-style staircase banister. Based on fragments of wallpaper, reproductions cover the walls. The chinoiserie-patterned wallpaper in the stairwell features an ancient symbol for good luck. The society purchased furniture to replicate the Beauchamps' nineteenth-century décor.

Upon arrival, a staff member explains the background of the house and its famous former occupant. Each room contains a display that provides additional information, alongside Mansfield quotations. The second floor has an extensive timeline of the author's life juxtaposed with her photographs. A reading corner is available where guests can sit and peruse Mansfield works.

The upper level also holds the children's bedrooms, where four antique dolls are on display. A hairbrush and a hand mirror sit on a dresser. One special artifact is a replica of the dollhouse from the classic Mansfield story. The dollhouse is spinach green with yellow windowpanes and a red roof. Inside is a miniscule amber lamp.

The museum includes interactive elements such as an example of the same model typewriter that the writer used. For those young enough to have never used a manual typing machine, they are welcome to try it out. A station provides tips for writing—advice gleaned from Katherine's letters. Space is also allocated to local artists.

Docents lead visitors to the scullery, furnished with steel pots, a meat grinder, and a wood shelf that holds a chalkboard, preserved fruit in jars, white canisters, and teacups. In the more formal kitchen, floral plates sit on a sideboard. The dining room has blue walls, a wooden table, and a cabinet that holds the good china. The green-painted drawing room holds a brown piano on which rests a display case with a bird inside—an apt metaphor for the home's famous daughter.

On the second floor is the Laurel Harris Room, a chamber devoted to an extensive timeline of Katherine's life with accompanying photographs. One jarring photo is of Granny Dyer holding the deceased baby Gwendoline, dressed as if she were alive, as was often customary for bereaved families in the early days of photography. The subtitle of the exhibit reads in red letters: "A Voyage Through Life, Loves, Literature..." On the next wall, under an oval portrait of the author as a young woman, is a quotation from a 1906 letter Katherine wrote to her cousin, Sylvia Payne, "Would you not like to try all sorts of lives—one is so very small—but that is the satisfaction of writing—one can impersonate so many people."

The front garden features the flowers Katherine mentioned in her stories: pot marigolds, cinerarias, and roses. The back garden holds indigenous shrubs and trees.

A quotation from Southern writer William Faulkner pertains to the life of the New Zealand author: "The past is never dead. It's not even past."

**Seen from Her Window:** In her final days, Katherine wrote of what she desired when she gazed from her window, "I want a garden, a small house, grass, animals, books..."

# CHAPTER 11

## *Beautiful*

*"Poetry elevates the mind to Heaven."*

**—ELIZABETH BARRETT BROWNING**

◇◇◇◇◇◇◇◇◇◇

### Casa Guidi

opened 1995 | Florence, Italy

An immortal sonnet begins, "How do I love thee? Let me count the ways." Elizabeth Barrett Browning's *grande amore* was her husband, Robert, and their Florentine home. To tread the halls of the literary couple, take a gondola ride to Casa Guidi.

When recalling the Victorian writer, most people envision Elizabeth as a princess locked in a tower until her rescue by her poet-prince, but she was far more. Elizabeth was born in 1806, the first of Mary and Edward Moulton-Barrett's twelve children. In a family fond of nicknames, Elizabeth was Ba, her sister was Addles, and her aunt was Bummy.

The Barretts' home, which bore the unsettling name Hope End, was a five-hundred-acre estate in Herefordshire that showcased their Moorish-style mansion, replete with minarets. The source of their lavish lifestyle was a Jamaican sugar plantation that made its profits on slave labor. Elizabeth later confided to art critic John Ruskin, "I belong to a family of West Indian slaveholders, and if I believe in curses, I should be afraid." Ensconced in a cocoon of childhood innocence, Elizabeth rode her pony, tended her white roses, and arranged theatrical productions with her siblings. Her teenage aspirations were to be the greatest female poet, liberate Greece from the Ottoman Empire, and have Lord Byron succumb to her charms. Edward proclaimed his daughter, "the Poet Laureate of Hope End" and he published fifty copies of her verses. She dedicated her poems to her adored father.

With the demise of slavery in the Caribbean, Edward's financial reversal led to the family's loss of Hope End, and the Barretts relocated to 50 Wimpole Street, in London. The ever more controlling Edward informed his children that he would disown them if they ever married. One theory concerning his bizarre request was his fear that an ancestor had fathered a baby with a Jamaican slave, and a dark-skinned child would make this manifestly evident.

When Elizabeth was fifteen, she, along with her sisters Henrietta, Arabella, and Mary, came down with an undisclosed illness, followed by a bout of measles. Elizabeth, the only sister who did not recover, suffered from muscular spasms and wore a spinal sling for nine months. She likened her symptoms to a cord tied around her stomach "which seems to break." Her medical treatment included opium, leading to a lifelong addiction. Due to her health issues and her overprotective father, Elizabeth seldom left the chaise lounge she shared with Flush, her cocker spaniel. Her canine companion was the subject of her poem, "To Flush, My Dog," as well as Virginia Woolf's *Flush: A Biography*. On no fewer than three occasions, the Barretts paid a ransom to thieves who had abducted their cherished pet.

John Kenyon, a distant cousin, popularized Elizabeth's writing, and her devotees included Victorian giants William Wordsworth, Samuel Taylor Coleridge, Alfred, Lord Tennyson, Thomas Carlyle, George Eliot, and Hans Christian Andersen. Although a stranger to romance, Elizabeth wrote of it in "A Woman's Shortcomings" with the poetic warning, "Unless you can die when the dream is past / Oh, never call it loving."

In 1844, Elizabeth published "Poems," an event that led to her nomination for poet laureate. Due to gender, the award of poet laureate went instead to Alfred, Lord Tennyson. England took another century and a half to appoint a female recipient. A feminist in a patriarchal society, Elizabeth detested the concept that women needed protection. In "An Essay on Women," the poet pondered, "Are vases only prized because they break?" Unlike her female contemporaries, Elizabeth published her volumes under her own name rather than a male pseudonym. Her innovative style impacted literary history, and the poet influenced writers Virginia Woolf, Oscar Wilde, and Rudyard Kipling. Her fame extended across the ocean to Amherst, Massachusetts, where fellow reclusive poet Emily Dickinson

*Poet of "Sonnets of the Portuguese" |*
*Wikimedia Commons,*
*Photographer: Unknown*

*Casa Guidi: Florence Home of the*
*Brownings | Wikimedia Commons, Sailko*

kept a framed portrait of Elizabeth in her bedroom. Emily said that her life "had been transfigured by the poetry of that Foreign Lady." Edgar Allan Poe dedicated "The Raven" to Elizabeth and wrote, "Her poetic inspiration is the highest—we can conceive of nothing more august." Harriet Beecher Stowe and Nathaniel Hawthorne travelled to Italy to meet the esteemed lady of letters.

At age thirty-four, Elizabeth lost her brother Samuel through a fever he had contracted at Cinnamon Hill, the family's Jamaican estate. To assuage her grief, to seek a cure for her illness, and to find a reprieve from Wimpole Street, a context she described as "the straitness of my prison," Elizabeth departed for the seaside town of Torquay in Devon, England. Her favorite brother, Edward, "Bro," accompanied her; the trip became a tragedy when Edward died in a sailing accident. Elizabeth remained in Devon for a year, where the sound of the waves reminded her of the "moan of a dying man."

Life forever changed when Robert Browning sent Elizabeth a fan letter declaring, "I love your verses with all my heart, dear Miss Barrett." Elizabeth's cousin, John Kenyon, doubled as Cupid when he arranged Robert's invitation to 50 Wimpole Street. Initially, Elizabeth put a brake on her heart as she could not understand how a man six years her junior could have feelings for a reclusive, thirty-nine-year-old, opium-addicted invalid. Nevertheless, a clandestine twenty-month courtship—to which her spaniel Flush was privy  followed, during which the couple exchanged 574 letters. In her poem, "First Time He Kissed Me," Elizabeth expressed her elation: "A ring of amethyst I could not wear here, plainer to my sight / Then that first kiss." For the only time in three decades, Elizabeth left her house; the eloping couple wed in a secret ceremony at St. Marylebone Church. Following in the footsteps of his hero, Percy Bysshe Shelley, Robert brought his bride to Italy, where he hoped the temperate weather would do more for her health than England's damp climate. The one blight on her happiness was that her father never forgave her. After Edward's death, among his effects were the letters from his disowned daughter—unopened.

When they arrived in Florence in 1847, the couple were enamored with its sublime beauty; Elizabeth described it as the "most beautiful of cities devised by man." They found their forever home in the fifteenth-century Palazzo Guidi—so named after its seventeenth-century owner, Count Camillo Guidi. Elizabeth rechristened it as the more personal Casa Guidi. She expressed her elation, "I am very happy—happier and happier." What made her even more ecstatic was that despite her illness, opium addiction, and miscarriages, at age forty-three, she gave birth to Robert Wiederman Barrett Browning, nicknamed Pen. Their rent included free admission to the nearby ducal Palazzo Pitti, where they strolled the bucolic gardens with their son. To the chagrin of her husband, Elizabeth dressed Pen in the fashion of a Renaissance prince, with velvet pants, embroidered blouses, and a wide-brimmed hat from which his long curls peeked through.

**Casa Guidi:** Visitors to this literary landmark can view the eight-room home with its high ceilings, now filled with reproductions of Victorian furnishings. The drawing room has seafoam green walls and heavy red curtains that cover tall windows, its colors in keeping with the Italian flag. On the top of the bookcase stand terracotta busts of Robert and Elizabeth. On the Brownings' first wedding anniversary, they watched from their balcony as 40,000 people paraded past their window in a political demonstration for the *Risorgimento*, the movement for Italian unification. The spectacle inspired Elizabeth's "Casa Guidi Windows," an impassioned plea for liberty. The poem became the country's anthem, and Italians viewed her as the poet of the Risorgimento. At their home, Robert and Elizabeth entertained fellow expatriates Anthony Trollope, John Ruskin, and Walter Savage Landor.

Casa Guidi was both the home where the Brownings' son Pen entered the world and where Elizabeth breathed her last. On the day of her funeral, the Via Maggio—the shopping district on the Brownings' street—was shut down. Mourners carried her coffin to the Protestant Cemetery of Florence, known as the English cemetery. Lord Frederic Leighton, the famous British artist, designed her marble tomb that rests on six pillars. Robert and twelve-year-old Pen left Italy, never to return. Before his departure, Robert commissioned George Mignaty to capture Casa Guidi on a canvas in memory of his fourteen-year sojourn.

Pen Browning eventually repurchased Casa Guidi and did his utmost to recover every relic that had once graced his childhood home. He became an artist, a pupil of Rodin, and yet never achieved his parents' acclaim. He ran up debts (which his father paid) and ran through his wife's money. Papa Robert's last words were of his adored son, "Oh, my dear boy, my dear boy."

On the exterior of Casa Guidi, a plaque is inscribed to "Elisabetta Barrett Browning / Who in her woman's heart reconciled / a scholar's learning and a poet's spirit / And whose poems forged a golden ring / between Italy and England," placed there in 1861 by "a grateful Florence." In her last moments, Robert held his beloved in his arms. Her final word: "Beautiful."

**Seen from Her Window:** When Roman soldiers founded Florence around 60 BC, they called it Florentina, which means "May she flourish." As Elizabeth gazed upon her adopted city, the name took on symbolic overtones, as she blossomed when removed from the confines of 50 Walpole Street.

# CHAPTER 12

# La Dame aux Camelias

*"We are the breakers of our own hearts."*

**—EUDORA WELTY**

◇◇◇◇◇◇◇◇◇

## Eudora Welty House & Garden

opened 2006 | Jackson, Mississippi

Although her home was where Eudora Alice Welty did her writing, it never
went by a literary name, as did Virginia Woolf's Monk's House, Louisa May
Alcott's Orchard House, or Jane Austen's Chawton House. Eudora referred to her
residence as "Tudor style with some timbering, you know, à la Shakespeare." To
learn about this literary landmark, set your compass to the Eudora Welty House
and Garden.

Along with contemporary writers such as Flannery O'Connor, William
Faulkner, Carson McCullers, and Tennessee Williams, Eudora shaped the
Southern Literary Renaissance. Eudora was the daughter of Methodist parents
Christian Webb Welty, a successful insurance executive, and Chestina Welty,
a teacher before marriage. The couple was thrilled with the birth of their son
Christian. But when the baby was fifteen months old, he and his mother became
ill. Chestina suffered from septicemia, a condition that resulted in the loss of her
long hair. Her husband placed the locks in a bag in a bureau drawer. Chestina
survived; her son did not. Before his burial, his grieving mother removed the two
polished buffalo nickels that covered his eyes and placed them in a cardboard box.

Joy followed loss with the 1909 arrival of Eudora.

In addition to a childhood enveloped in love, Eudora grew up within a milieu of books. Eudora later recalled the exhilaration of when she first fell under the spell of the written word, "It had been startling and disappointing to me to find out that storybooks had been written by *people*, that books were not natural wonders." A ritual, what she referred to as "a sweet devouring," was checking out books at the Jackson Public Library. Two things irked Eudora: The librarian, Mrs. Calloway, only allowed patrons to check out two books at a time, and they could not be returned the same day. Several decades later, the library bore the name of Eudora Welty. On Sundays, her father took her to his office, where she was allowed to use his typewriter. She reminisced, "It used to be wonderful to be in Daddy's office. That's where I fell in love with the typewriter." Young Eudora was in time joined by brothers Edward Jefferson and Walter Andrews Welty, and parents Christian and Chestina instilled the values of the New Testament in their children.

One day, Eudora discovered a cardboard box on her mother's bureau and from it removed the strands of russet-colored locks that reminded her of Rapunzel, a favorite fairy tale. In another box she found two buffalo head nickels, and she asked her mother if she could spend the coins. Chestina explained her refusal by telling her daughter about the baby brother who had died before she was born. The episode made a lasting impression on Eudora that would later infuse her stories: objects carried messages of love, loss, and the power of the past on the present.

Eudora attended the Mississippi State College for Women in Columbus, Mississippi—the first state college in the country to admit females, as well as one that required students to attend chapel. One student extracurricular activity was starting a literary magazine. She ended up obtaining her bachelor's degree in English at the University of Wisconsin in Madison, Wisconsin. Hell-bent on making her living as a writer, she never theless took her father's advice to pursue a practical career. She enrolled in an advertising/secretarial program at the Columbia University School of Business in New York, although it was a field that did not speak to her soul. Mrs. Welty, an avid gardener, sent Eudora boxes of camellias by train to Manhattan. Eventually, New York exerted a magnetic pull, and Eudora decided to remain after graduation. Fate, however, had other plans. She hurried back to Jackson when she heard her father was dying of leukemia. In the hospital, Eudora watched as her mother lay on a cot beside her husband, with a tube running from her arm to his as the doctors performed a blood transfusion. Christian passed away in September of 1931.

Eudora turned to writing to chronicle her truth: "My continuing passion was not to point the finger in judgment but to part a curtain, that invisible shadow that falls between people." In 1936, a magazine named *Manuscript* published her first short story, "Death of a Traveling Salesman," which recounted the last day of a lonely man taken in by two hillbillies in rural Mississippi. The year 1941 marked the release of a compilation of her short stories with an introduction by Katherine Anne Porter, author of *Ship of Fools*. Eudora's fictional world revolved around the historic forces that had shaped the South. The landscape of her birth dictated that yesterday shadowed the present. She once remarked that General Sherman had burned Jackson three times.

In 1936, Eudora obtained a position at President Franklin D. Roosevelt's Works Progress Administration that entailed travel throughout the Deep South. Distraught by the abject poverty she witnessed firsthand, she took photographs that she developed in her kitchen. The unstaged shots captured unemployed men slumped on park benches. Random House published her pictures as *One Time, One Place: Mississippi in the Depression.*

Gravitating to fellow writers, Eudora befriended Katherine Anne Porter, Elizabeth Bowen, and Robert Penn Warren. An enduring bond developed with her literary agent, Diarmuid Russell. An adherent of Southern hospitality, Eudora rarely turned down interviewers who enjoyed bourbon and a homecooked meal. However, when Henry Miller—with whom she shared a publisher—arrived in Jackson, Chestina refused to let him visit as she had heard that he wrote pornography. For the duration of his stay, Eudora drove him around in her family's Chevrolet, although she brought along chaperones in case he acted like one of his sex fiends in *The Tropic of Capricorn.* Eudora pronounced Henry the

*Eudora lived in her home for over seven decades* | Wikipedia Artist Tom Beck

dullest man she had ever met, one who "wasn't interested in anything outside himself." (In contrast, Eudora deeply disliked occasions when the conversation revolved around her.) As much as she did not care for Henry, she revered William Faulkner and was ecstatic when she received a letter from him in which he complimented her writing: "You're doing all right." Ecstatic at receiving a letter from Faulkner, Eudora sent it to a friend in Oxford. Later, the "friend" sold the letter to the University of Virginia for a "horrendous sum." The university sent Eudora a carbon copy. She framed another treasured letter, this one from writer E. M. Forster, and hung it in an upstairs room, later relocating it to the ground-floor sitting room. Eudora shunned public accolades, as evidenced at an appearance in 1990. At the podium of the Folger Theatre in Washington, DC, when 220 fans and fellow authors erupted into thunderous applause, she said, "Never happened to me before. I'm used to being last on the program because my name begins with a W."

During World War II, Eudora worked for *The New York Times Book Review*, contributing articles under the pseudonym Michael Ravenna, as the public felt ladies were not capable of serious commentary. She returned home to nurse her mother, who had lost both her husband and her younger son, Walter. One source of solace was her garden, which Eudora had embellished with an ornamental bench. In 1966, Eudora first lost her mother to illness, and then a few days later, her brother Edward, who died from injuries sustained in a fall.

In 1973, Eudora received a phone call from Frank Hains at the *Daily News*, who asked her, "How does it feel?" She was perplexed until she glanced out her window, where she saw two men approaching her door. Eudora had won the Pulitzer Prize for *The Optimist's Daughter*.

Though fortunate in her choice of friends, she was less lucky in the romantic arena. She had a decade-long friendship and relationship with John Robinson. He cared for her but often sent her mixed messages. The fly in the romantic ointment was when she discovered he was living with another man in Italy.

Another romance also came with a rub. In 1973, the Mississippi Arts Festival declared a Eudora Welty Day and asked the author to provide a guest list for her out-of-town friends. An acceptance arrived from author Kenneth Millar, who wrote under the pseudonym of Ross MacDonald. The two met after the deaths of Eudora's mother and brother and Kenneth's loss of his only child, Linda. In 1971, when Eudora was staying at the Algonquin Hotel in New York City and Kenneth had an adjoining room, he took her to a cocktail party his publisher, Alfred Knopf, threw in his honor. When he left, Kenneth sent Eudora a postcard that had a photograph of the Kissing Bridge in West Montrose, Ontario. On the other side was the message, "Treasuring fond memories of New York and you."

Despite their love, Ken never divorced his wife, Margaret. By 1980, Kenneth had developed Alzheimer's disease; Eudora wrote to him, "You're dear in every way to me, and I think of you in such concern and love." After his 1983 passing, Eudora attempted to write a story about the love triangle, but she admitted it was a tale she "could not and would not finish." Whether or not their love was consummated on the physical plane is a truth lost in the miasma of the Southern night, but passion there was. Kenneth told Reynolds Price, "You love Eudora as a friend. I love her as a woman." When asked about her single status, Eudora's response, "Marriage never came up." Even the buffalo nickels had not hinted at how tangled life could be.

As much as Eudora preferred staying out of the public eye, irate Northerners called in the middle of the night berating her for refusing to write about her region's rampant racism. Her counter was that authors were not required to preach from a political pulpit. However, when she felt strongly about an injustice, she used her pen to puncture the poison. When Byron De La Beckwith shot Black civil rights leader Medgar Evers in Jackson, on the night of the assassination, she began her story "Where is the Voice Coming From?" in which she explored the mind of a bigoted psychopath. She sent it to William Maxwell, the editor at the *New Yorker*. With the arrest of Beckwith, to avoid a libel suit, Eudora and the editors changed some details. Following publication, a journalist called Eudora and asked if anyone had burned a cross on her lawn. Her rejoinder, "The people who burn crosses on lawns don't read me in the *New Yorker*."

In recognition of her contribution to literature, accolades poured in. In 1962, Eudora presented fellow Mississippi writer William Faulkner with the Gold Medal for Fiction. Another Mississippi recipient was Tennessee Williams, who won it for drama. Her friend Katherine Anne Porter shared the same honor. In 1972, President Nixon appointed Eudora to the National Council for the Arts. Eight years later, President Jimmy Carter—whom she referred to as "one of my great Southern heroes"—awarded the grande dame of American letters the Presidential Medal of Freedom. The accompanying accolade stated that her fiction "illuminates the human condition," while her essays "explore mind and heart, literary and oral tradition." Ms. Welty collected awards just as Imelda Marcos collected shoes: Honorary ones arrived from Harvard and Yale. She was also the recipient of the Pulitzer Prize and France's Légion d'Honneur.

**Eudora Welty House and Garden:** Eudora observed, "A place that was ever lived in is like a fire that never goes out." Her words show her fealty to the Tudor-style home where she lived from age sixteen until her death at age ninety-two. In 1986, the author deeded her residence to the Eudora Welty Foundation, thus saving the organization from having to restore the structure to its historic condition. The Foundation's brochure refers to the residence as "one of the nation's most intact literary house museums." While many writers' residences' have a stuffy atmosphere, replete with ropes and hospital corner sheets on beds, the Welty home seems as if she has just stepped out to the Mayflower Café for a plate of fried catfish and butter beans.

Books are found in every room, on shelves, on her walnut dining room table, and even on stairs and couches. A charred set of Charles Dickens' novels carries a history: they had been a gift from Eudora's maternal grandfather, and Chestina had once rushed back into her burning home to rescue them from the flames. Bric-a-brac abounds, such as a gaudy bust of Shakespeare on the mantel. In her self-effacing way, Eudora kept her many awards in a cardboard box in an upstairs closet. Currently, they are found in the house next door that serves as the visitor center. Also on display are various literary awards, including her Pulitzer Prize.

Guests might experience a sense of déjà vu as some of the objects made their way into her work, such as the desk from *The Optimist's Daughter*; it may now be seen in her second-floor bedroom, one that was off bounds to visitors. At her desk, situated near a window, the author tapped away on her typewriter. (Those touring the home are permitted to try tapping some keys in the next-door visitor center; it is not an original model.) On her bureau rest perfume bottles, a jewelry box, and a comb. A wooden plaque reads: Eudora's Room.

The museum holds items that were near and dear to the author's heart; for example, her adored father's gold pocket watch and telescope, a favorite book from her childhood, the typewriter she took to Europe, and an RCA Victor vinyl album. An exhibit showcases photographs and news items of Medgar Evers detailing how his assassination helped fuel the Civil Rights Movement. The case displays a vintage watering can, tools, photos, and objects related to the cultivation of flowers.

If the house was Eudora's heart, her garden was her soul. When her night-blooming cereus yielded a flower, to partake of its beauty, Eudora threw a party that lasted from dusk to dawn. The Mississippi Department of Archives and History undertook the restoration of the gardens. They've recreated Chessie's trellises and arbors so visitors can enjoy what brought mother and daughter both joy and solace.

Eudora's attachment to her home can be understood with her words, "One place understood helps us understand all places." The Eudora Welty House & Garden provides insight into the South's own *Dame aux Camélias*.

**Seen from Her Window:** From her window, Eudora saw the oak tree her mother had planted. On the opposite side of the street was Belhaven College. Wafted on the southern breeze, music from the college students blended with the clack of Eudora's typewriter.

# CHAPTER 13

# A Grand Thing

*"Surely for everything you love,*
*you have to pay some price."*

## —AGATHA CHRISTIE

◇◇◇◇◇◇◇◇◇◇

## Greenway House

### opened 2009 | Devon, England

Agatha Christie's home is a mystery no more. Greenway, her pastoral retreat situated on a bluff overlooking the River Dart, is now part of Britain's National Trust. Gazing upon the meadows with their grazing sheep, visitors are astounded at how the estate's chatelaine birthed macabre ends for her cast of characters. The Queen of Crime's Greenway is as great a pilgrimage for literary fans as the King of Rock and Roll's Graceland is for the music mad.

Since the nineteenth century, Sir Arthur Conan Doyle's Sherlock Holmes has ruled the mystery novel roost. The advent of Dame Christie's spinster-sleuth, Miss Jane Marple, showed females also possessed the chops to be first-rate detectives. What remains an enigma is how Dame Agatha, who spent so much of her life in small English villages, was able to portray not only diabolical crimes but sleuths capable of shining a light through even the most tangled webs of criminal deceit.

The writer slated to become the Duchess of Death was born Agatha Mary Clarissa Miller in 1890; her home was Ashfield, the Miller mansion in the English seaside town of Torquay, Devon. Her father, Frederick Miller, an American with a trust fund, lived an indolent lifestyle that involved playing whist at Torquay's

Gentlemen's Club. Her mother, Clara, instilled a love of reading in her children, Louis Montant (Monty), Madge, and Agatha. Agatha reminisced, "One of the luckiest things that can happen to you in life is to have had a happy childhood." The bubble of contentment burst after investments went south, leaving the Millers with far less expendable income. When Agatha was eleven, her father Frederick passed away from pneumonia at age fifty-five.

In a boarding school in Paris, Agatha aspired to a professional life as a pianist, but excruciating shyness precluded a career on the stage. In a nod to her early creativity, she composed a piano waltz, "One Hour with Thee." In 1910, mother and daughter left for Cairo, at the time a European watering hole for husband hunting. Back in Britain, the teenaged beauty basked in three marriage proposals. At a gathering at Ugbrooke House, the belle of Torquay set her sights on the handsome Archibald ("Archie") Christie of the Royal Flying Corps. With the outbreak of World War I, he left for France; during a leave, Archie and Agatha married on Christmas Eve, 1914.

While her husband was overseas, Agatha volunteered at a Red Cross hospital dispensary; during breaks, she filled her notebook with stories and specifics on pharmaceutical prescriptions that doubled as agents of death. The experience led to *The Mysterious Affair at Styles*, whose dedication page bore the tribute, "To my Mother." By the time her book appeared, Agatha was busy with her baby, Rosalind, named after Shakespeare's heroine in *As You Like It*. Archie was busy playing golf. In 1922, Archie's job required a ten-month tour to strengthen trade relations between Britain and her colonies. Agatha accompanied him, leaving Rosalind with Clara. Upon their return, they settled in a twelve-bedroom house they named Styles, after Agatha's debut novel. A second book, *The Murder on the Links,* followed that bore the dedication: *"To My Husband.* A fellow enthusiast

*Greenway House, Agatha Christie's Vacation Retreat  |*
*Wikipedia Manhattan Research Inc.*

for detective stories and to whom I am indebted for much helpful advice and criticism."

As her literary star ascended, Agatha's life plummeted. Agatha's brother Monty failed at every quick money scheme he tried; unable to support himself, he returned to Ashfield. For entertainment, he fired bullets from his bedroom window. After shooting his pistol at one of his mother's friends, he explained to Agatha, "Some silly old spinster going down the drive with her behind wobbling. Couldn't resist it." To preserve their mother's sanity, Madge (who had married into wealth) and Agatha (affluent from her books) bought their brother a cottage named The Crossways and hired one Mrs. Taylor as his caregiver. As Agatha remarked, the "£800 for the Dartmoor bungalow was a cheap price for Madge and me to have paid." Matters further deteriorated in 1926, her *annus horribilis*. Clara, who suffered an agonizing end due to heart disease, passed away. Then Agatha discovered why Archie was always playing golf: he had fallen for a younger woman, fellow golf enthusiast Nancy Neele. The revelation might have made her want to include Archie in *Murder on the Links*.

There is only one "cold case" in the Agatha Christie canon; in 1926, Agatha became the original gone girl. The evening after Archie dropped the infidelity bombshell that shattered his wife, a despondent Agatha left Styles in the beloved green Morris Cowley roadster she had purchased with earnings from her novels. She left behind eleven-year-old Rosaline, as well as her terrier Peter. The following morning, the abandoned car lay near a body of water called "the Silent Pool"—a setting she had made use of in a novel. Her fur coat was on the seat; there was no trace of Agatha. A tabloid frenzy ensued, and police were joined by between 10,000 and 15,000 people, as well as bloodhounds and Peter, in the search. Sir Arthur Conan Doyle employed an occultist to help. The public's consensus was amnesia, suicide, or murder. When questioned as to whether he was seeing another woman, Colonel Christie stated, "My wife has never made the slightest objections to any of my friends."

The lady who vanished just as suddenly reappeared. Eleven days later, two members of a band from the Swan Hydropathic Hotel in Harrogate, Yorkshire, informed the police that a guest bore a striking similarity to the missing celebrity writer. She had registered under the name Teresa and the surname of the other woman, Neele. When Archie burst into the Swan, Agatha remarked, "Fancy, my brother has just arrived." The author refused to discuss the bizarre chapter. As she had once observed, "So, after illness, came sorrow, despair, and heartbreak. There is no need to dwell on it." Motives ascribed to her actions range from a publicity stunt to a fugue state caused by a concussion from the car crash to a nervous breakdown.

Their divorce two years later left Agatha at loose ends. Archie had two sons with his second wife; Rosalind rarely saw her father and never met her stepbrothers. During a dinner party, Agatha met a man who told her of his travels on the Orient Express. Although ladies of the era did not travel alone, Agatha booked her berth. Mutual friends Leonard and Katherine Wooley introduced Agatha to archaeologist Max Mallowan at a dig site near the pyramids. When their relationship took a romantic turn, Max said he hoped she would not be put off with his pursuit of a career centered on the study of crypts and burial grounds. The master of the murder mystery assured him, "I adore corpses and stiffs." Max and Agatha married six months later; their residence was the Winterbrook House in Oxfordshire. Her marriage to an archaeologist led to her quip, "An archaeologist is an ideal husband because the older you are, the more interested he is." Agatha refused a damehood so as not to outshine Max; however, when he became a knight, she became Dame Commander of the Order of the British Empire. There was however a fly in the marital home: Agatha's strained relationship with Rosaline, who felt her mother had paid more allegiance to her father, her stepfather, writing, and travel than to her. When asked about

Max, Rosaline offered, "He didn't beat me." In contrast, Agatha shared a loving bond with her grandson, Matthew Prichard, whom she took for drives in her Rolls Royce.

In 1971, Agatha was hospitalized with a broken hip. She spent her last Christmas at Greenway, the home closest to her heart. Only Shakespeare and the Bible have sold more copies than Dame Agatha Christie.

**Greenway House:** The estate where Agatha Christie dreamed up deadly deeds was the eighteenth-century Greenway House, nestled in a woodland garden with a view of the River Dart. She described her retreat as "the loveliest place in the world." Mrs. Mallowan, the name the villagers called her, vacationed in Devon with her family, where they played croquet and the chatelaine read aloud her latest mysteries. Greenway served as Agatha's muse, and she featured its boathouse in *Dead Man's Folly*.

The dominant feature of the morning room is a portrait of the author at age four holding her doll, Rosie, entitled *Lost in Reverie*. The actual Rosie—who hailed from France—sits under the portrait. Walking through the drawing room allows visitors to see items Agatha brought from Ashfield. Holding pride of place is a Steinway piano fashioned in the late 1800s. Agatha's bedroom has sweeping views of the River Dart and showcases a mother-of-pearl inlaid chest, a souvenir from Damascus. The library holds five thousand books and a frieze of history. During World War II, the British admiralty requisitioned Greenway; the United States Coast Guards stayed there until the D-Day invasion. Lt. Marshall Lee painted twelve murals on the library's cream-colored walls depicting World War II battles. Before their departure, the officer in charge offered to paint over it, but Max and Agatha decided to keep the historic memorial. However, Agatha did request they remove the fourteen latrines. The bathtub was where the author relaxed with a book and ate apples.

The collection of fascinating objects makes the house truly a museum. One startling piece is a skull-shaped tobacco jar with a ceramic frog on top of its lid, a memento from their archaeological travels. Agatha and Max brought home ancient artifacts such as ceramic pieces discovered in a buried temple at Tell Brak dating from 3500 BC.

One of Greenway's draws is that it is a repository of Agatha's youthful memories. She first become enamored with the estate when she saw it as a child, as it is situated fifteen miles from Ashfield. After she sold her family house, she brought its most cherished items to Greenway. While in its confines, the mansion served as a Proustian madeleine and conjured William Shakespeare's quotation from *Richard III*, "O, call back yesterday/Bid time return."

**Seen from Her Window:** Looking out of Greenway, Christie would have seen a clay tablet with cuneiform writing, unearthed by Max in West Asia, that is set on the outside wall.

# CHAPTER 14

# Still Somewhere

*"Sorrow lies like a heartbeat behind everything*
*I have written."*

**—P. L. TRAVERS**

◇◇◇◇◇◇◇◇◇◇

## The Story Bank

opened in 2019 | Maryborough, Queensland, Australia

If the east wind blows you into the town of Maryborough, visit the Story Bank to partake of heaping spoonfuls of sugar. The museum was the birthplace of P. L. Travers, the Australian-born creator of British nanny Mary Poppins.

Most people begin their lives in hospitals or homes, but this woman was not like most people. Originally named Helen Lyndon Goff (although she went by Pamela), she was born in 1899 on the second floor of the Australian Joint Stock Bank in Maryborough. The family's residence was a perk granted to her father, Travers Goff, for his position as bank manager. Dad and daughter shared a love of stories, though Travers was tightfisted with praise. A youthful Pamela penned a poem to which he responded, "Hardly Mr. Yeats." Her mother, Margaret, was related to a former premier of Queensland.

Unfulfilled and miserable as a banker, Travers sought solace in the bottle. Alcoholism led to his demotion to clerk and the loss of his residence. His death when Pamela was seven left her with a lingering trauma. Reminiscing about her childhood, she recalled, "I was his favorite child, and he was my beloved father. I brought him along with me all through my life." After her husband's passing, Margaret ran out of their house during a thunderstorm, threatening

*Bronze bust of P. L. Travers |*
*Wikimedia Commons, 14GTR*

to drown herself in the nearby river. For the sake of her two younger sisters, Pamela distracted them with the story of a flying white horse whose hooves pounded on their tin roof. Bereft of spouse and support, Margaret moved with her daughters to Bowral, New South Wales, the home of her maternal great-aunt, Helen Morehead, whom the children called Aunt Ellie. Helen Morehead served as the role model for Mary Poppins, as evidenced by her parrot-head umbrella, carpet bag, and oft-repeated phrase, "Spit, spot."

Lacking funds for university, Pamela worked as a secretary in a cashier's office till she quit to become an actress. She toured Australia with a Shakespearean company under the name Pamela Lyndon Travers. Due to her family's disapproval of her earning her livelihood on stage, and taking an opportunity to reinvent herself, she departed for England. Her altered autobiography held that her Irish-born father owned a sugar field plantation where she had grown up near the Great Barrier Reef. The former Helen Lyndon Goff, unlike the biblical Lot's wife, determined not to look back.

To support herself, Pamela contributed poems to the literary periodical *The Irish Statesman*, through which she met William Butler Yeats. With characteristic chutzpah, during a rainstorm in Dublin, Pamela gathered rowan bush branches from the Isle of Innisfree that she then presented to the poet. In return, Yeats showed her his canary's eggs. Her editor introduced Pamela to Madge, the daughter of Sir Francis Burnand, a playwright and former editor of *Punch*. In a seemingly romantic relationship, the women lived first in a London apartment, then in a nine-hundred-year-old thatched cottage mentioned in the *Domesday Book*. A revealing photograph taken by Madge while they were on a vacation shows Pamela on an Italian beach wearing only a floppy hat and shorts.

In 1934, Pamela was in her Sussex cottage when Mary Poppins, a character in search of an author, made her appearance: a nanny nonpareil. She delighted her young charges by sliding up banisters, taking tea on the ceiling, and pasting gold

**Birthplace of P. L. Travers** | *Wikimedia Commons, Heritage Branch Staff*

stars in the night sky. Her real purpose, however, was to fix the fractured Banks family. Decades later, Pamela elaborated, "I think the idea of Mary Poppins has been blowing in and out of me, like a curtain at a window, all my life." Unable to save her father, Pamela redeemed his fictional counterpart. Mr. Banks received his name after Travers' job as a banker.

Written under the pen name P. L. Travers, *Mary Poppins* sold millions of copies, with translations in twenty languages, including Swahili. Interestingly, her editor was Peter Llewelyn, the namesake of James M. Barrie's *Peter Pan*. After E. H. Shepard, the illustrator of *Winnie the Pooh*, turned down her request for collaboration, his daughter, Mary, supplied the drawings. Pamela's likeness appeared once in each of the six books of the series.

Ironically, while Mary Poppins was a child's dream nanny, Pamela's prickly personality would have inspired youngsters to play hide, without the seek. Setting her sights on motherhood, Pamela offered to adopt her teenaged maid. Despite Pamela's argument that the girl's parents had more than enough children and were without the means to support them, they demurred. On a visit to Ireland, Pamela heard about Joseph and Vera Hone, living with their four grandchildren in straitened circumstances. When Pamela held out an offer of adoption, the Hones thought the wealthy writer, author of the world's most nurturing nanny, the answer to their prayers. They proposed she take their six-month-old twins,

Camillus and Anthony. In a twist on the prayer, Pamela said she only wanted one. On the advice of her astrologer, and because she preferred his name over Anthony's, Pamela settled on Camillus. At her fictional No. 17 Cherry Tree Lane, medicine tasted like candy, but that was not the case in Pamela's upscale Chelsea home. Although life consisted of vacations on the French Riviera, time with Mama Travers was not a "jolly holiday." She was appalled when Camillus cried at night, and misbehavior resulted in the threat of the orphanage at Tunbridge Wells.

To escape the Blitz, mother and son left for the American Southwest, where they lived among the Navajos. The eccentric author took to wearing scarves, flouncy skirts, and armloads of silver bangles. Among her romantic relationships with both men and women, she fell for the Irish Francis MacNamara, father of Caitlin, who had married poet Dylan Thomas. Another chapter of her life was with the Russian George Gurdjieff; she sat at his feet as he spouted his mysticism. The grifter demanded money and sex from his flock.

At age seventeen, the twins discovered each other's existences and shared a reunion at a London pub. In the movie *Mary Poppins*, supercalifragilisticexpialidocious is defined as "something to say when you have nothing to say." The brothers might either have adopted that code of silence or used choice words regarding Pamela.

Worlds collided when, across the ocean, eleven-year-old Diane Disney told her father Walt about Mary Poppins, her favorite storybook character. Over the next decade, Walt made a Herculean effort to acquire the film rights. While most authors would be over the moon to have their novels turned into a Disney movie, Pamela balked. Her fear was the director would sugarcoat her work with such diversions as using anthropomorphic creatures with an uncontrollable urge to dance. But in 1959, with book sales drying up, Pamela relented. However, she did so with the provision that she was to receive script approval, $100,000 in advance, and a 5 percent cut of the gross, a deal that made her a multimillionaire. Walt discovered that working with Pamela was like swallowing a spoonful of bile. Perhaps he would have forgiven the harridan from hell had he understood that P. L. Travers hid Helen Lyndon Goff, or that Mary Poppins was her own lost Aunt Ellie.

Disney deliberately withheld an invitation for the 1964 premiere of the film; nevertheless, Pamela finagled her own way in and watched *Mary Poppins* as tears coursed down her cheeks...and not from joy. She explained, "They missed the point. It's not about sugar and spice, but something from which we grown-ups can learn."

In her nineties, frail and infirm, Pamela was housebound in her Chelsea home, a white Georgian town house with a bright pink door. (In 2019, her perfect former home went on sale for £4.85 million.) Journalists who paid a visit had to follow guidelines: Read her latest book beforehand, and refrain from asking personal or stupid questions.

**The Story Bank:** Like the moon, people have a dark side that no one can see. However, the best place to discover Pamela is her childhood home in the 1882 bank in Maryborough. Once the venue of finance, the bank is now a museum dedicated to the author and her beloved characters. In the entrance to the Story Bank, the Bird Woman sits on a bench, feeding her pigeons, selling breadcrumbs to passersby for a tuppence. Behind her is a masterful rendition of St. Paul's Cathedral. Another statue is of a bronze Mary, a magnet for selfies. A brick wall displays a black sculpture of a hat and purse with the sign Cherry Tree Lane. Inside Mary-land is a cornucopia of whimsey: Mary, Jane, and Michael perch on a banister, while above the trio dangles a chandelier made of teacups. The historic heritage building holds movie memorabilia such as figurines encased in shadow boxes, posters, and props. There are also black-and-white framed photographs such as pictures of Pamela with Walt Disney and Julie Andrews. The walls display quotations, a painted hat rack with an actual hat, and a bathroom door sign bearing the words: Chimneysweeps & Servants Only. Maryborough continues the whimsey with traffic lights displaying Mary with umbrella down for stop, umbrella up for go.

Before the west wind took Pamela at age ninety-six, she remained as elusive as ever and wrote, "Mary Poppins is not lost. She is still somewhere. You only have to go and find her."

**Seen from Her Window:** Surely Pamela, who became the world-renowned author P. L. Travers, would have looked out from the Story Bank to behold what her irresistible character Mary Poppins proffered: "Here is the world at your feet."

# PART II

# The Artists

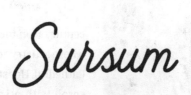

# CHAPTER 15

*"Shall not our dwellings, our public buildings,*
*our factories, our gardens, our parks, reflect in reality*
*the loveliness of our artistic dreams?"*

**—ELISABET NEY**

◇◇◇◇◇◇◇◇◇◇

## Formosa: The Elisabet Ney Studio and Museum

### opened 1911 | Austin, Texas

A plaque located at the home museum of Susanna Dickinson in Austin, Texas, declares she was the "toughest woman on the Texas frontier, survived the Battle of the Alamo and five husbands." After escaping the fort, Susanna delivered the news of its defeat to Sam Houston, leading to her renown as the "Messenger of the Alamo." Austin's other woman's home museum is dedicated to art rather than war. To travel to Texas' past, head to Formosa: The Elisabet Ney Studio and Museum.

Where, under one roof in Texas, do notables such as King Ludwig II of Bavaria, Jacob Grimm, and Stephen Fuller Austin congregate? The common denominator amongst the royal, the writer, and the statesman is the German-born Elisabet Ney.

The woman who sculpted American heroes was born in 1833 in Münster, Westphalia, Prussia (now Germany), and was named at birth Franzisca Bernadina Wilhelmina Ney, daughter of Johann Adam and Anna Elizabeth Ney. Johann enjoyed a comfortable livelihood supplying the local cemetery with funeral statues. While other girls played with dolls, little Elisabet fashioned clay models of her dog, Tyrus. Her mother told her daughter the legend of the fourteenth-

*Portrait of Elisabet Ney with the bust of*
*King George V of Hanover |*
*Wikimedia Commons,*
*Artist Friedrich Kaulbach*

century sculptor Sabina von Steinbach, whose artistry adorned the Strasbourg Cathedral. Her statue of St. Joan held a scroll with a Latin inscription that translated to, "Thanks be to the holy piety of this woman, Sabina, who from this hard stone gave me form." Anna Elizabeth had related the tale as a lesson in piety, but the realization that a girl could be a stone-carver was what captivated Elisabet.

The youthful Elisabet had two goals, and one was "to know great persons." She achieved this aspiration through her great-uncle, Michel Ney, Napoleon's Field Marshall, who met his end by firing squad. Her second was to study art in Berlin; her parents were against this as they felt it immoral to leave home before marriage, especially to live in a Protestant city. Dreading the "sweet, uneventful life of a German hausfrau," Elisabet embarked on a hunger strike that ended with Bishop Müller's compromise that she would be permitted to attend the Catholic Munich Academy of Art, where she became its first female student. On an excursion, Elisabet met Edmund Duncan Montgomery, the illegitimate son of a Scottish baron, a medical student at the University of Heidelberg. Her biographer, Bride Taylor, wrote that he seemed "to her romantic soul like a hero just stepped out of the pages of some splendid book." A further joy was acceptance to the Berlin Art Academy. Bishop Müller granted Elisabet her first commission: a statue of St. Sebastian. Another request came from the chronicler of fairy tales, Jacob Grimm. A student of philosophy, Edmund encouraged Elisabet to sculpt Arthur Schopenhauer. Although an avowed misogynist, Arthur nevertheless served as her model. During his sitting, he stared at the artist and commented, "I am trying [to see] if I cannot discover a little moustache. It becomes to me each day more impossible to believe that you are a woman." Upon completion of his bust, due to lack of space, the artist had

***Elisabet Ney Home and Studio*** | *Wikimedia Commons, Bryan Rutherford*

engraved his name as "Ath. Schopenhauer." She was however able to amend it to "Arth."

King George V of Hanover hired her to create an oversized bust. Pleased with the work, Queen Marie gifted Elisabet a diamond bracelet. King George hired Friedrich Kaulbach to paint a full-length portrait of Elisabet that depicted his subject with sculpting tool in hand, arm resting upon a table which holds the king's bust. Friedrich christened his work *L'artiste*. Both the sculpture and the painting are on display in the Niedersächsisches Landesmuseum in Hanover.

After a decade, Edmund convinced Elisabet to become his wife. In 1863, the couple wed in Madeira in the British consulate. She insisted on retaining her maiden name, claiming she was "no man's property," and her husband always referred to her as Fraulein Ney. She called him "my best friend." They settled in a villa they christened Formosa, Portuguese for "beautiful." One of the works she created in her studio portrayed two young boys, one holding the torch of knowledge, the other grasping a key. She explained her work's theme as "Learning is the Key to Success." She also worked on a portrayal of the god who stole fire from the gods, a work she named "Prometheus Bound." A second summons arrived from a royal when the King of Prussia commissioned Elisabet to fashion a bust of Count von Bismarck, known as the Iron Chancellor. The work was part of the Paris Art Exposition. A further royal order arrived from King Ludwig II of Bavaria, known as Märchenkönig, the Swan King or the Mad King, whom she depicted in the garb of a Knight of St. George.

Although Europe had showered Elisabet with acclaim and wealth, wary of Germany's political intrigues—in which she had participated—the couple left for America. Initially, they settled in Georgia, joining a utopian community where they built a log castle they shared with sons Arthur, named after Arthur Schopenhauer, and Lorne, named after the Marquis of Lorne, the son-in-law of Queen Victoria. As the commune did not prove the envisioned paradise, they relocated to Hempstead, Texas, where they hoped the weather would alleviate Edmund's tuberculosis. They purchased a Greek revival house, Liendo Plantation; during the Civil War, it had served as a base for prisoners of war, Sam Houston had been a guest, and it had been General George A. Custer's military base. Lore holds that when Elisabet first saw Liendo, she stood on the second-floor balcony and rejoiced, "Here is where I shall live and die." Upon her arrival, her adopted city looked askance at the foreigner with the outlandish clothes and unconventional lifestyle. Despite causing a tempest in a Texas teapot, Elisabet refused to hearken to anyone other than her own drummer. When asked why she had forgone her flourishing career, she explained motherhood was her priority and that she was "busy with a more important art of molding flesh and blood." Sorrow struck Liendo when Arthur passed away at age one from diphtheria. His grieving mother made a plaster cast of his body. Putting the letter 's' before the word mother, Elisabet obsessed over her remaining child. After Lorne had beat up three tutors, his father, over his wife's objections, sent him to a boarding school. Lorne turned into the Texas Casanova and ran through three wives with whom he had six children. He joined Teddy Roosevelt and fought with the Rough Riders. A lifelong grief was estrangement from her son.

In later life, Governor Roberts requested Elisabet sculpt statues of Samuel Houston and Stephen Austin for display at the Texas Pavilion at the World's Columbian Exposition in Chicago. She portrayed the men in buckskin, Houston with a saber, Austin with a rifle. The statues reside in the rotunda of the Texas Capitol building while replicas are in the US Capitol. In reaction to a criticism that the Houston rendition was too tall and the Austin one too small, Elisabet responded, "God Almighty makes men. I only copy his handiwork. I suggest you take your complaint to God." In tribute to Bishop Müller, Elisabet created a colossal head of Jesus. Her final work was an echo of her father's funeral works: a winged cherub for the tombstone of Elisabeth Emma Schnerr. In need of a room of her own to sculpt, Elisabet designed and built a studio-home that resembled a Greek temple, which she also named Formosa. Her fame turned her studio into a salon for Austin's artistic and intellectual community, and she entertained luminaries such as Enrico Caruso and Anna Pavlova.

In 1907, Edmund came from Liendo to say goodbye to his best friend. In honor of her request, "There must be no mourning when I am put out to sea," there was no funeral. A stone placed over her grave bore the inscription, "Elisabet Ney, Sculptor." Four years later, Edmund passed away; his casket held Arthur's ashes. In 1913, Lorne died due to a fall from which he sustained a spinal injury. He chose interment in Arlington National Cemetery.

**The Elisabet Ney Studio and Museum:** The Madame Tussaud's of Texas is Formosa, with one difference: Instead of wax figures, there are those of stone. Following Elisabet's death, her friends and admirers turned the studio into the Elisabet Ney Museum; the Austin limestone castle is the oldest artist's studio in Texas. The picturesque site is enhanced by nearby Waller Creek. On display are casts of hands, feet, a human skull, an ear, and a nose, alongside the artist's tools. While most of the works depict the famous, some held purely sentimental value. A plaster head of "the young violinist" portrays the fifteen-year-old Lorne.

Formosa holds the largest collection anywhere of Elisabet Ney's works of both European and American origin. The marble statue she completed near the end of her life was of Lady Macbeth, vainly trying to rub the blood from her hands. The original is in the Smithsonian, while an earlier plaster mold is in her studio. What distinguishes the Elisabet Ney Museum from a typical museum is the presence of the sculptor's furnishings and personal effects, such as Elisabet's clothes, jewelry, and perfume bottles. She often slept on her studio's roof, provided with a view of the Capitol and the University of Texas, to which she ascended through a trapdoor she called "the sky trap." A disciple of philosopher Jean-Jacques Rousseau, Elisabet rejected conventional landscaping and left the indigenous plants to flourish. Liendo Plantation is the final resting place of Elisabet and Edmund; their graves are no longer open to the public.

The cornerstone of Formosa carries a Latin engraving that is also the name of the sculpture of the two boys: "Sursum," which translates to "Arise."

**Seen from Her Window:** Looking out at the Austin landscape, despite all her Texas tribulations, brought Elisabet the satisfaction that she had escaped the life of a German *hausfrau.*

# CHAPTER 16

# *Don't Forget Me*

*"I am happy to be alive as long as I can paint."*

**—FRIDA KAHLO**

◇◇◇◇◇◇◇◇◇◇

## Museo Frida Kahlo

opened in 1958 | Coyoacán, México

I n the early and mid-twentieth century, Coyoacán was Mexico City's equivalent of Montparnasse, Greenwich Village, and Haight Ashbury as artists congregated in its free-spirited enclave. The queen of Boho, Frida Kahlo reigned from her eclectic blue Casa Azul (its blue a nod to the cultural tradition that the color wards off evil spirits), now the Museo Frida Kahlo.

A cult of Fridamania has sprung from the artist; her image appears on fridge magnets, and she has inspired an Oscar-winning film starring Salma Hayek, a Barbie doll (although one that came without a black unibrow or moustache and was far too thin for verisimilitude), a cartoon skeleton in the Pixar movie *Coco*, and endless Etsy tchotchkes. One thousand fans gathered at the Dallas Museum of Art in Frida drag. Posthumously, she has garnered more than 800,000 Instagram followers. Frida, dressed in her bright Tehuana outfits, is as ubiquitous in Mexico as Marilyn, sheathed in her sequined gown, is in the United States.Artists are known for their tortured psyches, and Magdalena Carmen Frida Kahlo y Calderón was the patron saint of suffering. At age six, Frida contracted polio that made her right leg shorter than her left, leading to her classmates' taunt, "Peg-Leg Frida." At age eighteen, a tram collided with the bus where she was a passenger, leaving her with severe lifelong injuries. Confined to a full body cast during a yearlong convalescence, she turned to painting. She filled her canvases with self-portraits,

images of violence and vulnerability, and the blending of gender norms. Her father, a German-Jewish photographer who had adopted the name Guillermo, took a picture of Frida wearing a three-piece man's suit. A revelatory canvas portrays the artist as a deer pierced by arrows, wearing a crown of thorns, hemorrhaging from a pregnancy. Frida underwent thirty operations, including the 1953 amputation of her right leg due to gangrene. Transforming pain into art, Frida decorated her prosthetic and boot in red ribbon and silk.

Frida met her destiny at the Escuela National Preparatoria when its directors commissioned Diego Rivera to paint a mural above the stage of her school's auditorium. The sixteen-year-old Frida became infatuated with the thirty-six-year-old Mexican Michelangelo. She confided to her friend that she planned to have Diego's baby "as soon as I convince him to cooperate." Thus began the Latin Beauty-and-the-Beast love story.

Two years later, Diego paid a visit to Casa Azul, where they shared their first kiss. After obtaining a divorce—his second—he proposed. While Guillermo was pleased with his daughter's match to the acclaimed painter who, after Matisse, was the second artist to have a solo exhibition at the Museum of Modern Art, her mother was against her marrying a divorced man twice her age and the father of three. She refused to attend their 1929 wedding.

Diego's three hundred–pound frame dwarfed his diminutive wife, but she held her own. While dining in Detroit in 1932, she turned to car czar Henry Ford, known for his virulent anti-Semitism, and asked, "Mr. Ford, are you Jewish?" Eschewing designer clothes, Frida wore floor-sweeping skirts and blouses fashioned after traditionally dressed women from the matriarchal Tehuantepec region of Oaxaca where her maternal family had roots. The long flowing skirts illustrated pride in her culture and camouflaged her limp. Diego was pleased with this choice of clothing as it served as a rebuke of the rich who emulated Parisian

*Casa Azul (Blue House)* | *Wikimedia Commons, Rod Waddington*

couture. A *Vogue* magazine spread helped alter "Madame Diego Rivera's" status from that of the wife of a prominent artist to one in her own right.

In 1941, the couple moved into Frida's childhood home. While Guillermo had designed his residence in a European style, Frida and Diego transformed it into an ode to Mexico's past. They filled their home with folk art, papier-mâché skeletons, and Mesoamerican sculpture. Through their door came fellow Communist Party members, artists, wealthy art collectors, and movie stars. To help ease the pain of infertility—the result of injuries sustained in the accident—Frida filled her garden with a menagerie of pets, including monkeys, a deer, and Xoloitzcuintli (hairless dogs). From the courtyard, her tequila-imbibing parrot squawked, "*No me pasa la cruda*"—an idiom translating to "I can't get over this hangover." Art historian Luis-Martín Lozano wrote that La Casa Azul was not just Frida's cobalt compound but served as the "artistic and aesthetic universe that nurtured Kahlo's work."

A thorn in their marriage was the way in which Diego expressed himself with more than his paintbrush. Frida's younger sister, Christina, began appearing in her brother-in-law's murals...and in his bed. Wounded after the dual betrayal, Frida claimed custody of their spider monkey. Of her heartache, she stated, "I suffered two grave accidents in my life: one in which a streetcar knocked me down and the other was Diego. Diego was by far the worse." The blue walls did not deter the evil spirits. The couple divorced in 1940; they remarried the following year in

San Francisco. She explained her forgiveness, "I do not think the banks of a river suffer by letting the water run." Refusing to placidly accept the role of the woman scorned, Frida embarked on heterosexual affairs as well as same-sex ones with Mexican film stars Dolores del Rio and Maria Felix. Professionally Frida became more than the wife of Diego Rivera. She was the first Latin American woman to have a painting in the Louvre; André Breton described her art as "a ribbon around a bomb." Her last self-portrait, *Diego and I*, depicts her shedding three teardrops while her forehead bears the image of her husband. Sotheby sold the painting for $34.9 million, a record-breaking highest sale for a Latin American artist.

In a life of surreal proportions, it would have been hard to lower the bar of bizarre; Frida managed. In 1937, Frida and Diego used their political clout to influence the Mexican government to grant asylum to the exiled communist revolutionary Leon Trotsky, who started life as Lev Davidovich Bronstein in the Ukraine. For seventeen months, Trotsky and his wife, Natalia, made their home at Casa Azul. In its sunshine-hued kitchen, Trotsky sat at the table drinking tea Russian style: He sipped the hot beverage while holding a sugar cube between his teeth. Mexican asylum also apparently consisted of adultery; the fifty-eight-year-old Trotsky and twenty-nine-year-old Kahlo began an affair. Aware that hosting the fugitives put them in danger, Frida and Diego covered their windows with brick and erected a security tower. Eventually, Diego, fed up with the live-in adultery, demanded Leon and Natalia find new living quarters. The Trotskys moved to a nearby gray cement fortress-like house on Rio Churubusco where an agent of Stalin's secret police eventually assassinated Leon with an icepick blow to his head. The address is now the León Trotsky Casa Museo.

Relying on tequila and painkillers, Frida held her first Mexican solo exhibition, which she attended on a stretcher. Eleven days before her death, sitting in a wheelchair with Diego by her side, she made an appearance at a rally to protest American intervention in Guatemala. Frida passed away at the Casa Azul, officially of pneumonia, though rumors of suicide swirled. A Soviet banner covered her coffin on its way to the crematorium. Such were the times that her 1954 *New York Times* obituary heralded, "Frida Kahlo, Artist, Diego Rivera's Wife."

**Museo Frida Kahlo:** It is fitting that the home museum for artist Frida Kahlo is located in her beloved Casa Azul as it was in important ways her soul's home rather than merely a residence. Casa Azul is full of bright colors, including the red letters that proclaim the Museo Frida Kahlo. An inscription on the courtyard's wall reads, "Frida y Diego vivieron en casa 1929–195." The words "lived here" is an understatement, considering the soap opera sagas that unfolded between these two artists, who if nothing else, lived large. Another wall gives Frida's year of birth as 1910; she changed it from her actual birthdate so that it would coincide with the start of the Mexican revolution. Thousands make pilgrimages to Coyoacán to learn about the woman behind the movie, the magnets, the myth. Scattered throughout the house are retablos (holy pictures representing salvation) and dozens of paintings on tin that line the staircase, together with masks and ceramic animals. Glass cases display Frida's embroidered dresses, fringed shawls, and long petticoats. An address book is open to "Marcel Duchamp" at 14 Rue Hall, and his painting hangs on the museum's wall. The dining room's floor is painted bright yellow. The kitchen's centerpiece is a blue-and-white stove; miniature pots spell out Frida and Diego with an outline of two doves tying a love knot. The master bedroom, on the ground floor, took on single occupancy status when marital discord seeped in. Diego's hat remains on the coat rack.

Features of Casa Azul far afield from those of traditional museums include Frida's wheelchair, seen in front of an adjustable stand that holds a painting of a still life. On her bed is the artist's death mask wrapped in a shawl. In a diary entry penned a few days before her death, she wrote, "I hope that the exit is joyful, and I hope never to return."

Frida's upstairs bedroom was not always a serene retreat for painting. Her affair with sculptor Isamu Noguchi ended when Diego, an enraged bull, caught the couple in bed. As Noguchi scrambled for his clothes, a hairless dog pounced on his sock. Forgoing the sock, Noguchi fled from the window, scrambled up a patio orange tree, and fled over the roof.

Frida's bedroom holds a plaster corset decorated with images from her crippling afflictions. The mirror under the canopy of her bed allowed her to document her pain; fifty-five of her 143 paintings are self-portraits. A canvas of a dead child hangs above the headboard, juxtaposed with a frame that holds photographs of Marx, Mao, Stalin, Lenin, and Trotsky. A lace-trimmed pillow bears the embroidered words, *"No me olvides amor mio."* "Don't forget me, my love."

**Seen from Her Window:** Overlooking the garden is a stone studio Diego added so Frida would have a room of her own. From the studio, she looked upon a scaled rock pyramid that displayed a collection of pre-Columbian art.

# CHAPTER 17

# *The Next Morning*

*"My life is full of mistakes.*
*They're like pebbles that make a good road."*

**—BEATRICE WOOD**

◇◇◇◇◇◇◇◇◇

## The Beatrice Wood Center for the Arts

opened in 2005 | Ojai, California

In medieval Florence, Beatrice Portinari served as Dante Alighieri's guide in his masterpiece, *The Divine Comedy*. In twentieth-century California, Beatrice Wood served as James Cameron's inspiration in part for the character of Rose in his blockbuster movie, *The Titanic*. Her spirit yet resides in the Beatrice Wood Center for The Arts.

Upon reading Beatrice's 1985 autobiography, *I Shock Myself* (which she had written with encouragement from author Anaïs Nin), director James Cameron contacted the author about using her as the inspiration for *Titanic*'s female lead character, Rose Dawson Calvert. Beatrice's response was, "Oh, I couldn't possibly do that because I'm only thirty-five." (She was 102 at the time.) James also suggested Beatrice play the role of the elderly Rose, but due to her hearing loss, she declined. Illness prevented the acclaimed artist from attending the movie's premiere. On her 105th birthday, James presented Beatrice with a pre-release recording of the film. She later admitted that she had not finished watching it because of its tragic ending, declaring, "It is too late in life to be sad."

A bohemian was born in 1893 San Francisco; when Beatrice was five, the Wood family moved to an exclusive zip code on Manhattan's Upper East Side.

*Beatrice Wood, Marcel Duchamp,
and Francis Picabia, 1917 |*
*Wikimedia Commons,*
*Photographer: Unknown*

Her childhood entailed a year in a convent school in Paris, enrollment at a finishing school, and summer trips to Europe. Realizing that her headstrong daughter's dream was to become a painter rather than a society wife, her mother sent her—nanny in tow—to France to study at the Académie Julian. Never short on nerve, Beatrice peered through a hedge to watch Claude Monet painting in his Giverny garden. (In *Titanic*, Rose mentions Monet as Jack paints her wearing nothing but the magnificent gem, "the Heart of the Ocean.")

Finding her classes tedious, Beatrice ran away from her chaperone and moved into an attic room accessible only by a ladder. To alleviate the gloom, she filled its walls with her canvases. When her mother discovered she had run away, she came for her incorrigible daughter. Beatrice recalled, "And I still can see her, climbing this ladder with her high-heel shoes. She was very elegant, with a black satin dress with real hand embroidery at her throat and a wonderful hat with feathers. And she said, 'Look at the cobwebs.'" When Mrs. Woods and daughter returned to Paris, Beatrice announced she had switched her field of interest to theater. She took dance lessons with members of the *Comédie-Française* and appeared on stage with Sarah Bernhardt. When Isadora Duncan showed appreciation of Beatrice's handmade dyed scarves, she gifted the dancer several. After the dancer met her tragic end in the Riviera when her long scarf became entangled in her sport car's rear wheel, Beatrice always made it clear that her present had not been *that* scarf. As she explored her own devotion to dance, one of her teachers was Ivan Clustine, choreographer for Anna Pavlova. Vaslav Nijinsky, considered the greatest male dancer of the twentieth century, watched Beatrice perform. Beatrice in her turn attended the 1913 debut of Igor Stravinsky's "Rite of Spring" that featured Nijinsky.

With the gathering storm clouds of World War I, Beatrice returned to the States and continued her acting career. Theater lost its luster because, "Acting is very fascinating. But being an actress is not, because you become so concentrated on yourself. And your smile and the way you move your head and the way you look. And really, it's a pain in the ass." She continued to accept roles, since she wanted an independent income. She recalled her desire for a room of her own, a refuge from the Wood residence: "I was a good little girl. Nothing is more revolting."

A friend told her of a French composer, Edgarde Verèse, confined to a hospital with a broken leg; as he did not speak English, she paid him a visit. Through Edgar, Beatrice met Marcel Duchamp, best known for his painting *Nude Descending a Staircase*. The avant-garde artist introduced her to Henri-Pierre Roché, a writer who became her first lover...and the first to break her heart. Her romantic cross was she "was a monogamist woman in a polygamous world." Her next romance was with Duchamp, whom she considered the most intelligent, talented, and handsomest man in the world. She recalled, "We immediately fell for each other, which doesn't mean a thing because I think anybody who met Marcel fell for him. He was an enchanting person." Marcel shocked Beatrice with his assertion that sex and love were two different things. She disagreed; their love affair ended, but their friendship endured. Through Duchamp, Beatrice became a regular guest of an exorbitantly wealthy art patron couple, Walter and Louise Arensberg. Her fascination with modern art began in their home when she saw a Matisse painting that "almost put her into a trance."

Roché, Duchamp, and Wood published the avant-garde journal *The Blind Man* that ultimately resulted in Beatrice's appellation, "the Mama of Dada." For the publication, Beatrice drew the symbol of The Blind Man, depicting a stick figure thumbing his nose while taking a step forward. Her father described the magazine as "a filthy publication" and warned if she distributed the smut by mail, she would end up behind bars like birth control activist Margaret Sanger. After Roché's novel regarding a ménage à trois, *Jules and Jim,* inspired François Truffaut's 1961 film of the same name, the common consensus held that the featured female was Beatrice. To stop the rumor mill, Beatrice denied she was involved in a love triangle with Roché and Duchamp, insisting she was a serial monogamist.

At age twenty-three, to escape her mother's meddling, Beatrice eloped with her friend Paul Renson, a theatrical manager, and the newlyweds departed for Montreal, Canada. The relationship was one of convenience, never consummated.

*The Beatrice Center for the Arts* | *Permission of Beatrice Wood Center for the Arts*

Paul looked upon his wife as a cash register since her savings supported his gambling. Highly suspicious of their son-in-law, the Woods hired a private investigator who uncovered the unsavory news that Paul had a wife and child in Belgium. In a nod to art imitating life, in *The Titanic*, a PI investigates Jack Dawson's past when Rose and Jack began exchanging looks of love. After the annulment of her marriage, Beatrice returned to the Big Apple, a move that proved unsatisfying: The Dada Movement had died down, Marcel was in Europe, and Roché had returned to Paris. What alleviated the gloom was Reginald Pole (the future father-in-law of Anaïs Nin). Beatrice reminisced, "We were so much in tune that our communication was almost telepathic." But Reginald broke her heart when he became telepathic with an eighteen-year-old future Mrs. Pole. Beatrice decamped for Los Angeles, where she married for a purely practical reason. After a flood destroyed the house she shared with her friend, Steve Hoag, in the belief the Red Cross provided more aid to married couples, she headed for the registry office. In her autobiography, Beatrice clarified, "I never made love to the two men I married, and I did not marry the men I loved. I do not know if that makes me a good girl gone bad, or a bad girl gone good." Later in life, Beatrice delivered a commencement address where she stated that one should not focus on simply being good—as that will result in being good for nothing.

To be near her disciple, the Indian guru J. Krishnamurti, with money realized from the sale of a Duchamp drawing, Beatrice secured her forever home in cacti-covered Ojai, California. The name Ojai derived from a word of the indigenous Chumash Tribe that translates to "Valley of the Moon." Beatrice's dearest friend, Rosalind Rajagopal, along with Krishnamurti, and with input from author Aldous Huxley, created the Happy Valley School, which focused on small classes, the Socratic Method, and a no-grades policy. The artist's final romantic relationship was with an East Indian scientist with whom she fell in love at age sixty-eight while on a trip to India. He said of their affair's ending, "Our trains move in opposite directions." Beatrice's take on romance: "If a man says he loves me, I fall into his lap like a ripe grape." This East Indian romance resulted in her 1992 book, *33rd Wife of a Maharajah: A Love Affair in India.*

When Krishnamurti was at Castle Eerde (a gift from a devotee), Beatrice flew to the Netherlands to attend his lectures. The trip changed her life, and not because of her guru's words. Beatrice purchased a set of baroque dessert plates with a luster glaze; unable to locate a matching teapot, she enrolled in an adult education class at Hollywood High School to learn to create her own. The experience led to her passion for pottery that held shades of Dada, eroticism, and satire. Entranced by the quirky and quaint, from her Ojai studio, she produced images of Queen Elizabeth I. As an explanation of the lure of the royal, on a brochure for one of her exhibitions, she wrote, "Did you know what Queen Elizabeth I did with ambassadors? Each had to spend a night with her, and those with the best qualifications got the job." Further imperial figures caught in clay were the Duke and Duchess of Windsor. Other creations were of bordellos and Madonna—the singer, not the saint. Endlessly experimental, the master ceramist remarked, "Knowing what one's about to take out of a kiln is as exciting as being married to a boring man." Beatrice signed her pieces with her nickname, Beato. A 1948 sign outside her studio door bore the message, "Beatrice Wood—Fine Pottery: Reasonable and Unreasonable."

In 1961, the American State department invited Beatrice to visit India on a fourteen-city tour. The experience proved transformative, and she took to dressing exclusively in saris and wearing Indian jewelry.

Visitors to Beatrice's studio were privy to the barefoot centenarian ceramist with hip-length hair styled in a long, thick braid, her arms adorned with a challenging amount of silver and turquoise jewelry. Rings accentuated her scarlet-painted toes, which complemented her brightly colored saris. For her hundredth birthday celebration, Beatrice had two birthday cakes, lemon chiffon with blueberries and chocolate with raspberries, with frosting that depicted The

Blind Man. When asked about the key to her longevity, Beatrice attributed it to "art books, chocolate, and young men." Governor Pete Wilson of California declared her a "California Living Treasure." Forever youthful in terms of romance, Beatrice shared, "I still would be willing to sell my soul to the devil for a nice Argentine to do the tango with." At age 103, Beatrice wrote to her friend, "I hang onto the statement of scientists that there is no time. Therefore, join me in telling everyone you are thirty-two. This allows me to go after young men and plan grabbing husbands from my girlfriends. Choosing to live in the timeless, I am now at the easiest and happiest time of my life."

The legendary lady befriended Brancusi, danced for Nijinsky, and shared a gynecologist with Edna St. Vincent Millay. Beatrice's birthday bash drew 250 guests, among them James Cameron and Gloria Stewart, who had portrayed *Titanic's* elderly Rose. The titanic lady of the avant-garde, Wood passed away shortly afterwards in her home; her last view was of her beloved Topatopa mountains. Her friends scattered a portion of her remains near the Weeping Mulberry Tree across from her studio. The remainder of her ashes ended up mixed with a glaze that artists used to create ceramic stones. Her beloved studio, home, and grounds became the contemporary museum in a transition made possible through the efforts of the Happy Valley Foundation.

**The Beatrice Wood Center for the Arts:** The Center promotes self-expression through the media of ceramics, painting, music, film, photography, and woodworking. Of Beatrice's pottery, Anaïs Nin wrote, "[she] combines her colors like a painter, makes them vibrate like a musician. They have strength even while iridescent and transparent. They have the rhythm and luster of both jewels and human eyes. Water poured from one of her jars will taste like wine." The gallery preserves its founder's legacy through her pottery, international collection of folk art, extensive library, and healing crystals. The original sign in her studio remains, "Reasonable and Unreasonable;" visitors may make their own conclusion. Her bright pink mailbox—which for decades appeared alongside the highway—is now stored at the center, its logo of The Blind Man forever thumbing his nose. The succulents in her garden hold the ceramic stones sprinkled with Beatrice's ashes, thereby making her one with the land and home she loved. Guests often came bearing gifts of chocolate and left with copies of *I Shock Myself*, which she sold as a memento of their time in Ojai.

A plethora of objects await visitors: The 1926 self-portrait with Reginald Pole, the 1936 King Edward VIII and Wallis Simpson plate, the 1969 Rainbow Luster Chalice, and a nod to whimsical artistry: Mr. & Mrs. Teapot ceramic. A shelf holds artifacts relating to her magical mystery tour in India, a photograph, a mask, a gem-studded necklace.

A display case holds Beatrice's eclectic silver jewelry, accompanied by an explanatory text that includes her quotable statement, "Ever since I was a little girl I have loved jewelry, and have never gone out without a necklace and a bracelet. I have never paid attention to fashion."

The center's photographs of Beatrice Wood provide a visual diary of the original hippy chick. One is dated 1917, Coney Island. Beatrice is seated on a fake ox, with Duchamp behind her in a cart. Of the magical memory, Beatrice wrote, "With Marcel's arm around me, I would have gone on any ride into hell with the same heroic abandon as a Japanese lover standing on the rim of a volcano ready to take a suicide leap."

A visitor can take home several gifts bearing the stick figure of The Blind Man as it is emblazoned on aprons, journals, and caps. One also leaves the Beatrice Wood Center with a kaleidoscope of brightly colored images, a shifting scene of Dada's Duchamp, the spiritualist Krishnamurti, the author Aldous Huxley, and the ceramist herself, the *grande dame* of Ojai.

A Beatrice Wood quotation sums up her life's philosophy, "There are three things important in life: Honesty, which means living free of the cunning of the mind. Compassion, because if we have no concern for others, we are monsters. Curiosity, for if the mind is not searching, it is dull and unresponsive."

Despite the passionate life she lived, true love proved elusive for the artist. She rued that the Topatopa Mountain range the only partner she could count on "to be there when I go to bed at night and still be there when I wake up the next morning."

**Seen from Her Window:** On clear nights, Beatrice was privy to "the pink moment," the phrase the residents of Ojai use to describe their city's spectacular sunsets reflected on the Topatopas.

# CHAPTER 18

# Black-and-White Gold

*"[Being a great photojournalist is] a matter of getting out on a damn limb and sawing it off behind you."*

## —LEE MILLER

◇◇◇◇◇◇◇◇◇◇

## Farleys House & Gallery

### opened 2006 | East Sussex, England

In his play *As You Like It*, William Shakespeare wrote, "One man in his time plays many parts...." And one woman who played many parts was Lee Miller, whose intrepid spirit lives on in her country retreat, a music box that recalls its chatelaine and the era of surrealism in a Sussex setting.

Her father, Theodore, was an engineer; her mother, Florence, was a nurse from Canada who struggled with her mental health. Theodore's hobby was photography, such as his work "December Morn," that revealed his seven-year-old daughter standing in the snow wearing only bedroom slippers. His interest in photographing his child, as well as later pornographic photographs he took, suggest he had a prurient interest in his daughter. In a horrendous sexual assault, a family friend raped Lee shortly before her eighth birthday, leaving her infected with gonorrhea that entailed agonizing treatments. This traumatic experience may also have contributed to later behavioral difficulties, as several private schools expelled Lee; a teacher described her as "an idle student and an active rebel." Another issue the family faced was in the 1960s when John, Lee's brother,

*Lee Miller |*
*Wikimedia Commons, U. S. Army Official*
*Photograph*

began to cross-dress. Always supportive, Lee would send him clothes, such as a fur coat. In 1964, police arrested John—a.k.a. Felicity—near his home in New York state for violating a vagrancy law prohibiting people from disguising themselves in a manner that would conceal their identities. Consequently, he lost his job as a pilot with Eastern Airlines. (Current federal law would have protected him, but at the time, many laws criminalized expression of gender identity not matching gender assignment at birth.)

After a stint at Vassar College, Miller enrolled at the Art Students League of New York. While crossing a street, she literally stumbled into her professional modeling career when Condé Nast, the founder of *Vogue*, pushed her out of the way of an oncoming vehicle. Due to her ethereal beauty, Lee made her debut on the cover of *Vogue* in 1927. Her image of the sexually liberated flapper with the blond bob launched dozens of plum photo shoots. She rapidly became a fixture on the social scene, partying with luminaries such as Josephine Baker and Dorothy Parker. Although she was initially thrilled with being the It Girl of Manhattan, disillusionment soon set in, and she departed for the Bohemia of Paris.

Montparnasse was the neighborhood of surrealist photographer Man Ray, the Jazz Age's rendition of Andy Warhol, who had started life as Emmanuel Radnitzky from Brooklyn. Lee showed up at Ray's favorite café, Le Bateau Ivre ("The Drunken Boat"), where she introduced herself as his new apprentice. Dumbstruck, he told her, "I'm leaving for a holiday in Biarritz." "I know you are, and I'm coming with you," was her response. The thirty-nine-year-old Ray and the twenty-year-old Lee embarked on a road trip the next day. The Americans in Paris developed a strong bond, and Lee Miller served as Man Ray's protégée, muse, collaborator, and lover.

Dozens of celebrities had posed for Ray, including Wallis Simpson, Coco Chanel, and Virginia Woolf; however, his most magnetic muse was Miller. He

*Farleys House, Farley Farm, East Sussex, England by Tony Tree |*
*©Lee Miller Archives, England 2024, All Rights Reserved. (Leemiller.co.uk)*

delighted in concentrating on various parts of her anatomy and produced Lee Miller's Legs with Circus Performer, Miller's Lips, Observatory Time, and La Priere, which showcased her backside. Jean Cocteau, a flamboyant member of the Paris avant-garde, coated her body in butter and transformed her into a plaster cast of a classical statue for his film, *The Blood of a Poet.* A glass manufacturer sold champagne flutes modeled after her breasts. One of her lovers, Pablo Picasso, painted six portraits of her; the most memorable portrayed her with a green mouth and a vagina resembling an eye. Celebrity and fashion photographer Cecil Beaton altered her gender to dovetail with his homosexual proclivities, and only lusted after the model by convincing himself that she resembled a "sun-kissed goat-boy on the Appian Way." Theodore Miller arrived in Paris from Poughkeepsie and took pictures of his nude daughter.

After years of posing for men: her father, *Vogue* photographers, the surrealists, Lee decided "she would rather take a picture than be one," and she obtained a position at French *Vogue.* Her subjects included Charlie Chaplin, Colette, Marlene Dietrich, and Maurice Chevalier. On vacation in Paris, she met railroad magnate Aziz Eloui Bey, who left his wife to marry Lee. Man's reaction to Lee's desertion was a self-portrait where he portrayed himself sitting in a chair, noose around his neck, gun in hand. As the mistress of a beach house in Alexandria as well as a mansion in Cairo, she oversaw a fifteen-member staff. Her hobbies were snake-charming lessons, camel racing, and desert safaris. Another pastime was scandalizing the stuffy Cairo bourgeoisie, and she announced, "If I have a letch for someone, I hop into bed with him." When not using her camera to capture the pyramids, sphinx, and the desert near Siwa that René Magritte used as inspiration for his 1938 painting, "Le Baiser," she had to keep her demons at bay. She described her interior landscape as, "a water-soaked jigsaw puzzle, drunken bits that don't match in shape or design."

To escape the heat and her husband, Lee took a solo trip to Paris; at a party, she met the artist and art collector Roland Algernon Penrose, whose right hand and left foot had been dyed a vibrant blue to match surreal artist Max Ernst's blue hair. At the time, Penrose was separated from poet Valentine Boué, and he soon shared Lee's bed. Her betrayal of her husband, Bey, led to her confession, "My 'always' don't seem to be much, do they?" Despite respective faraway spouses, the couple summered in a Cornish farmhouse with pal Henry Moore and joined Picasso outside Cannes.

The idylls of the surrealists ended the day Hitler invaded Poland, and the lovers departed France for Hampstead, London. British *Vogue* commissioned her to document war chic, and she snapped shots of women in factory overalls and turbans. In frustration, she wrote her parents, "It seems pretty silly to go on working for a frivolous paper like *Vogue*. Tho it may be good for the country's morale, it's hell on mine." The war became her muse, and Lee turned her lens on Blitz-ravaged London. Upon earning accreditation as a war correspondent and after ordering a uniform from a pricey Savile Row purveyor, she followed the Allied armies, "What's a girl to do when a battle lands in her lap?"

Her lens captured the bizarre family portrait of the Nazi treasurer of Leipzig surrounded by his wife and daughter, all dead from suicide, while another photograph was of an SS prison guard floating underwater in a canal. Besides capturing the customary carnage of battle such as the D-Day aftermath, she also took shots of civilians, such as French female collaborators with shaved heads and the corpse of a German woman. The war photographer trailed the Allied advance throughout Europe; the blonde Venus huddled in a foxhole shocked the soldiers. The GIs liked her as she was intrepid under fire—and could match them swear word for swear word.

After trudging through the newly liberated concentration camps at Dachau and Buchenwald, Lee wrote, "I could never get the stench of Dachau out of my nostrils." The day Hitler and Eva committed suicide, Lee was in Munich, where the Army's 179th Regiment had established its headquarters in the dictator's apartment on the *Prinzregentenplatz*. Lee wiped her boots, thick with the cremated ash of Dachau, on the bathroom mat. Lee and photographer David E. Scherman placed a photograph of the Fuhrer in the bathtub beside the soap dish. Scherman then photographed Lee in the tub. She remarked, "Mein host was not at home." Another image captured Lee smoking in Eva Braun's bed in her nearby home. Tormented by what she had witnessed, Lee holed up in the Hotel Scribe in Paris to process the horror of the Holocaust, along with the terror of the foxholes.

On a train headed for an assignment in Switzerland, at age forty, Lee discovered she was pregnant, a situation she regarded as scarier than the Front. The bohemian Miller and Penrose took the bourgeoisie road of marriage to legitimize their son, Antony. Her trepidation of impending motherhood is reflected in Penrose's painting of his pregnant wife with her fetus portrayed as a green lizard. In 1947, the couple purchased Farley Farm, a residence that proved to be their forever home.

After Penrose's knighthood, Lee became Lady Penrose; she referred to herself as Lady Penrose of Poughkeepsie. Suffering from postpartum depression and post-traumatic stress disorder, she self-medicated with alcohol. Placing her yesterday under wraps, she tried to distance herself from her mine-laden past. Nevertheless, she remained in contact with Man Ray, who was often a guest at Farley House. In 1975, she attended her old friend's exhibition at the Institute of Contemporary Arts. The meeting was bittersweet for the former first couple of the Paris surrealists. Lee's beauty had diminished; Ray was in a wheelchair.

Fighting her demons, Lee was not always the perfect parent, and Antony was embarrassed by his outspoken mother. He remarked that what was on her mind was what was in her mouth. Cooking provided a creative outlet, and Lee earned a Cordon Bleu diploma and created culinary oddities: blue spaghetti, green chicken, pink cauliflower. Dinner guests were luminaries such as Henry Moore, Sonia Orwell, (George's widow), Picasso, Dora Maar, and Françoise Gilot. Post dessert, guests indulged in communal baths. After his mother's passing from cancer in 1977, Antony said of her, "She was way, way beyond difficult. I mean, God, she was impossible."

Shortly before Lee's passing, there had been a mother and child reunion; a posthumous bond arrived when Antony's wife, Suzanna, discovered Lee's wartime mementoes in the attic. The photographs served as a diary that helped Antony make peace with his mother's memory. The epiphany changed Antony from a dairy farmer to the curator and chronicler of Lee's life. He had gained insight into his mother's tortured memories, ones that she referred to as her "winged serpents."

**Farleys House & Gallery:** Peering through the keyhole of Farley Farms, in the hamlet of Muddles Green, Sussex, is to partake of a surreal world nestled in the British countryside. The museum's guest book is a who's who of twentieth-century artists; a page holds Picasso's signature with the date of his visit, November 11, 1950. The farm is a curiosity shop where a Picasso gravy jug rests alongside mugs by local artists and thrift store finds such as stuffed owls. A cabinet holds a mummified rat that Penrose discovered on a hot water pipe alongside a two-thousand-year-old Mayan sculpture. The dominant feature of the dining room is the fireplace that Penrose painted with the protective deity of Farley Farms: a sun with human attributes that matches the hue of the walls. The kitchen still retains Lee's mixing bowls, cookbooks, and recipes. The backdrop to the stove is a Picasso painted tile, a glazed colorful face. Docent Antony Penrose commented of the tile, "It has survived 60 years of bacon fat." The house also holds another Picasso tile in which a man fondles a woman's left breast. Among the unique Farley Farms bric-a-brac is a figure of a wooden lady, which used to be the figurehead of a ship, a transplant from a Cornish shipyard. What might have proved disconcerting for Antony was his home's large nude photograph of his mother.

Inscribed on the stairs is a poem by poet Paul Eluard. In the ground-floor sitting room are mementoes of the war years: a gunner's binoculars, a fabric Star of David, an Hermès Baby typewriter still holding a sheet of paper, and a Rolleiflex camera. The most startling photograph is of Lee in Hitler's bathtub, her boots still bearing the filth of Dachau.

The garden holds the sculpture *The Fallen Giant*, a work that appears to be the remnants of a man buried in the perfect English garden. Antony scattered the ashes of Sir and Lady Penrose in the grounds: on the giant, in the vegetable patch, and under an ancient chestnut tree. In the fairy tale, the miller's daughter spun straw into gold. The twentieth-century Miller's daughter, through her photographs, created black-and-white gold.

**Seen from Her Window:** A favorite sight was the Long Man of Wilmington, a 227-foot chalk giant lying on the South Downs, holding two walking sticks. Penrose reproduced the image on the fireplace, adjacent to the sun god.

# CHAPTER 19

## Divine Affection

*"Art is a tyrant. It demands heart, brain, soul, body...I wed art."*

**—ROSA BONHEUR**

◇◇◇◇◇◇◇◇◇◇

### Château de Rosa Bonheur

opened 2017 | Thomery, France

Visitors to artist Rosa Bonheur's estate in France never knew if they might encounter an exotic creature around any corner as her residence was not only a repository of animal art, but a menagerie of pets both tamed and untamed, foreign and domestic. To view her paintings and learn about an artist who took the road less travelled, proceed to the Château Musée Rosa Bonheur.

The fictional Dr. Doolittle could talk to the animals, a trait shared by Marie Rosalie (Rosa) Bonheur, born in Bordeaux in 1822 to mother Sophie and the portrait painter Raimond Bonheur. In pursuit of commissions, Raimond moved his family to Paris in 1829, where the family frequently changed addresses to evade creditors. Rosa recalled, "In my early years, we used to migrate with the birds." For a period, Raimond found steady employment with Étienne Geoffroy Saint-Hilaire, the founder of the Jardin de Plantes Zoo, who hired him as an illustrator. One fringe benefit for Rosa was she could roam the zoo's grounds.

A dreamer and idealist, Raimond, despite his Jewish religion, fell under the influence of the Christian utopian socialist Saint-Simon sect that promised planetary harmony. A tenet of their philosophy was gender equality, and as such, they created a pants-dress for women. Her grandfather referred to Rosa's odd

*Portrait of Rosa Bonheur with Bull* |
*Wikimedia Commons, Edouard Louis Dubufe*

manner of dressing as, "a boy in petticoats." The cult initiated Rosa in a bizarre nocturnal ceremony that involved cloaks and candles. Raimond's enthrallment with the Saint-Simon sect was apparent with his pronouncement of its leader, "I believe in you as I believe in the sun." Earning a living fell mainly on Sophie's shoulders, who gave piano lessons and took in sewing. Tragedy intruded when the eleven-year-old Rosa lost her mother; Raimond buried his wife in a pauper's grave. Describing Sophie's premature death, Rosa wrote, "My mother, the most noble and proud of creatures, [succumbed] to exhaustion and wretched poverty, while my father was dreaming about saving the human race."

When Rosa was nineteen, she shared a small Paris home with her father and three siblings, Isidore, Auguste, and Juliette, as well as her menagerie, consisting of a squirrel named Kiko, rabbits, and assorted birds and butterflies. On the terrace, she kept a sheep, and when it appeared lonely, a billy goat joined the household. Rosa brought the sheep and billy goat down five flights of steps to graze in the nearby Plaine Moneau Park. Raimond gave his daughter drawing lessons, since the art academies did not admit female students. As a teen, Rosa occupied herself by copying paintings at the Louvre, mainly of Dutch masters. She filled her sketchpad with images of photographic precision. A firm believer that animals had souls, she portrayed them staring at the viewer, their eyes radiating emotion. Male art students mocked her as "the little hussar."

At age nineteen, Rosa held her first exhibit at the Paris Salon, where she displayed *Rabbits Nibbling Carrots*. Although her work initially failed to attract attention, by 1845, her canvases were flying off her easel, and she won a third-place medal. The following year, her painting *Sheep* prompted the critic Théophile Thoré to write, "Mlle Rosa Bonheur's flock of sheep makes one want to be a shepherd, with a crook, a silk waistcoat, and ribbons." He ended with the era's ultimate compliment, "She paints like a man." Rosa also began dressing like a man. To study animal anatomy in the all-male domain of slaughterhouses, Rosa

*Portrait of Rosa's Studio* | *Wikimedia Commons, Stumpsnbails*

circumvented an 1800 law that made it illegal for women to don men's attire. The Paris police granted her a *"permission de travertissement"* allowing her to wear pants in public. Unwilling to be molded by social mores, Rosa refused to ride sidesaddle, cut her hair short, told bawdy jokes, and indulged in after-dinner Havana cigars, even though smoking was associated with prostitution. During a performance at Opéra Comique, Rosa attended clad in her trademark blue painter's smock. The lady also preferred ladies. As she expressed her preference, "As far as males go, I only like the bulls I paint." The Napoleonic Code of 1804 refrained from punishing acts of private female sexuality.

A turning point in Rosa's career occurred in 1848 when she received a gold medal from judges Delacroix and Ingres, followed by a three thousand-franc commission for her canvas *Ploughing in the Nivernais,* which portrayed two teams of oxen pulling heavy ploughs. Paul Cézanne commented, "It is horribly like the real thing." Another critic observed the painting showed "much more vigor...than you normally find in the hand of a woman." She used part of the proceeds to cover the cost of her father's funeral. By 1951, using inspiration from the equine engravings on the Parthenon frieze, Rosa completed her largest and most famous work, *Marché aux chevaux de Paris* or *The Horse Fair.* The eight-foot canvas depicts the Paris horse market as a battle scene enacted on the tree-lined Boulevard de l'Hôpital. When the canvas had a British showing, Queen Victoria received a private viewing. Art critic John Ruskin suggested the French woman use watercolors and add some purple. *The New York Times* wrote, "She has taken London by storm by her skill and happy talent." Nevertheless, the Bordeaux

Museum refused to purchase the canvas, and Cornelius Vanderbilt II acquired it in an 1887 auction for $53,000–$1.6 million in contemporary currency. The Gilded Age millionaire bequeathed the painting to the Metropolitan Museum of Art in New York. Occasionally, Rosa painted people, most notably Wild West legend Buffalo Bill, who was in Paris for the 1889 Universal Exposition, as he posed on his horse in a buckskin jacket.

Château de Rosa Bonheur: In 1859, the girl who had suffered from a nomadic youth purchased the Château de By, a three-story, seventeenth-century manor house built on the remains of a 1413 manor house. The estate is located at the outskirts of a forest, close to the Château de Fontainebleau—a castle that served as the summer hunting lodge for eight centuries of French kings. Rosa declared her home "the domain of Perfect Affection." A staggering statistic is that the keys to the Château weigh almost eleven pounds. The home and garden became the stomping grounds of Margot the mule, Jaques the stag, Roland the horse, Rastata the monkey, and Wasp the Cairn terrier. To feed Nero, the lion, servants pushed twenty pounds of raw beef through the bars of its cage. He eventually proved so unmanageable that Rosa sent him to the Jardin des Plantes; years later, when she visited, he responded to her call. Other pets included a Bengal tiger, three panthers, and polar bears. On a trip to the Pyrenees, Rosa returned with a pet otter that escaped its enclosure and found its way into her bed. A distinguished visitor to her far from humble home was the Empress Eugénie, the wife of Napoleon III, who pinned on Rosa's chest the Légion d'Honneur, making her the first woman to receive the medal. On the occasion, the empress remarked, "Genius has no sex." Another royal guest was Queen Isabella of Spain. Imperial accolades arrived from Emperor Maximilian of Mexico and King Alfonso XII of Spain. Tsar Nicholas II and Empress Alexandra of Russia met Rosa at the Louvre. The British author George Eliot, after viewing "The Spanish Muleteers Crossing the Pyrenees," remarked, "What power! This is the way women should assert their rights." A German manufacturer marketed a porcelain doll with the artist's image for Christmas gifts. Not all were in Camp Rosa; her detractors referred to her as "that Jewess," a barometer of the era's anti-Semitism. She filled her estate with sheep, monkeys, dogs, birds, and horses. She also shared the château with Nathalie Micas, who she had known since age fourteen, and, for a time, her lover's liberal mother. Of her companion, Rosa declared, "Had I been a man, I would have married her. I would have had a family, with my children as heirs, and nobody would have had any right to complain." After the two shared life together for forty years, Nathalie passed away. The next occupant was the American painter Anna Klumpke, who Rosa referred to as "my wife."

Despite the estate's grandeur, it retains a homey feel from touches such as a paint-dappled blue smock that rests on an upholstered chair alongside brown leather lace-up boots and an umbrella. A carved oak case holds Rosa's tools of her trade: paint tubes, palettes, and paintbrushes. Next to the easel sprawls the golden skin of Fatma, Rosa's pet lioness. In a nod to kitsch, a puppet is clothed in Rosa's military-style black jacket done in miniature, which displays her Légion d'Honneur cross. One can view the buckskins, a gift from Buffalo Bill. Her cross-dressing permit from the Paris police hangs in the drawing room. Resting on an easel is an oversized unfinished canvas of horses in motion that Rosa was working on when the Grim Reaper intruded. The walls display the animalier's canvases, interspersed with items such as horns, antlers, and a Scottish bagpipe. What might take visitors aback are the stuffed and mounted animals: a crocodile displays the taxidermist's art, along with the heads of a deer, an antelope, and a horse. A black crow with flapping wings is reminiscent of the one in the Poe poem, "The Raven."

Two portraits of the artist stare at her guests: In one, Rosa is dressed in her knee-length blue smock and black trousers, posing with her palette and her work in progress. Her devoted dogs, Charlie and Daisy, sit by her feet. In the other canvas, painted by Édouard Dubufe, Rosa's hand rests on a bull; she vetoed Dubufe's image of a "boring table" and took it upon herself to paint the animal. A photograph reveals Rosa and Anna's close relationship. In the second-floor salon is a desk and glass-doored cabinet that holds Baccarat glasses, white teacups and saucers, and in a nod to realism, an ashtray with cigarette butts.

While France has many storied hotels where one may lay one's head, such as the Ritz, associated with Ernest Hemingway and Princess Diana, the Château Rosa Bonheur offers guests an unforgettable overnight experience. The museum's website offers the tantalizing invitation, "Who hasn't dreamed of sleeping in the room of an illustrious figure, dining at their table, and listening to the music they loved, all the while contemplating the artworks, drawings, and objects that made up their daily life? It is this rare experience that the Château offers its guests." After visiting the museum, guests can slip into Rosa's monogrammed sheets, once also shared by Nathalie and an otter. The parquet floors are worn by age and the footsteps of former occupants. One can also enjoy Rosa's original furniture. The tearoom is a culinary treat and offers homemade pastries served on Limoges plates. The museum includes an outdoor theater and chamber music performances.

On the grave of Rosa Bonheur, buried between her beloved Nathalie and Anna in Père Lachaise Cemetery, their shared headstone bears the inscription, "Friendship is divine affection."

**Seen from Her Window:** Looking out from her estate over the Seine, Rosa must have marveled that the girl who had "migrated with the birds" had transformed to the chatelaine of a castle.

**PART III**

# The Entertainers

# CHAPTER 20

## No Regrets

*"Every damn thing you do in this life,*
*you have to pay for."*

### —ÉDITH PIAF

◇◇◇◇◇◇◇◇◇◇

### The Musée Édith Piaf

opened 1977 | Paris, France

The blind poet, John Milton, illustrated insight into the human condition with his statement, "The anguish of the singer makes the sweetness of the strain." One particular chanteuse who proved his words was an alchemist whose songs dwelled on the permanence of love, the impermanence of lovers. To step into her world, enter the Musée Édith Piaf.

Édith remains as symbolic of France as baguettes, berets, and the Left Bank. One of her lyrics was, "My heart is at the corner of a street / And often rolls into the gutter," and the gutter was where she arrived. Lore suggests that after a horse-drawn ambulance failed to arrive on time, two policemen delivered Édith on the pavement. Another story contends she was born in the hallway of an apartment on 72 Rue de Belleville. A plaque on the cracked marble doorstep states, "On the steps of this house on December 19, 1915, was born into the greatest poverty Édith Piaf, whose voice would later move the entire world." A far more prosaic account holds that the Hôpital Tenon in Paris issued her birth certificate. Her father, Louis Gassion, an acrobat, married her mother, Annetta, a café singer, before he left for the trenches of World War I. The army issued him a leave to attend his wife's labor; when he failed to show up, Annetta bitterly remarked, "I'll

*Known as Little Sparrow* |
*Wikimedia Commons, Permission*
*Studio Harcourt*

bet he wasn't late for happy hour—la buvette—at a train station bar." The baby's name was supposedly inspired by Edith Clavell, the British nurse shot by the Germans for aiding the escape of French prisoners.

When petite Édith was only two months old, her maternal grandmother became her guardian when the twenty-year-old Annetta deserted her family, partially as her drug habit kept landing her in jail. (She later died of a drug overdose in 1945.) Upon Louis' return, shocked at his child's skeletal frame, he took her to Bernay to live with Acha, his mother, the madame of a Normandy brothel. When Édith suffered from blindness, her grandmother and the eight prostitutes, rosaries in hand, embarked on a pilgrimage to the nearby shrine of Saint Thérèse in Lisieux. Six days later, when her eyesight returned, the town declared it *miraculée*, an experience that left Édith deeply religious. Another explanation is a doctor delivered the cure.

At age seven, Edith rejoined her father, where she accompanied him in his livelihood. Louis performed acrobatic tricks while she waited for the clink of coins on the cobblestones. Soon she took over as a singer; the voice that emerged from her four-foot eight-inch frame was, in Louis' words, powerful "enough to drown out the lions." For seven years, father and daughter slept on park benches or in cheap hotels until she took off with her friend, Simone Berteaut (Mômone), who later claimed to be Édith's half-sister. While Édith sang on the streets of Belleville, Mômone collected tips. They slept in cellars, taking turns warding off the rats. After a fling with a delivery boy nicknamed P'tit Louis, seventeen-year-old Édith gave birth to Marcelle (Cécelle). By 1933, as her Achilles heel was men in uniform, she left her baby's daddy and, along with Mômone and Cécelle, performed in the army barracks of Paris. Furious at her desertion, Louis absconded with their daughter, who died from meningitis before her second birthday. Another cryptic chapter is told of how the bereft mother slept with a man in exchange for ten francs to bury her baby. Later in life, Édith claimed she received the money, but that the man did not demand anything in return. Although she had not undergone a baptism, Édith was certain Cécelle had gone to heaven.

In 1933, Édith migrated to Pigalle, Paris' red-light district, where she became a singer for Lulu's, a lesbian dive. Two years later, while performing near the Champs-Élysées for tips, in Hollywood fashion, Louis Leplée hired her on the spot to work at Le Gerny's, his prestigious, mob-frequented café. He became Édith's Pygmalion and took her shopping for a black dress, a style that became her signature fashion. Her eighty-five-pound weight reminded him of a bird, and he dubbed her Piaf (French slang for *little sparrow*). His nickname for her was "La Mome" or "the kid." She referred to him as Papa. She made her debut in his nightclub, where Maurice Chevalier proclaimed, "That Kid Sparrow tears out your guts." By the end of the year, she had starred in a film and made her first recording. When a mob bullet—fired into Leplée's eye—ended his life, suspicion fell on his protégée. She weathered the scandal and ultimately became the country's highest paid entertainer.

During World War II, Édith toured the Stalag III-D camp near Berlin, where the camp commander allowed her to be photographed with French prisoners of war. The Resistance used the pictures to create false identification cards that proved instrumental in aiding the escapes of over a hundred inmates. In 1947, Édith performed in America at the Versailles, an East Side nightclub where she met Marlene Dietrich, who called Édith "the soul of Paris." The relationship between the Blue Angel and the Little Sparrow made for a lifelong bond. After the club refused to admit African American Lena Horne, the Little Sparrow unleashed her fury.

And then, *mon Dieu*, there were the lovers; no one, including the chanteuse herself, knew their number. The possessor of a Geiger counter for Mr. Wrong, Édith fell in love with middleweight boxing champion, Marcel Cerdan, who was inconvenienced with a wife and children. When the Moroccan Bomber ignored his fear of flying to surprise his lover in New York, his Air France Lockheed Constellation jet crashed over the Azores, killing all forty-eight on board. Scheduled to perform at Versailles the night his plane went down, the audience, aware of the tragedy, applauded her entrance. She shared with her fans her heartbreak, "No, there must be no applause for me this evening. I am singing for Marcel Cerdan and him alone." Overcome with the tragedy, Édith collapsed on

*Plaque on Musée Édith Piaf* | *Wikimedia Commons, Amadalvarez*

stage. Several of her letters to her love are on display at the Hôtel de Ville. His loss plunged the singer into an abyss of alcoholism, morphine, and depression. In addition, she suffered from crippling arthritis, exacerbated by injuries inflicted by several car accidents. By the 1950s, the Little Sparrow looked twenty years older than her age; her frizzy red hair revealed her scalp; her face looked like a mask accentuated by penciled-in brows.

Édith passed away, destitute, from liver cancer in 1963 at age forty-seven. Writer Jean Cocteau stated, "Ah, la Piaf est morte. Je peux mourir aussi," which translates to, "Ah, Piaf is dead. I can die also." Her deathbed adornment was an emerald cross necklace, a present from Dietrich that the pope had blessed. While the Little Sparrow had always embroidered her biography, her final act needed no embellishment. After the media posted her obituary, mourners purchased 300,000 of her records. Her final resting place is Père Lachaise Cemetery, situated ten blocks from where she was born; her black marble tomb is near Gertrude Stein's. At the foot of her monument are the words, "God reunites those who love each other." In tribute, 40,000 Parisians wept at her grave where Marlene Dietrich delivered her eulogy. The Archbishop of Paris denied her a funeral Mass as he pronounced her lifestyle "irreligious." In contrast, the French government allocated her the honor of placing a tricolor flag over her coffin for her wartime valor.

**Musée Édith Piaf:** To make certain Édith would not endure a second death—one of oblivion—Bernard Marchois founded the Musée Édith Piaf and has served as its curator for over half a century. The museum is in the apartment where Édith lived in 1933 when she sang in the streets of Belleville for her supper. As visitors walk down the hallway, they hear the strains of a Piaf song such as "La vie en rose." The museum consists of two small rooms in a fourth-floor apartment that adjoins the docent's own living quarters. Stepping across the threshold, one is greeted with a life-size cardboard cutout of the diminutive songbird. A pair of boxing gloves that belonged to Marcel Cerdan rest on a small round table that holds both their photographs. He had been the inspiration for "Hymn à l'Amour," the song she sang on stage on the evening of his death. Almost the same size as the former occupant, on a rocking chair rests a teddy bear, a gift from her second husband, Theophanis Lamboukas. The red walls are adorned with floor to ceiling framed letters such as those from Jean Cocteau, photographs, and album covers.

Throughout are the former occupant's china plates, papers such as her birth certificate, and awards. There are also portraits of the diva, mouth open in the agony of song. Petite headless mannequins model her black dresses; nearby are her Cinderella-sized shoes, gloves, and crocodile-skin Hermès handbag. Bernard says the haphazard placing of the items was intentional as he did not want a traditional, everything-in-its-place museum. He preferred to make it seem as Édith was still present. The heavy furniture came from the apartment where she lived during her final years. When asked why he did not move to a larger space, Bernard responded, "You'll have to ask Édith yourself." He said his feelings for Édith were platonic, and this is the reason why he closes the doors between their apartments at night. He elaborated, "She has her rooms, and I have mine." Before bidding guests adieu, Bernard looks pointedly at the donation bowl. Making their way down the hallway, visitors are oftentimes accompanied by the strains of "Je Ne Regrette Rien," "No Regrets."

**Seen from Her Window:** When Édith looked from her window at her beloved Paris, its streets reflected her metamorphosis from the Little Sparrow to the International Nightingale.

# CHAPTER 21

# Loved By Others

*"I believe in the idea of the rainbow. And I've spent*
*my entire life trying to get over it."*

**—JUDY GARLAND**

◇◇◇◇◇◇◇◇◇◇

## Judy Garland Museum

### opened 1994 | Grand Rapids, Minnesota

I n Frank L. Baum's novel, *The Wonderful Wizard of Oz*, Dorothy tells the Scarecrow, "There is no place like home." For Judy Garland, the star of the movie adaptation of the novel, home was in the picturesquely named city of Grand Rapids. To pay tribute to the actress and to the childhood classic, one can follow the yellow brick road to the Judy Garland Museum.

Few films—no matter how much time goes by—bring to mind as many memories as does *The Wizard of Oz*. The 1939 classic evokes images of ruby slippers, a gingham dress, witches both good and evil, Munchkins, flying monkeys, and a once in a century voice. The movie also recalls young Dorothy Gale and her heartfelt wish to escape to the land over the rainbow.

A star was born in 1922 as Frances Ethel Gumm (called Judy) joined sisters Mary Jane and Dorothy Virginia Gumm. Their parents, Frank and Ethel Gumm, were vaudeville performers who put their daughters on stage at the family's New Grand Theater, where musical acts coincided with silent films. Her 1924 stage debut occurred when her two siblings stepped aside to reveal the two-year-old Baby Gumm, who belted out "Jingle Bells." Frank carried his toddler off the stage as she kicked and shouted, "I wanna sing some more." After a theater marquee

inadvertently spelt out Glumm instead of Gumm, upon the recommendation of George Jessel, the family went by Garland. The name Judy derived from a Hoagy Carmichael song.

As the movie industry was pushing vaudeville toward its swan song, in 1926, Ethel, children in tow, moved to the West Coast. The essence of the pushy stage mother, Ethel doled out pep pills "to keep those girls going!" followed by evening sleeping pills. An adult Judy referred to Ethel as the "real Wicked Witch of the West." While his wife booked performances and pushed pills, Frank propositioned boys in the back rows of his theater. The child-star sang, "Zing! Went the Strings of My Heart" on Los Angeles radio while her father was in the hospital with meningitis. Frank died the next day, leading Judy to remark, "It was the most terrible thing that ever happened to me in my life."

In *A Star is Born*, actor James Mason told Judy Garland, "I never heard anybody sing...just the way you do." At age thirteen, MGM studio bigwig Louis B. Mayer cried upon hearing Judy's perfect pitch and signed her on the spot. Of her God-given voice, she observed, "I have a machine in my throat that gets into people's ears and affects them." Because of Mayer's badgering "to reduce," while she sang of lemon drops in character as Dorothy, Judy's diet consisted of chicken broth and black coffee. There was a price to pay to fit her four-feet eleven-inch frame into her blue-and-white gingham dress. Sleeping pills, diet pills, and a starvation diet made for a dangerous cocktail. A grueling schedule led Judy to remark, "I started to feel like a windup toy from FAO Schwarz." Further problems arrived with rumored sexual harassment from MGM executives.

Her 1939 role in *The Wizard of Oz* made the Minnesota girl the North Star in Hollywood's firmament. Dorothy and Judy had similar lives: Midwesterners transported to lands of fantasy that only appeared beautiful while wearing green-tinted glasses. Judy received a special Juvenile Academy Award Oscar that she

*Judy Garland Museum | Permission of the Judy Garland Museum*

christened her Munchkin Award. The same year, she left her hands and footprint in Grauman's Chinese Theatre.

Judy's romantic life offered little respite. In the Emerald City, Dorothy exclaimed, "My! People come and go so quickly here," and the same could be said for Judy's husbands. She had five unfulfilling trips down the aisle. Her marriage to director Vincente Minnelli resulted in the birth of Liza, christened after an Ira Gershwin song, "Liza All the Clouds'll Roll Away." Judy kept Ethel away from her grandchildren. Marriage to director Sidney Luft produced Lorna and Joe. The star lamented she longed for the love of a man rather than the applause of thousands.

Self-medication took its toll; after fifteen years, MGM removed the legend who had become a liability. The self-admitted "queen of the comeback" rallied, appearing in an acclaimed role in the 1954 film *A Star is Born*. When Grace Kelly won for *A Country Girl*, Groucho Marx reportedly sent her a telegram, "Dear Judy, this is the biggest robbery since Brinks."

Playing the role of Sally Bowles in *Cabaret*, Liza won the Oscar—the award that had eluded her mother—where she reminisced about a prostitute named Elsie. She sang, "The day she died the neighbors came to snicker: 'Well, that's what you get from too much pills and liquor.' " In 1969, Judy passed away from the same affliction that plagued Elsie; the difference was, rather than snickers, her death launched an avalanche of grief. For hours, 20,000 fans waited in line behind police barricades at the Frank E. Campbell Funeral Home to gaze their last upon the actress in her white and gold coffin. Bouquets arrived from Fred Astaire, Irving Berlin, and James Stewart. A huge wreath of peonies shaped like a rainbow made for a heart-rending arrangement. Attending the funeral service were Lauren Bacall, Katherine Hepburn, Mickey Rooney, Frank Sinatra, and Cary Grant. In 2017, her children arranged for their mother's remains to be exhumed from the Ferncliff Cemetery north of New York and reinterred at the Hollywood Forever Cemetery. The Judy Garland Pavilion is in the vicinity of fellow celebrities ranging from Rudolph Valentino to Hattie McDaniel.

**Judy Garland Museum:** Fans of the icon can head to the home where Judy spent her first four years. Although she rarely returned to her Minnesota hometown, in a 1958 movie magazine interview, she stated, "Basically, I am still Judy Garland, a plain American girl from Grand Rapids, Minnesota, who's had a lot of good breaks, a few tough breaks." Although later the resident of pleasure domes in Los Angeles, Malibu, London, and Manhattan, there was no place like the home of her birth at 435 Hoffman Avenue in Grand Rapids, Minnesota. The Gumms/Garlands lived in a charming, late nineteenth-century, white clapboard house. New York based interior designer (and Judy enthusiast), Marc Charbonnet explained, "This little farmhouse has been blown around like the house in *The Wizard of Oz*." The 1892 structure had been situated in two other addresses after the family sold it: In the 1930s, it moved to a site a dozen blocks away; then in the 1990s, to its present location at 2727 S. Pokegama Avenue.

Charbonnet spent two years acquiring period furnishings, wallpaper, fabrics to make the house appear as it did when the Gumms walked its halls. Some vintage artifacts located in the house: Singer sewing machine, small grand piano, Underwood typewriter, and camera. The staircase landing holds the ghosts of the three sisters who stood on them to entertain while their mother accompanied them on the piano. Her family understood Baby was a prodigy when the two-year-old stood by the railing and belted out "My Country, 'Tis of Thee." In the upstairs master bedroom is Judy's crib, with a doll, teddy bear, and quilt. A walled-in side porch holds a scooter and roller skates, the sisters' variation of Rosebud.

Adjacent to the residence is a museum, a shrine to Garland and *The Wizard of Oz* whose pathway is a yellow brick road. Behind plexiglass is Dorothy's blue-and-white check gingham dress, and on a wall is an Andy Warhol serigraph bearing an image of the silver screen queen and the phrase, "What becomes a legend most?" A green-hued room displays the carriage from *The Wizard of Oz* film on a rotating stand, the vehicle that carried the four friends around the Emerald City. A Winkie spear from the witch's castle is seen nearby. Among other treasures is a first edition of *The Wonderful Wizard of Oz* signed by Jack Haley, Ray Bolger, Bert Lahr, and Judy Garland. Another sacred artifact is an original script from *A Star is Born*. In 2014, the museum merited mention in *The Guinness Book of World Records* when 1,093 people dressed in Oz costumes congregated on the premise.

In 2005, John Kelsch, the founding director of the Judy Garland Museum, had just stepped out of a shower when he received horrifying news in a call from Kathe Johnson: "They're gone!" Feeling as if he were caught up in a cyclone, John arrived at the museum to discover all that was left of the original ruby slippers was a single red sequin. A donor offered a million-dollar reward for the shoes, valued at between $3.5 to $6 million. But it took far more than three clicks of the heels to bring the revered memorabilia home. After eighteen years, the police recovered the slippers in a discovery that resulted in the arrest of Terry Jon Martin. Janie Heitz, the executive director of the museum, explained Martin thought the shoes were made from rubies, thereby proving the thief was in need of what the Scarecrow wanted from the Wizard.

Viewing her life through the lens of her fractured family and broken romances, Judy rued she had never attained the land where the bluebirds sing. Tragically, she should have heeded the wisdom of the Wizard, "A heart is not judged by how much you love, but by how much you are loved by others."

**Seen from Her Window:** Standing on the balcony of her childhood home, Judy would have seen the 1895 Old Stone School, so called because the builders made it from stone from the Grand River. Frances Ethel Gumm would have been part of its student body had her voice—the source of her triumph and tragedy—not transformed her destiny.

# CHAPTER 22

# "J'ai Deux Amours"

*"I don't lie. I improve on life."*

## —JOSEPHINE BAKER

◇◇◇◇◇◇◇◇◇◇

## Château & Jardins des Milandes

### opened 2001 | Castelnaud-la-Chapelle, France

"Un coup de coeur" loosely translates to "love at first sight." This French expression well describes how Josephine Baker felt upon first gazing at what she called Sleeping Beauty's Castle. To experience the enchantment, step back in time and enter the Château des Milandes.

The entertainer who gave bananas a niche in the pantheon of entertainment and who trod the path from ghetto to castle, wore many lavish hats. "A Black childhood is always a little sad," Josephine remarked; hers began in 1906 in St. Louis, Missouri, as Freda Josephine McDonald. Her teenaged washerwoman mother, Carrie, called her chubby baby "Tumpy" in a play on Humpty Dumpty, a nickname that stuck even after poverty made her daughter rail thin. Carrie beat her daughter and informed her that her birth had been an accident. By age eleven, Josephine was working as a maid for a white family where her employer, Mrs. Keiser, burned her hands with scalding water for using too much laundry soap.

Shedding the name Freda, at age thirteen, she wed Willie Wells, a man twice her age, who hit her on her head with a bottle during an argument. She fared no better with her second husband, railroad porter William Howard Baker, whom she wed at age fifteen. Josephine fled from William and St. Louis, desperate for a fresh start.

*Josephine Baker clad in her trademark banana skirt |*
Wikimedia Commons, Lucien Waléry

Josephine booked a one-way ticket to New York, where she electrified Black Broadway in her role in *Shuffle Along*, a performance that thrust her into the Harlem Renaissance. In 1925, Anita Loos published *Gentlemen Prefer Blondes*, a title the nineteen-year-old Josephine refuted when she became one of the world's most popular entertainers. In Paris, Josephine starred in the production, *La Revue Nègre*, at the Théâtre des Champs-Élysées. The finale was the "Danse Sauvage," where Josephine performed nude except for a pink flamingo feather between her legs. While the hit song of 1923 had been, "Yes, We Have No Bananas," Josephine had sixteen gold ones on her infamous banana skirt. Her sexual gyrations ushered in France's love affair with the dancer Parisians dubbed "The Bronze Venus." The crowds cheered for "La Ba-kir" then, simply, "Jasephine." Ernest Hemingway declared her, "The most sensational woman anyone ever saw." Pablo Picasso dubbed her "the Nefertiti of now." Alexander Calder created a sculpture of her in wire. Her role in the 1927 film *Siren of the Tropics* made her the first Black woman to star in a movie. Dolls bore her likeness, clad in her banana skirt. The girl who had started out on the wrong side of the tracks wore couture by Balenciaga and walked Chiquita, her pet cheetah, who sported a diamond-studded leash. The star socialized with Picasso, Colette, and Hemingway.

Not everyone was in Camp Jasephine. The Catholic Church condemned her blatant sexuality and hounded her stiletto-heeled footsteps. Austrian headlines denounced the "Black Devil." The Third Reich's propaganda minister, Joseph Goebbels, held her up as an example of degenerate, *untermenschlich* art.

With a dread of sleeping alone, Josephine had a relationship with a Spanish gigolo, as well as the self-styled Italian Count Abatino who served as her manager. Cohabiting with "the Count" did not preclude affairs with an Indian maharajah, a Swedish prince, and alleged liaisons with Colette and Frida Kahlo. A third trip down the aisle was with the French Jewish industrialist, Jean Lion. Despite the appeal of his surname for the animal-loving star, Madame Lion filed for divorce due to his infidelities.

When the Nazis goosestepped into France, Josephine enlisted in the—as she referred to it in her heavily accented French—"Rey-zis-tonce," trading in her banana skirt for a uniform. Her country castle, the Château des Milandes, which had once been a fifteenth-century fortress, became a fortress once more, harboring fugitives and arms. When Nazi officials arrived at her door with a search warrant, the château did not give up its resistance fighters. One mission entailed smuggling military intelligence using invisible ink on her undergarments. In case of capture, she carried a cyanide pill. After the war, President Charles de Gaulle pinned the medal of the Rosette of the Resistance on her uniform.

In 1947, Josephine married her bandleader, Jo Bouillon; after a miscarriage, she opened des Milandes to orphans of various countries, such as Korea, Finland, Algeria, Columbia, Japan. In a Christmas card, she wrote of "twelve tiny tots who were blown together by a soft wind as a symbol of universal brotherhood." She dressed her "Rainbow Tribe" in their native garb and maintained their birth religions. She tried to provide them with the happy childhoods she had never experienced; however, as she was kept busy operating des Milandes as a theme park, nannies often served as nurturers. Josephine commissioned a wax statue of herself as the Virgin Mary surrounded by her children. When their offspring numbered a dozen, Bouillon bid adieu.

Despite her fame, Josephine still faced racism. In the United States, she refused to perform in segregated clubs, and historians credit her activism with the desegregation of Las Vegas casinos. When Manhattan's Stork Club refused service, she made a show of walking out in the company of Grace Kelly, who had overheard the confrontation. The NAACP formed a picket line in front of the restaurant, and Josephine filed legal charges. J. Edgar Hoover placed Josephine on the FBI watch list; the Ku Klux Klan left threatening calls.

As the organizers of the 1963 March on Washington did not allow women as keynote speakers, Josephine addressed the crowd before the official program. On that historic occasion, there was no banana skirt nor rhinestone-studded microphone. Instead, she wore the uniform of the Free French Air Force that displayed her Legion of Honor Medal. In contrast to her flamboyant dance moves,

*Josephine's Sleeping Beauty Castle Château des Milandes* | *Wikimedia Commons, Bthv*

her speech was spartan, "I have walked into the palaces of kings and queens and into the houses of presidents. But I could not walk into a hotel in America and get a cup of coffee..." Before she concluded, she looked out over the quarter-of-a-million-strong, multiracial crowd and stated, "Salt and pepper, just what it should be." After the march, Josephine wrote a letter to Dr. Martin Luther King Jr. that she signed, "Your sister in battle."

Belying the expression "cheaper by the dozen," the cost of caring for her children and the upkeep of her castle dissipated her fortune. During a rainstorm, gendarmes physically evicted a hysterical Josephine from her adored Milandes. Financial assistance from Princess Grace and Brigitte Bardot allowed for the purchase of a Monaco villa. The last performance of her half century long career took place at the Club Bobina, where the diva drove a motorcycle across the stage. In attendance were Sophia Loren, Diana Ross, and Liza Minnelli. A few days later, Josephine passed away from a cerebral hemorrhage; glowing reviews of her show lay on her bed. Twenty thousand mourners lined the streets to bid farewell to "Jasephine."

**Château des Milandes:** This 1489 castle that overlooks the Dordogne River and Valley was the home and fortress of the Caumont family until the French Revolution. François de Caumont christened it mi-landa, "among the moors." In

1950, Josephine installed a ground-floor mosaic featuring the Caumont's coat of arms, which includes three gold leopards that also appear above an oversized fireplace. Medieval mementoes are much in evidence: stained glass windows, turrets, and gargoyles. The chapel served as the venue for Josephine's 1947 marriage to Jo Bouillon, and it is where she baptized those of her adopted children who hailed from a Roman Catholic heritage. During a 2017 renovation, builders unearthed paintings by Renaissance artists as well as a crypt. The current owner is Angélique de Saint-Exupéry, whose husband is a relative of Antoine de Saint-Exupéry, the author of the famed story *The Little Prince.*

Josephine employed ten gardeners to maintain the three-hundred—acre estate, whose path leads to a riverbank. Within the grounds' six parks are Ural owls, white-tailed eagles, and hedgehogs. Guests can participate in the medieval sport of falconry. One can imagine Josephine's menagerie walking its grounds: her Great Dane, Bonzo, her monkey, Glouglou, and her pig, Albert.

Josephine created Jorama, a wax museum that showcased her in various incarnations; one such was a life-size Josephine in her scandalous *La Revue Nègre* costume, lounging before an Art Deco backdrop. The museum's grand salon has velvet-covered walls and houses dozens of the star's costumes and dresses, most involving crystals, all in size remove-a-rib. The library holds the crown jewel: the gold banana skirt-encased in glass, with descriptive text that touts it as "the most famous costume in show business." A bathroom resembles a bottle of Arpège by Lanvin, her favorite scent; accents are gold-plated taps, Murano glass mosaics, and a green porcelain tub. The Resistance Room has exhibits depicting Josephine's valor, including a letter from President Charles de Gaulle. The only photograph of Josephine in distress is one of her 1969 eviction where she is sitting on her home's front steps in the rain, refusing to relinquish Sleeping Beauty's Castle.

Forty-six years after her death, members of the French Air Force carried Josephine's flag-draped coffin—that held soil from St. Louis, Monaco, and the Château des Milandes—into the Panthéon, making her the first Black woman to be honored in the hallowed tomb. Per the request of her family, her body remains in a Monaco cemetery. The backdrop of the ceremony was the cadence of Josephine's signature song, one that could have symbolized her adoration of France and Milandes: "J'ai Deux Amours," which translates to "I Have Two Loves."

**Seen from Her Window:** The view from Josephine's castle encompassed the expanse of the Dordogne Valley and magnificent gardens. Josephine's "Sleeping Beauty" castle surpassed the dreams of the girl from the St. Louis projects as she looked upon her rainbow tribe, animal menagerie, and legendary guests.

# PART IV

# *The Scientists*

# CHAPTER 23

# *Ethereal Blue Light*

*"I don't know. You can ask my husband."*

## —MARIE CURIE'S

response when a journalist asked
how it felt to be married to a genius

◇◇◇◇◇◇◇◇◇◇

## The Maria Sklodowska-Curie Museum

opened in 1967 | Warsaw, Poland

O ne is as likely to witness a blue moon, find a hen's tooth, or catch a glimpse of bigfoot as one is likely to encounter a Nobel Prize recipient in everyday life. Miraculously, one family garnered five of the coveted awards between them. Two memorial museums are dedicated to an acclaimed scientist: Paris's Musée Curie and Poland's Maria Sklodowska-Curie Museum.

The crown princess of science bequeathed the world a treatment for cancer, two new elements on the periodic table, and the Atomic Age. Marya (whose family called her Manya, although history remembers her as Marie) was born in 1867, the fifth and last child of Wladyslaw Sklodowska, a teacher, and his wife Bronislawa Sklodowska, a headmistress of a girls' school. The national sorrow was the loss of Polish freedom under Tsarist Russia. The family's private pain derived from the deaths of oldest daughter, Zofia, from typhus and then Bronislawa from tuberculosis.

Marya Sklodowska's evolution into Marie Curie came about because of Warsaw University's ban on female students. As voracious for knowledge as Dr. Faustus, Marie participated in her city's Flying University, an underground women's school. Desirous of a degree, Marie and her sister Bronia plotted to enroll

*Dr. Curie 1903
Nobel Prize Portrait |
Wikimedia Commons,
Nobel Foundation*

in the Sorbonne. Marie agreed to finance her sister's medical training; in turn, Bronia would support her when she became a physician.

Marie worked as a governess, and in a letter to her family, she wrote of her despair of "ever becoming anybody." Consolation arrived when she fell for her wealthy employer's son. As Marie was not of their social class, the relationship ended. For distraction, her father sent her complex mathematical problems to solve. Five years later, after Bronia had received her MD—one of three women among thousands of men—she sent a one-way ticket from Poland to Paris. Marie made the trip while sitting on a stool in the train's fourth-class section, as she could not afford a seat. The young woman displayed fortitude by travelling alone, an act at the time typically associated with prostitutes.

In Paris, the workaholic rented a sixth-floor garret in the Latin quarter. Thrilled when she came in first in her physics examinations, she berated herself over her second place in mathematics. Four years later, Marie met Pierre Curie, whom she fell for upon hearing about his quadrant electrometer. What woman could resist? They had found their soulmates and were married in 1895 in a civil ceremony for which the bride wore a cotton blue dress. The honeymoon revolved around cycling.

Consumed by their experiments, meals consisted of bread and coffee. Wanting to work as much as possible, after the birth of her daughter, Irene, Marie relegated childcare to her recently widowed father-in-law, Eugene, a retired physician. Pierre, who worked as a physics professor, knew his colleagues viewed his wife as a "Marie Marie Quite Contrary," like "Mary" of nursery rhyme fame, because she preferred holding a beaker to holding a baby bottle. The Curies conducted their experiments in a shed described as "a cross between a stable and a potato cellar." The walls consisted of rough planks, and the glass roof

*Marie Curie's Birthplace* | Wikimedia Commons, Tilman2007

bore makeshift patches that let in the rain. Inside were three battered tables, a few chairs, and a potbellied stove. The asphalt floor had a few coarse mats. Yet in these inauspicious surroundings, Marie and Pierre made a groundbreaking scientific breakthrough.

While the Curies christened their daughters Irene and Eve, they also named their discoveries: One was a radioactive element they called radium from the Latin for "ray," while the other was the element polonium, christened as a tribute to Poland.

Of the ethereal beauty of their radiation, Marie mused, "The glowing tubes looked like faint, fairy lights." The substance served as a novelty that appeared on watch faces, cream and lipstick jars, toothpaste, and laxatives. But the element that emitted a fairy light had insidious effects. By the time Pierre had received a chair at the Sorbonne, he limped from bone deterioration.

In 1903, the Curies received the Nobel Prize in physics, making Marie the first woman in history to garner the gold standard of awards. As a female, Marie was not permitted to speak during the ceremony. The President of the Academy delivered a biblical quotation that downplayed Madame Curie's contribution, "It is not good that man should be alone. I will make a helpmeet for him." Pierre's counter was his wife was far more than a mere helper. Fame dogged their footsteps, and journalists even reported on their black-and-white cat.

Tragedy followed triumph. Three years later, as Pierre absentmindedly stepped off the curb, a horse-drawn wagon crushed him under its wheels. Two years later, the president of France, the French Cabinet, the president of the University of Paris, and scientists from three continents gathered in the Sorbonne. The occasion for the august meeting was that Marie Curie had assumed her late husband's chair in physics, making her the first female Sorbonne professor. On the auspicious occasion of her first lecture, she wore a plain black dress, bowed, and waited for the applause to die down. Professor Curie addressed her audience, "Pierre Curie has prepared the following lesson for you."

Far from being a merry widow (Albert Einstein commented that he found her "as cold as a herring"), a tsunami erupted with the news that madame liked sex as well as science. The object of her passion was Pierre's former student, Paul Langevin, with whom she rendezvoused in an apartment near the Sorbonne. Paul's wife, Jeanne, the mother of his four children, dished the dirt to the press. Paris branded Marie the Polish Jezebel; Paul fought a duel against the journalist. The Swedish Academy, which had just nominated Marie for her second Nobel Prize for chemistry, did not appreciate the scandal. A letter from Stockholm urged Marie not to accept her award in person so as not to force her presence upon King Gustaf V. Madame responded, "There is no connection between my scientific work and my private life." Shortly after the ceremony, she suffered a nervous breakdown.

Redemption arrived with World War I when Marie established the first mobile radiological center, whose X-rays located shrapnel wounds. She worked with her daughter, Irene, who, along with her son-in-law, Frédéric Joliot-Curie, earned the Nobel Prize for their discovery of artificial radioactivity. Interestingly, Irene's daughter married Paul Langevin's son. Her younger sister, Eve, quipped that she was the only one of her family not to have won a Nobel Prize. However, her husband, Henry Richardson Labouisse, as the executive director of UNICEF, accepted the Nobel Peace Prize on the organization's behalf.

Further acclaim arrived in 1921 when Madame Curie made a trip to the United States, where American women raised $100,000 to purchase a grain of radium, with President Harding presenting the donation. Eight years later, President Hoover awarded her $50,000.

Marie had dedicated her life to science; what remains murky is if she knew she had also sacrificed her body. Long exposure to radiation had taken its toll; at age sixty-six, basically blind from cataracts, lesions covered her body. She sought treatment in a remote sanatorium in the French Alps under the shadow of Mont Blanc. The martyr to radium died in 1934, poisoned by the very substance that had gifted her immortality. Eve and Irene accompanied their mother's body to a crypt twenty miles from Paris, where they laid her to rest next to Pierre. The few other mourners laid roses on her casket. The international press carried the news of her passing. In 1995, President François Mitterrand arranged for her entombment in the Panthéon. She was the first woman to receive the honor based on her own, rather than a husband's, merit. President Lech Walesa of Poland was present at the ceremony. Although her life held many honors, she summed up her biography, "I was born in Poland. I married Pierre Curie, and I have two daughters. I have done my work in France." Irene and Frédéric died from the same scourge. Frédéric deemed it "our occupational disease."

**The Maria Sklodowska-Curie Museum:** The Polish Chemical Society founded this museum in Marie's eighteenth-century family home on the centenary of her birth. In tribute, her countrymen affixed an honorary plaque on its exterior. During the 1944 Warsaw Uprising, Nazis had targeted the building, but the plaque remained intact. On display in the home museum is an elephant figurine that President Herbert Hoover presented to Madame Curie in 1929 during her visit to the White House. One of the five rooms is a recreation of Marie's Parisian laboratory; another showcases photos and personal effects.

A difference between the Polish and Parisian museums is that the French one houses papers, furniture, and books that, even after a century, remain radioactive. If visitors want to investigate madame's possessions, they must wear protective clothing and sign a waiver of liability. The warning makes sense: Radium-226 has a half-life of 1,601 years.

For those who see with analytical eyes, the Maria Sklodowska Curie Museum showcases the remnants of a remarkable life. But for those who observe with an eye attuned to the supernatural, the rooms are suffused with an ethereal blue light.

**Seen from Her Window:** If young Marya Sklodowska, who became Dr. Marie Curie, had possessed a crystal ball, she would have seen in its depths two Nobel Prizes, her beloved Pierre, and her interment in the Panthéon.

# CHAPTER 24

# *By the Seashore*

*"The world has used me so unkindly,
I fear it has made me suspicious of everyone."*

## —MARY ANNING

◇◇◇◇◇◇◇◇◇◇

### Lyme Regis Museum

opened 1921 | Lyme Regis, England

The museum is built on the site of Mary Anning's home

(not in the original structure).

After visiting Lyme Regis, the seaside town overlooking the English Channel, Jane Austen mined the ancient site for locations to use in her novel, *Persuasion*. The author wrote, "A very strange stranger it must be, who does not see the charms in the immediate environs of Lyme." But the charms sought by the celebrated Victorian fossil hunter, Mary Anning, were the skeletal remains of ancient creatures hidden in the Jurassic Coast. To partake of her expeditions into a vanished world, visit the Lyme Regis Museum.

A saying holds that the times make the man; yet it is equally true that environment shapes destiny. Mary Anning was born and spent her life in nineteenth-century Lyme Regis, Dorset, England. The isolated town received its name from its location on the Lyme River; in 1284, King Edward I granted it a royal charter that resulted in the addition of the royal Regis to the town's name. The village's beach consists of hundreds of rocks lashed by the waves of the English Channel. Standing sentry are the Blue Lias (blue from its blue-gray color, Lias from the word for layers pronounced in a Dorset accent), in whose limestone and

shale cliffs reside creatures that swam the seas when dinosaurs roamed the Earth. The area is known as the Jurassic Coast after its geological history, which stretches back 205 million years.

While Jane Austen was writing tales of husband-hunting heroines, Mary was knee-deep in clay, on the prowl for prehistoric bones. Born in 1799, her parents, Richard, a cabinetmaker, and Mary, a lacemaker, were Dissenters, a term referring to those who had separated from the Church of England. In addition to their poverty, the couple endured the loss of eight of their ten children. Their only remaining offspring were Joseph and Mary; her name was the same as a sister who had died from burns when her clothes caught on fire. When the future paleontologist was fifteen months old, Elizabeth Haskings, a family friend, along with two companions, brought the baby to an outdoor festival. After a storm erupted, lightning killed the three women, miraculously sparing the infant.

Richard supplemented his income by selling fossils that he referred to as curiosities. Jane Austen visited Lyme Regis twice and in one instance interacted with Richard Anning. In a letter to her sister, Cassandra, she explained that she had taken a box with a broken lid to the local carpenter for repair but had declined his services as she felt five shillings was "too steep a price." The author used the locale as a backdrop for a scene in her novel *Persuasion*. In her book, Louisa Mulgrave fell off the steps of the Cobb—a man-made fourteenth century harbor wall—and into Captain Wentworth's arms. Several television adaptations used the landmark when filming Austen's novels. In tribute, Lyme Regis holds an annual Jane Austen pilgrimage. Outfitted with a child's chisel, Mary accompanied her father to the inhospitable beaches in search of the Channel's ancient offerings. One winter night, Richard slipped while across the top of the Black Ven (black from its color, Ven from the word for fen in the Dorset dialect). Eleven-year-old Mary was devastated with Richard's death, due to his injuries compounded by consumption (tuberculosis). His pregnant widow—the baby died shortly after birth—had to accept charity. To contribute, Mary, not yet a teenager, sold fossils to the tourists from Bristol, Bath, and London.

The year after Richard's passing, Joseph uncovered the head of a creature with huge eyes and a mouth that could hold two hundred teeth. For the next few months, Mary—along with quarrymen—scoured for the remainder of the skeleton. On a typical day, she usually exposed an area half the size of her hand. Removing the debris of 200 million years from fossilized remains was an arduous endeavor.

Tenacity paid off when Mary unearthed an Ichthyosaurus, or "sea-lizard," that had appeared years before dinosaurs had left their first footprints. News spread of the twelve-year-old girl from Lyme Regis who had discovered a sixteen-foot, prehistoric skeleton of a hitherto unknown creature. In a nod to Mary's remarkable find, the Geological Society of London convened to discuss the excavation. The discovery stirred up a tempest in a science teapot, as it challenged the prevailing belief that God's creatures were immutable and eternal. In 1818, the reptile was in the possession of Sir Everard Home, an anatomist at the Royal College of Surgeons. While the body of the prehistoric creature has been lost, the skull still exists.

Throughout her sojourns, Mary, who never married or had a child, had a constant companion in Tray, her devoted dog. In her only known portrait, he (or perhaps another one of her canine companions) is lying at her feet. In 1833, a landslide had claimed the life of Tray.

Other fantastic finds followed: the first complete Plesiosaur and the first British Pterosaur. From her store, situated in the Anning home, Mary sold her wares, and scientists from London came to meet "the fossil girl." One of her customers, Richard Owen, had coined the word "Dinosaur." The king of Saxony also stopped by, and Mary informed him, "I am well known throughout the whole of Europe."

With the exacting standards of a professional paleontologist, Mary illustrated and labeled her specimens. To her great dismay, because of her gender, religion, regional dialect, and socioeconomic standing, she did not receive official status as an expert on the subject. A contemporary wrote, "Men of learning have sucked her brains and made a great deal by publishing works, of which she furnished the contents, while she derived none of the advantages."

**Modern Museum Building** | *Reproduced with permission © Lyme Regis Museum*

Shortly before Mary's passing from breast cancer in 1847, acknowledgment arrived when naturalist Louis Agassiz named two different species of fossil fish after her. Mary's interment was in St. Michael's Parish Church; the Fellows of the Geological Society contributed funds for a stained glass window bearing her likeness.

Another eminent resident of the same coastal village, John Fowles, was the author of *The French Lieutenant's Woman,* whose protagonist was a fossil hunter. The film version, starring Jeremy Irons and Meryl Streep, used Lyme Regis as its setting. John Fowles stated, "One of the meanest disgraces of British paleontology is that although many scientists of the day gratefully used her finds to establish their own reputation, not one native type bears the specific *anningii*." However, the former museum curator was incorrect. There are many species that bear the name *anningii,* including one described in 1847.

It took two centuries, but Mary finally received the full recognition she so richly deserves. London's Natural History Museum designated an area as "The Anning Rooms," a movie starring Kate Winslet as Mary came out in 2020, and the Royal Society named her as one of the ten most important British women in science. On the 223rd anniversary of her birth, an artist created a bronze statue of the paleontology princess, with Tray at her feet, overlooking the Black Ven cliffs.

**The Lyme Regis Museum:** Another memorial to Mary is the Lyme Regis Museum, which Sir David Attenborough pronounced, "A remarkable museum, a gem." The museum is situated on the spot where Mary's first modest home and shop once stood. In this charming emporium, visitors can experience 200 million years of history.

What lends the structure a unique architectural appearance is the juxtaposition of the original 1902 building, red in color, with the 2017 Mary Anning Wing, constructed of glass and zinc, the latter the color of the local Blue Lias stone. Visitors can enjoy a spectacular view of Lyme Bay where the coastlines of Dorset and Devon converge on the Jurassic Coast World Heritage Site. The lamp posts on the beach are designed after the shape of ammonites. The wing consists of an interactive geology gallery that shares its namesake's biography and the story of her fascinating fossils.

The gallery consists of several thematically organized areas. The Geology Gallery features several varieties of ammonites together with innumerable other fossils. A wall holds an Ichthyosaur, "Kevin," of which there are only skeletal remains. The curators mounted the specimen on a board along with a painted outline of its original eighteen-foot five-inch frame. Dominating another wall is a diorama based on Henry de la Beche's 1830 watercolor *Duria Antiquior* ("a more ancient Dorset"); the artist donated the sale of prints of the work to Mary, his childhood friend. He explained that the painting had been made possible due to her treasure hunt in a prehistoric world. The scene depicts prehistoric life based on Lyme Regis fossils. In the foreground, an Ichthyosaur bites the neck of a Plesiosaur. Staring out from a glass case is the skull Joseph Anning had discovered two hundred years earlier; however, most of the displays were the finds of Mary Anning.

Mary Anning succeeded as a scientist despite all odds. The tongue-twister that seems to refer to her is apocryphal; however, it is accurate in one respect: the paleontologist was far more that "the girl who sold seashells by the seashore."

**Seen from Her Window:** If Mary could rise from St. Michael's Church Parish and return to her home, she would look out once more on the Lyme Regis Bay and its surrounding cliffs, where, in the company of Tray, she resurrected ancient reptiles.

# PART V

# The Religious Ladies

# CHAPTER 25

# Of Their Number

*"Afflictions are the steps to heaven."*

**—MOTHER ELIZABETH ANN SETON**

◇◇◇◇◇◇◇◇◇◇

## The National Shrine of Saint Elizabeth Ann Seton

opened 1965 | Emmitsburg, Maryland

It may surprise many to find out that the first American saint recognized by the Vatican was a woman, particularly since the vast majority of Catholic saints are in fact male. It might be even more surprising when one considers she was born not only well-to-do but not Catholic. To learn about the woman who traversed the road from socialite to saint, head to Emmitsburg, Maryland, the site of the National Shrine of Saint Elizabeth Ann Seton.

In 2015, when Pope Francis visited America, he became a septuagenarian superstar. *Time* magazine featured the Bishop of Rome on its cover, his Holiness' fame thereby surpassing that of Syrian President Bashar-al-Assad, whistleblower Edward Snowden, and pop star Miley Cyrus. This surge of devotion to the Holy Father illustrated how far the United States had come from its historic roots where Protestantism ruled the roost. Anti-Roman Catholicism in America was a cross Mother Seton bore.

Born in the colony of New York in 1774, Elizabeth Ann Bayley was the second daughter of Catherine and Dr. Richard Bayley, socially prominent Episcopalians. Dr. Bayley was a professor of surgery and autonomy at King's College, now Columbia University. In the spring of 1777, when Elizabeth was two years old, her mother Catherine died soon after the birth of her third daughter. The baby passed away a year later. Dr. Bayley's second wife, née Charlotte Amelia

*Miniature of Elizabeth, a gift from her husband on their wedding day. The portrait is the only likeness painted during her lifetime* | Courtesy of the National Shrine of Saint Elizabeth Ann Seton

Barclay, was a granddaughter of Jacobus Roosevelt, founder of the Hyde Park branch of the political dynasty. Maria and Elizabeth never warmed up to their stepmother, whom they addressed as Mrs. Bayley. To ease family tensions, Richard sent his two eldest children to live with their Uncle William and Aunt Sarah in New Rochelle, a city the girls' forebears had founded. In one indelible childhood memory—although the story may be apocryphal—fourteen-year-old Elizabeth was standing on Wall Street amidst the celebration of George Washington's appointment as the nation's first president.

When Elizabeth met William Magee Seton, heir to a Manhattan mercantile fortune, he called her Eliza; like the fictional Eliza Doolittle, she could have danced all night. Nineteen-year-old Elizabeth married William in a small ceremony at the home of her sister, Mary Post. The Right Reverend Samuel Provost, the first Protestant Episcopal Bishop of New York, officiated. The bride's adornment was a family keepsake, a gold filigree brooch. The Setons moved into a Wall Street house where their neighbors were Alexander and Elizabeth Hamilton. The Setons' residence echoed to the strains of Elizabeth's piano and William's violin, one that he had purchased in Cremona, Italy—the first known Stradivarius in America. The instrument remained in the family as an heirloom until a grandson left it on a train. In pride of place was a silver tea set that bore the Seton motto, "Hazard Ye Forward." In 1797, Elizabeth's father-in-law, William Seton the elder, was high enough on the societal hierarchy to help organize a ball for President Washington's sixty-fifth birthday.

Life was wonderful until the Setons encountered a period that could be described as,"these are the times that try men's souls." By 1800, William's shipping business went bankrupt due to piracy and conflict in Europe. The couple lost their home and most of their valuables. The financial blow was made even more dire considering William was supporting not only his immediate family but also his six younger stepsiblings. Further heartbreak followed: Dr. Bayley passed away from yellow fever; William came down with tuberculosis.

Praying Italy's warmer climate would provide a cure, William and Elizabeth set sail on *The Shepherdess* to Leghorn, Pisa, with their oldest daughter Anna. Italian officials assumed William suffered from yellow fever and ordered the family into the lazaretto, a dungeon-like quarantine center. William passed away in 1803 at age thirty-five; his widow arranged his burial in the graveyard at St. John's Anglican Church. Elizabeth began to dress in traditional Italian widow's garb—a black dress with a ruffled cap—and continued with it all the days of her life. While waiting for a return passage, mother and daughter stayed with Antonio and Amabilia Filicchi, with whom they toured Florence. Visiting the city's ancient churches, Elizabeth underwent an epiphany: Roman Catholicism "was the one, true Church."

While Elizabeth's conscience was at peace with her decision, her circle was incensed. Elizabeth received the sacrament of Confirmation from the Bishop of Baltimore, the Right Reverend John Carroll, the only Catholic bishop in the country. She wrote to Amabilia, "God is mine, and I am His."

After a year in Baltimore—as Maryland was the state most receptive to Catholics—Elizabeth travelled to Emmitsburg (ten miles south of Gettysburg, Pennsylvania) in a covered wagon. Home was a residence she and her sisters dubbed Stone House—since it was stone cold as drifts of snow entered the decrepit structure. Sixteen women slept in four rooms. Her next residence, dubbed the White House, provided far better accommodation. In Emmitsburg, Elizabeth founded St. Joseph's, the nation's first Catholic school run by an order of sisters. She also established the first order of sisters in the United States, the Sisters of Charity of St. Joseph's. Elizabeth was devastated at the loss of two daughters from tuberculosis: Anna, at age sixteen, and Rebecca, at age fourteen. She interred them under the oaks in a cemetery she christened God's Little Acre. Rather than giving way under the weight of the loss of her husband and two children, Elizabeth remained steadfast to the Seton family motto, "Hazard Ye Forward."

Intrepid to the end, in 1821, as Elizabeth lay dying from the dreaded disease that had stalked her family, she wrote her friend, "Death grins broader in the pot every morning, and I grin at him and show him his Master." Her passing saved her from enduring the horror of her son Richard's death at sea two years later.

*The National Shrine of Saint Elizabeth Ann Seton | Courtesy of the National Shrine of Saint Elizabeth Ann Seton*

A century and a half after Elizabeth's death, Pope Paul VI announced the canonization of Saint Elizabeth Ann Seton. Among the 100,000 onlookers were Carl Kalin and Ann O'Neil, both of whom had recovered from life-threatening illnesses after asking for Mother Seton's intercession; the church deemed their cures miracles. After the canonization ceremony, the words "American saint" were no longer an oxymoron. Another first was the Sistine choir including Americans, such as members of the Emmitsburg Community Chorus. The seventy-seven-year-old pope spoke "ex cathedra," meaning "from the chair," when he proclaimed in English that Blessed Elizabeth Ann Seton to be Saint Elizabeth Ann, forever afterwards to be hailed as "a citizen of Heaven and worthy of veneration by the Universal Church." The ceremony took place against the backdrop of the world's largest church, with the display of a six-yard-long tapestry of Saint Seton in her black habit, standing on a cloud over a globe with North America bathed in sunlight. The canonization represented the result of a century of effort by American Catholics who had lobbied for Elizabeth's sainthood. After her beatification, Catholic Churches could display her statue and could bear her name, both of which transpired in the National Shrine of Elizabeth Ann Seton.

**The National Shrine of Saint Elizabeth Ann Seton:** On the museum's grounds, the visitor can experience Elizabeth's Stone House, whose period furnishings transport one back to the early 1800s. In 2015, President Barack Obama presented Pope Francis with the original key to Elizabeth's first Emmitsburg home. A house reconstructed in historic style on the grounds known as the White House holds a piano from a later period, in a room like the one where Elizabeth taught French and catechism. Another room still displays students' slates of the type used in that period—though not those of the original students—maps, and rows of little chairs. In the corner is where Elizabeth passed away; she met death just as she had met life: unafraid.

The Seton Shrine Museum, refurbished for four million dollars, is a structure of marble and mosaics, stained glass windows and cathedral ceilings. The museum features an enormous painting of St. Seton floating above the Earth, as well as a white statue that originated in Italy. The Basilica, with its monumental dome, includes the Altar of Relics where the patron saint's remains rest in a copper casket.

Through her personal belongings, Elizabeth is resurrected. The museum holds her little red book, a tiny tome that held messages of motherly wisdom to her daughter Catherine. Sentimental objects include the hand-painted wedding porcelain miniatures that depict Elizabeth and her husband. On the back of her miniature portrait are strands of her hair, while the back of her husband's displays his initials. Further bridal mementoes are her gold filigree bridal brooch and cream-colored shoes. Elizabeth's black widow's cap with its ruffled frill is especially moving. Other family mementoes are Catherine's christening gown, locks from her daughters' hair, and her father's tea chest, which still holds remnants of tea leaves. The religious relics of yesteryear: her red glass bead rosary and crucifix, bearing a skull and crossbones. For over two centuries, a large woodcarving featuring the scene from Calvary hung over the fireplace on the White House wall. The artifact, likely a gift from the Filicchi family, is now in the Servant Gallery of the National Shrine.

For her life of selfless devotion, when the saints went marching in to heaven, no doubt Mother Seton was of their number.

**Seen from Her Window**: If Mother Seton could have gazed from Stone House to the National Shrine of Saint Elizabeth Ann Seton, this New Testament quotation could have come to mind: "God moves in a mysterious way, His wonders to perform."

## CHAPTER 26

# *Remained to Pray*

*"I am not a healer. Jesus is the healer. I am only the*
*office girl who opens the door and says, 'Come in.'"*

**—AIMEE SEMPLE MCPHERSON**

◇◇◇◇◇◇◇◇◇◇

### Foursquare Heritage Center—
### The Parsonage of Aimee Semple McPherson

opened 2006 | Los Angeles, California

It can be a daunting endeavor for Canadians to achieve acclaim in the United States, but a few have managed to make their mark. One of the successful who transformed herself into America's evangelist was born Aimee Elizabeth Kennedy in Ingersoll, Ontario. Her spirit resides in the Parsonage of Aimee Semple McPherson.

Sister Aimee was the most colorful and controversial of evangelists. She was born in 1890, the only offspring of Methodist James Kennedy; he wed wife Mildred (known as Minnie) when he was fifty and his bride was fifteen. A prodigy at prayer, at age four, Aimee could recite all the books of the Bible, taught her dog, Jip, about the Lord, and preached to the barnyard animals. The twelve-year-old's oratory mesmerized a crowd of 15,000 in her province's fabled Albert Hall.

Aimee attended a revival conducted by an Irish immigrant Pentecostal preacher, Robert Semple; she went on to marry him just before her eighteenth birthday. The Semples headed to China as missionaries; in Hong Kong, Robert died from malaria, leaving his widow in Asia without money and pregnant with their daughter, Roberta Star Semple.

*Aimee Semple McPherson preaching at the newly built Angelus Temple* | Copyright Protected. Used by express consent of the International Church of the Foursquare Gospel

Mother and baby headed for New York, where Aimee's mother Minnie had moved. After Aimee wed Harold McPherson, they held tent revivals on the East Coast. The life of itinerant preachers proved daunting as they washed diapers in streams and spent nights in tents fighting off mosquitoes. Harold abandoned his wife and their son, Rolf, and returned to his grocery business. At the wheel of her jalopy, Aimee drove throughout the country preaching fundamentalist salvation in teachings she christened the Foursquare Gospel. The name alluded to four cornerstones: regeneration, baptism in the spirit, divine healing, and the Second Coming.

The nomadic life ended when Aimee received a divine message "that bade me build a house unto the Lord." She arrived in Los Angeles with ten dollars and her tambourine; with donations from the faithful, she purchased a property that faced Echo Park. There she founded the Evangelistic and Missionary Training Institute, which attracted fifty students on its first day. As it was too small for the school, Aimee transformed the parsonage into her home, where she lived for the next fourteen years. In the lot next door, she founded the 5,300-seat Angelus Temple; it included a dome that became a local landmark, crystal doors, and a lighted cross on the rooftop visible from fifty miles away. The Angelus Temple housed KFSG (with "FSG" representing the name Foursquare Gospel), one of the first religious radio stations that delivered "the word" from Australia to Africa. Upon paying off the $1.5 million mortgage on New Year's Eve, Sister Aimee burned the real estate document in a huge urn on the temple's dome. Klieg lights spotlighted the evangelist as she lit a match while 15,000 onlookers cheered and white-clad clergy with white cloth wings danced on the dome.

With a Bible under one arm and red roses in the other, Sister Aimee promised salvation. Amongst the congregation were thousands of the ill and the crippled, all begging to be healed. With a flair for the theatrical, dressed as a policewoman, she

*The Foursquare Heritage Center* | Steve Zeleny

rode a motorcycle across her stage and cried out, "Stop! You're speeding to Hell!" Actresses Clara Bow and Jean Harlow studied her performances. Allegedly, Aimee inspired Cole Porter's aptly named song "Anything Goes." Her children, Roberta and Rolf, rode horses at actor Tom Mix's stable, while Aimee drove a black sedan painted with white letters: "Jesus is Coming Soon—Get Ready." Aimee visited leper colonies and provided succor to the women in the floating brothels on the Cantonese River. In an era rife with discrimination, Aimee held an egalitarian philosophy. Actor Anthony Quinn stated that without the church's intervention, the Mexican community would have starved during the Depression. While her fellow fundamentalist white Protestants maintained racial segregation, Aimee welcomed Black preachers to her pulpit. An early proponent of gender equality, she ordained female ministers.

Sister Aimee's life was a nod to the Byronic "stranger than fiction," and her popularity surpassed that of P. T. Barnum, Harry Houdini, and President Teddy Roosevelt. In 1926, upon returning from a trip to Palestine, Aimee was at Ocean Park Beach, California, where the evangelist, in a green bathing suit, swam out past the pier. Afterwards, news of her death dominated the headlines, while the Angelus Church Temple's faithful held a month-long beachside vigil. Thirty-six days later, Sister Aimee reappeared in Agua Prieta, Mexico, across the border from Douglas, Arizona, explaining desperadoes had abducted her for a $500,000 ransom. Escape from an isolated shack was achieved by cutting through her restraints with the jagged edge of a syrup can and walking for seventeen hours. News of her resurrection led to a media frenzy. Her flock was ecstatic; her critics, skeptical. The police questioned her abduction because her dress and shoes were pristine and she was neither sunburned nor dehydrated. Rumor held that the celebrity evangelist had been on a romantic tryst in a Carmel cottage with the married Kenneth Gladstone Ormiston, a KFSG engineer, who was AWOL at the same time. Aimee told reporters, "That's my story, boys, and I'm sticking with it." The Los Angeles district attorney ordered Aimee's arrest on charges of "corruption of public morals, and obstruction of justice." A judge eventually dropped the charges.

From that point on, Sister Aimee spent time battling in courts of law as well as battling the court of public opinion—and battling her mother. Minnie and Aimee fought over the management of the temple; in one argument, Minnie claimed her daughter punched her in the nose. Ma retaliated by dishing dirt on Aimee's finances. In a 1930 reconciliation, the two travelled abroad, where Aimee preached beside the Sea of Galilee, visited Parisian nightclubs, and had a facelift. The next year, Aimee eloped to Yuma, Arizona, where she married choir singer David Hutton. Post nuptials, David and Aimee cooed over the radio from the bridal boudoir in the evangelist's home and signed off with a wet smack. The following day, Pasadena nurse Myrtle Joan Hazel St. Pierre sued the "Big Boy" (David topped three hundred pounds) for breach of promise and eventually won. When Aimee learned of the lawsuit, she fainted, with a fall that caused a skull fracture serious enough she bled from her nose and ears; nevertheless she recovered. On the subject of another foray into matrimony, Aimee declared, "*Jamais encore*," which translates to "Never again." Daughter Roberta brought a suit for slander against her mother that ended with a two-thousand-dollar judgment against Aimee. One afternoon, Aimee appeared in three different courtrooms in one day, for which she wore three different suits. A news photograph covered the event with the caption, "Her Life's Just One Suit After Another." Throughout her travails, Aimee, head held high, stated, "I only remember the hours when the sun shines." Ignoring hostility, she founded a branch of her Foursquare ministry in the Amazon.

For the woman who led a storied life—as the chatelaine of a Temecula Castle, hobnobbing with the famous and experiencing fabulous fortune—her final days in 1944 were a denouement. She was in Oakland, California, where she had ridden in a horse-drawn buggy to an auditorium to conduct a revival sermon, the last time she shouted out "Hallelujah!" At age fifty-three, Sister Aimee passed away, likely from an accidental overdose of barbiturates, in the arms of her son, Rolf. She left him her church, which now claims ten million followers in 150 countries and property valued at $1.3 billion. To her ma, she left ten dollars.

**Foursquare Heritage Center—The Parsonage of Aimee Semple McPherson:** If there were such an award, the Oscar for best home parsonage would surely go to the Aimee Semple McPherson Parsonage in the aptly named Echo Park as it retains echoes of the era the evangelist ruled from the pulpit. If the walls could talk, the living room would whisper about celebrities such as neighbor Charlie Chaplin. A 1927 Fisher player piano is heard—via an iPad—echoing Aimee's original songs. A case holds her tambourine; on its back is her name and her self-designed coat of arms bearing the Latin motto "Res Non Verba," which means, "Do it, don't just say it." In a corner resides Aimee's white-covered Bible and a 1924 Rose Bowl Trophy garnered from the occasion the Angelus Temple float won first prize. Seemingly incongruous, sits a pair of wooden shoes. Aimee wore them, dressed in traditional Dutch attire, when she delivered her sermon, "A Leak in the Dike." Nearby, on a stand, is a white dress that she bought in which to preach in Rhode Island. She found the dress in a store's section devoted to servants' clothing. She felt the garment was apropos as she was a servant of the Lord. The white was a nod to the biblical dove. The fireplace mantle displays a photograph of Robert Semple; by the door is one of Aimee and her ma.

The dresser in Aimee's bedroom retains a handkerchief sprayed with her signature scent, Quelques Fleurs. A Corona typewriter with a paper in it with words to a sermon rests on her bed. Her painting is on the wall, alongside purple drapes.

The staircase's handrail has a ball that contains a streetcar token; a nod to the time parishioners needed carfare. Leading up the stairs are photographs of Aimee in various countries, as well as mementoes of her international ministries such as tribal masks from the Belgian Congo in Africa, traditionally worn by men who had killed an enemy tribal member. Another area showcases photographs of the famous whose paths crossed Aimee's, such as Mahatma Gandhi, President Reagan, and Clark Gable. Souvenirs from those congregants saved by Aimee are in a display case that holds crutches, casts, and braces. A silver tray showcases donations from the faithful, including objects such as silverware, jewelry, gold teeth, wedding rings, bridgework, and a pistol. The fate of Aimee's original 1918 Oldsmobile gospel car remains a mystery. The Foursquare Church occasionally exhibits a 1921 Oldsmobile Eight touring car identical to the earlier model. In a nod to verisimilitude, the Church painted it with the slogan: JESUS IS COMING SOON—GET READY.

Although there is debate as to whether Sister Aimee was a saint or sinner, during her ministry, Los Angeles was a little closer to the meaning of its Spanish name ("the Angels"). The eighteenth-century Irish poet Oliver Goldsmith's words proved prescient: Those "who came to scoff, remained to pray."

**Seen from Her Window:** From her second-story window, Aimee could view the Echo Park Lake and may well have wondered at the extraordinary fate that took her from a farm in Canada to an empire in Los Angeles.

**PART VI**

# The Activists

# CHAPTER 27

# *The Devil's Brew*

*"I believe in being everlastingly on the warpath."*

## —CARRY A. NATION

◇◇◇◇◇◇◇◇◇◇

## Carry A. Nation Home & Museum

### opened in 1950 | Medicine Lodge, Kansas, United States

Pete Seeger and the Weavers' famous folksong held the lyrical promise, "If I had a hammer, I'd hammer in the morning..." Carry A. Nation's choice of instrument of social justice was, rather than a hammer, a hatchet. (Although the legal spelling of her name was "Carrie," she used the spelling "Carry," which is reflected in the name of the home museum in her honor.) In the Carry A. Nation Museum, one can learn about the activist who was never temperate in terms of the Temperance Movement.

Before becoming an avenging angel against alcohol, Carrie Amelia Moore was born in Garrard County, Kentucky, the eldest of six children. Her father, George Moore, owned a plantation that depended on slave labor; her mother, Mary Moore, was convinced she was Queen Victoria. (Mary ended her days in an insane asylum.) A formative influence on Carry was the South's tent-based evangelists, who preached the gospel of hellfire. Although temperance was the cornerstone of the religious revivalists, booze was a constant presence in the Moores' home. Neither her father nor her grandfather, despite the fact that he was a deacon in the Baptist Church, were ever far from a bottle. Falling on hard times, in 1854, the family relocated to Belton, Missouri.

At age twenty-one, Carry married Dr. Charles Gloyd, a lodger who rented a room from the Moores. Haunted by the horror of battlefield amputations, Charles

*Temperance Activist Carry A. Nation |*
*Wikimedia Commons, White Studio*

traded his medical career for one as a teacher. As their Puritan courtship had afforded Carry and Charles little time in each other's company, she did not realize her fiancé sought anesthesia in alcohol. The groom was inebriated while taking his vows in front of the fireplace in the Moores' Missouri parlor. Married life consisted of her husband spending his nights downing drinks at the local Masonic hall. In desperation, a pregnant Carry returned to her parents' home. Charles died of alcohol-related symptoms sixteen months after their wedding, leaving his widow to raise their baby daughter, Charlien. (Charlien's future would also entail time in an insane asylum, following in the footsteps of her grandmother Mary Moore.)

Carry's second husband, David Nation, was a widower nineteen years her senior. After struggling to make ends meet, David accepted a job as a preacher in Medicine Lodge, Kansas, where Carry taught Sunday school. Her second marriage also proved joyless, and she took refuge in founding a chapter of the Women's Christian Temperance Union. The organization's mission statement was from the Greek philosopher, Xenophon, "Moderation in all things healthful; total abstinence from all things harmful." Denied the vote, women stood outside taverns reciting hymns and holding placards proclaiming, "The lips that touch alcohol shall never touch mine."

Fanatically opposed to liquor, Carry's habitual greeting to saloon owners was, "Good day, you donkey-faced bedmate of Satan." Although Kansas was a dry state, the law turned a blind eye to enforcement. She also abhorred tobacco and snatched cigars out of men's mouths by declaring, "If the Lord had wanted you to smoke, he'd have put a chimney on your head." In a prequel to feminist movements regarding feminine styles, she exhorted women to shun corsets and tight clothing. The social reformer established a shelter for the wives and children of men in the grips of addiction. The crusader never pointed the finger of blame at the inebriated; she reserved her fury for those who sold liquid brimstone.

In 1900, Carry loaded her buggy with rocks and bricks and set out for Dobson's saloon in nearby Kiowa. While singing the hymn, "Who Hath Sorrow? Who Hath Woe?" the reformer smashed the bottles behind the bar while the cowering Dobson looked on. When her ammunition ran out, Carry utilized billiard balls. She recalled of her literal baptism during her battle against booze that beer "flew in every direction, and I was completely saturated." A future target was the Hotel Carey in Wichita, a venue that also stoked her ire with its life-size nude painting entitled *Cleopatra at the Bath*. Her rock tore through the canvas and shattered a huge mirror along with several bottles. On this occasion, she carried an iron rod as a weapon of destruction because, "I found out in Kiowa that I could use a rock but once." Her husband joked that next time, she should carry a hatchet for maximum effect. Carry responded, "That is the most sensible thing you have said since I married you." She later called her hatchet-wielding tactic "hatchetations." To finance her cause, Carry sold pewter hatchet shaped pins with her name inscribed on the handle. Saloons took to sporting signs, "All Nations Welcome But Carrie." Retaliation often proved grim. In Enterprise, Kansas, a saloon owner's wife horsewhipped the avenging angel in retaliation for the damage to her husband's business. Carry remained indefatigable, "I never saw anything that needed a rebuke or exhortation or warning but that I felt it was my place to meddle with it."

Seven years later, Carry left for Washington, DC, where she demanded a meeting with President Theodore Roosevelt. After guards barred her entry, she made her way to the lawn and railed against the president for allowing wine in the White House. The press had a field day; the firebrand insisted that photographers only take pictures of her holding her Bible. The police escorted her from the White House grounds, and the court fined her twenty-five dollars. The temperance titan described herself as "a bulldog running along at the feet of Jesus, barking at what He doesn't like."

After thirty-two arrests and national notoriety, David divorced Carry on the grounds of desertion, as he termed her absences when she travelled throughout the country spreading the gospel of abstinence. Carry was grateful to David; his surname had afforded her the slogan that defined her crusade: "Carry A. Nation" to the Promised Land of Prohibition. (The reason she had tweaked Carrie to Carry was for its publicity appeal.) In New York City to campaign against alcohol, she heard an officer warn her, "Some of these days you'll get into jail and never get

*Nickname: Hatchett Hall* | *Wikimedia Commons, Ammodramus*

out." Ms. Nation's retort was, "And some of these days you'll get into hell and never get out." The officer's words almost proved prescient as she narrowly escaped a lynching. At the same juncture, after damaging a Coney Island cigar store, Carry found herself behind bars. For the rest of her life, she continued to terrorize American whiskey drinkers and saloon owners.

Due to her failing health, after her 1910 speaking tour, she purchased property in Eureka Springs, Arkansas, which included a farm she dubbed Hatchet Hall. The following year, while delivering a lecture, the temperance leader collapsed; her final words were, "I have done what I could." The phrase was from the Book of Mark, wherein Jesus stated that Mary "has done what she could" by washing his feet. The Women's Temperance Christian Union erected a granite headstone over her gravesite in Belton, where her burial site is adjacent to her mother. The monument bears the inscription, "Faithful to the Cause of Prohibition, She Hath Done What She Could." Eight years later, the Eighteenth Amendment passed, making Prohibition the law of the land.

**Carry A. Nation Home & Museum:** The home Carry shared with her second husband has white pillars and a large second-floor balcony. The structure's pleasant exterior is in jarring juxtaposition to its sign: *Hatchet Hall*. The Women's Christian Temperance Union purchased Carry's home, and in 1976, the site became a US National Historical Landmark. Visitors can view artifacts such as her desk, a pump organ, a walnut dresser, an oak bed, a suitcase, a hat, and hatchet pins. The most memorable souvenir of Carry's crusade is her actual hatchet, protected under a glass enclosure.

Located next to the museum is the Medicine Lodge Stockade, a reproduction of the original 1874 stockade, whose function was to protect settlers from attack by Native Americans. The building houses historical artifacts and antiques including the peace pipe used in the signing of the 1876 Medicine Lodge Peace Treaty. Despite their being separately owned, one ticket grants the visitor access to both museums.

One of the exhibits behind the stockade's walls is the Old Steel Jail, a replica of the one that used to be situated in the basement of the 1886 Medicine Lodge Courthouse. The prison housed a total of eighteen murderers in its time, including the one who shot a local lawman, Sheriff Enos L. "Bud" McCracken. When the authorities installed running water, they added a tub. The last prisoner who used it died the day after taking a bath. The doctor said he had died of pneumonia, but lore held he had passed from shock, as it was the first time he had ever bathed.

While Pete Seeger and the Weavers sang of "the hammer of justice," Carry wielded the hatchet of sobriety in her quest to serve as savior from "the Devil's Brew."

**Seen from Her Window:** Perhaps when standing on her second-floor balcony, at times Carry was able to envision an America where Prohibition was the law of the land, a land free of the scourge of addiction and the evil of bootleggers.

# CHAPTER 28

# Seen the Glory

*"The best and most beautiful things in the world cannot be seen or even touched—they must be felt with the heart."*

**—HELEN KELLER**

◇◇◇◇◇◇◇◇◇◇

## Ivy Green

### opened 1954 | Tuscumbia, Alabama

One would likely find it difficult to refrain from crying while watching the movie *The Miracle Worker*. Tears flow along with the water from the pump as Helen cries out, "Wah! Wah!" The house of Helen Keller's birth, Ivy Green, holds powerful testimony to prevailing over seemingly impossible odds.

Mark Twain compared Helen Keller to Joan of Arc, and deemed her "fellow to Caesar, Alexander, Napoleon, Homer, Shakespeare and the rest of the immortals." The story of Helen and Ivy Green began with Kate Adams, a relative of General William Tecumseh Sherman. At age twenty-two, she married Captain Arthur Henley Keller, two decades older, a widower, and a second cousin of General Robert E. Lee. The Kellers lived in a cottage on Ivy Green, "The Little House," until the 1880 birth of their daughter, Helen Adams Keller.

At nineteen months, Helen contracted what doctors diagnosed as "brain fever," most likely scarlet fever or meningitis. The illness left the toddler blind, deaf, and unable to formulate articulate speech. Kate's life in Ivy Green was no ivory tower. The Kellers had a strained relationship, one exacerbated by their daughter, who possessed the social skills of a feral child. She threw tantrums,

*Helen Keller* |
*Wikimedia Commons,*
*Photographer: Unknown*

snatched food from others' plates, and smashed lamps. On one occasion, she locked her mother in a pantry; jealous of her younger sister Mildred, she overturned her cradle. Relatives suggested the "mental defect" be placed in an institution. Mother Kate privately confided to a friend, "Fate ambushed the joy in my heart when I was twenty-four and left it dead."

The Kellers took Helen to the inventor of the telephone, Dr. Alexander Graham Bell, whose practice centered on deaf patients; his mother and wife shared the same affliction. He suggested Arthur and Kate contact the Perkins Institute for the Blind in Boston. One of the school's teachers, Dr. Samuel Gridley Howe, whose wife, Julia Ward Howe, had penned *The Battle Hymn of the Republic*, had wrought wonders with the deaf-blind Laura Bridgman.

Dr. Bell's son-in-law, Michael Anagos, the director of Perkins, recommended twenty-year-old Anne Mansfield Sullivan as Helen's tutor. At age five, Anne had contracted trachoma, an illness that had diminished her eyesight, and she was familiar with both Braille and the manual alphabet.

For a salary of twenty-five dollars a month, Anne arrived at Ivy Green, where chaos ruled the Keller roost due to Helen's outbursts. On her first encounter with her charge, Helen ransacked Anne's purse for candy; finding none, she threw a punch that knocked out one of the stranger's teeth. The first order of business was to move with Helen to the Little House, away from her overprotective parents. The plan for unlocking language was to let Helen feel an object, followed by Anne signing into her palm.

The magic moment occurred in 1887 at the pump in Ivy Green's yard when Helen made the connection between the feeling of the water and her memory of one of her early words, learned before she had contracted her illness—"Wah! Wah!" The water pump had been transformed into her Tree of Knowledge. The adult Helen recalled, "I knew that w-a-t-e-r meant the wonderful cool thing that

*Ivy Green: Helen Keller's birth house | Wikimedia Commons, Calstanhope*

was flowing over my hand. That living word awakened my soul, gave it light, hope, joy, set it free." After mastering her first word, Helen pointed to Anne, who spelled "teacher," and teacher she was for the remainder of her days.

Just a few months later, Anne shared with Anagnos that Helen had learned approximately four hundred words, a fact he reported to a Boston newspaper that referred to the prodigy as "the wonder child." By age twelve, five years later, Helen had read John Milton's *Paradise Lost*. She wrote of the books wherein she could visualize a world closed to her, "Literature is my utopia... Here I am not disenfranchised." President Grover Cleveland invited the teacher and her singular student to the White House; over the course of her life, Helen met with thirteen presidents. She was acquainted with writers Oliver Wendell Holmes, John Greenleaf Whittier, and Mark Twain, as well as celebrities such as Charlie Chaplin, Enrico Caruso, Sophie Tucker, Eleanor Roosevelt, and Harpo Marx.

If fate had woven a different scenario, Helen would have likely trod the same path as her sister Mildred: marriage, motherhood, and a life as an Alabama matron. Instead, Helen went on to attend Radcliffe, even though higher education was still mainly the domain of men. Since the Kellers could not have afforded the tuition, Mark Twain introduced Helen to Standard Oil magnate Henry Huttleston Rogers, who financed her studies. Helen distinguished herself as the only deaf-blind student in the school's history, and its only published author. On her Hammond Braille typewriter, Helen wrote *The Story of My Life*; it bore the dedication, "To Alexander Graham Bell, who has taught the deaf to speak and enabled the listening ear to hear speech from the Atlantic to the Rockies."

Tuscumbia's daughter had scaled remarkable heights: graduation cum laude, an event that garnered international headlines, and an autobiography that appeared in fifty translations. She had touched the faces of royalty, travelled the world, and danced with Martha Graham. And yet sadness seeped in; in 1922, she wrote, "I have desired the love of a man." She found her soulmate in journalist Peter Fagan, who acted as her secretary when Anne took ill. The couple's attempted elopement collapsed when a newspaper reported they had taken out a marriage license. Ever the overprotective mother, Kate ordered Fagan to stay away. Helen remarked that if she could see, "I would marry first of all."

As life had denied Helen not only sight and sound but husband and child, she turned to social causes. Because she was an early opponent of Nazism, Joseph Goebbels consigned her books to the bonfire. In response, Helen penned a letter to German students, "You can burn my books and the books of the best minds in Europe, but the ideas in them have seeped through a million channels..." Helen's remarkable achievements flew in the face of Hitler's Akton T4, a program of euthanasia for those who had physical or mental handicaps. The courageous crusader cofounded the American Civil Liberties Union, was an early supporter of the NAACP, and championed birth control. J. Edgar Hoover kept a file on Helen due to her leftist leanings.

In 1936, as Anne Sullivan lay dying, Helen held the hand that had been her lifeline to the world for fifty years. Thirty-two years later, Helen, who had begun life in Ivy Green, Alabama, died in 1968 at her Connecticut home, Arcan Ridge, named after a Scottish village Helen had once visited. Death held no terror as it signified a reunion with her beloved Anne, and Helen's acceptance of it is revealed in her words, "Death is no more than passing from one room into another. But there's a difference for me, you know. Because in that other room I shall be able to see." Officials from the National Cathedral in Washington, DC, held a commemorative service and interred her ashes next to Anne Sullivan's remains.

Myriad laurels had graced Helen's brow. In 1966, President Johnson had presented Helen with the Presidential Medal of Freedom. Alabama placed her likeness on the state quarter, the only coin to feature Braille, with the caption: "Spirit of Courage." A fifteen-cent postage stamp of Anne holding her student's hand debuted on the hundredth anniversary of Helen's birth. Amidst these memorials, perhaps the greatest one is her home museum.

**Ivy Green:** To serve as backdrop, several historic markers are scattered throughout the Keller home. One of these bears the inscription, "Ivy Green—The family home of Captain Arthur M. & Kate Adams Keller was built in 1820, being the second house erected in Tuscumbia. Here on June 27, 1880, was born America's first lady of courage, Helen Adams Keller." The white-framed house with the dark-green shutters nestles in a grove of oak trees. The "whistle path" connects the main house to the kitchen located at the rear of the home. Helen's denunciation of Margaret Mitchell's *Gone with the Wind* shows that unlike her pro-slavery father, she condemned the race-based injustices of pre-Civil-War Alabama.

The highlight of the museum is the iron pump that unveiled the secret of language. To commemorate the watershed moment, there is an all-white three-dimensional depiction of Helen and Anne at the pump. Visitors can view the family's original furnishings, including personal mementoes, Helen's Braille typewriter, and her library of Braille books, as well as photographs, such as one where Helen is touching President Eisenhower's face, paintings, letters, dishes, and clothing. The Little House consists of one room with a bay window and playroom. A walk in the extensive grounds may include the sight of a Japanese garden that includes a hand-carved gate made by the Māori, donated by the Lions of New Zealand, in memory of Helen's visit to their country. In the summer months, there are outdoor performances of *The Miracle Worker*.

**Seen from Her Window:** When Helen stood at Ivy Green's window, no doubt memory conjured Anne Sullivan. She wrote, "The most important day I remember in all my life is the one in which my teacher came to me. It was the third day of March, 1887." Helen said the date was her soul's birthday.

# CHAPTER 29

# *The World Entire*

*"There is no pit so deep that God's love*
*is not deeper still."*

**—CORRIE TEN BOOM**

◇◇◇◇◇◇◇◇◇◇

## Corrie ten Boomhuis

opened 1988 | Haarlem, Holland

A quotation attributed to Edmund Burke states, "The only thing necessary for the triumph of evil is for good men to do nothing," a philosophy to which Corrie ten Boom adhered. Upon visiting the Corrie ten Boomhuis, one feels her commitment to humanity.

Tick...tick...tick...echoed through the watch shop located on Barteljorisstraat 19, called by its shortened version, the Beje. Casper ten Boom (known as "Opa," Dutch for grandfather) inherited the store from his father, who founded the firm in 1837. The second and third floors served as the residence for the family, which included Casper's wife, Cornelia (called Cor), and their children, Elisabeth (Betsie), Willem, Arnolda (Nollie), and Cornelia (Corrie) Arnolda Johanna ten Boom, who arrived on April 15, 1892. In the evenings, Casper read biblical passages to his family such as the Psalm, "You are my hiding place and my shield. I hope in Your word."

At age fourteen, Corrie met Karel, with whom she later had a romance that ended when he introduced her to his fiancée. As Corrie knew she would never love another, when her only brother Willem joined the ministry, she determined to become the practitioner of the family craft in the third generation of Ten Boom

*Heroine of the Holocaust* |
*Wikimedia Commons,*
*Photographer: Unknown*

*"Engelenbak" "The Angel's Den"* |
*Courtesy of the Corrie ten Boomhuis*

watchmakers. As the only places that offered classes in horology (the study of watchmaking) were in Switzerland, the cost was prohibitive. A source recounts— though it may be apocryphal—how Corrie read a magazine article about Emperor Karl I of Austria, whose gold pocket watch played "Ranzdes Vaches," a Swiss folk song. After the Emperor's abdication, master watchmaker Caspar oversaw its sale, and his commission on the transaction financed his daughter's dream. In 1921, Corrie became the first licensed female watchmaker in Holland, a joy darkened by her mother's passing from a stroke.

In 1937, Holland celebrated the marriage of Crown Princess Juliana to the German prince Bernhard of Lippe-Biesterfeld, and the Ten Booms held a party to mark the hundred-year anniversary of their family business. Shortly afterwards, Jewish customers who turned in their timepieces for repair failed to reclaim their property.

The horror of the Third Reich arrived in the Netherlands in 1940 with the Luftwaffe bombing of Holland that included the Schiphol Airport, situated five miles from the Ten Boom residence. The Occupation dictated Jews had to wear a yellow Star of David. Father Casper stood in line to receive his star; if all the Dutch wore them the invaders would have trouble identifying their prey. He said of the Nazi invaders, "I pity the poor Germans. They have touched the apple of God's eye."

Desperate Jews arrived at the Ten Booms' door, and the Beje was transformed to "De Schuilplaats," a name that translates to "The Hiding Place." What elevated the risk was the fact that the home was situated half a block from the Haarlem police headquarters. Corrie obtained black market ration cards that she camouflaged in a cubbyhole in the stairwell. She devised a code: If a wooden Alpina Watch sign was visible from the dining room window, it was safe to enter; its absence signified danger. A mirror set up outside the shop warned if friend or foe approached. Hidden in a grandfather clock, the Dutch Resistance smuggled in bricks and mortar they used to build a secret compartment in Corrie's bedroom where six adults could hide in an upright position. Access to the space behind the fake wall was through a wooden linen closet with a removable bottom panel. The family christened the space "Engelenbak," which means "The Angels' Den." Hundreds of people survived due to the Ten Booms' "station on the underground railroad."

In 1944, a Dutch collaborator informed the Nazis of suspected illegal activities in the Ten Boom residence. As the police led Corrie away, she pretended to trip, thereby knocking down the Alpina sign, but the ruse did not work. Due to Casper's advanced age and sterling reputation, a Gestapo officer offered to release him if he swore he would not cause further trouble. Casper replied that if he went home the next day, he would still open his door to anyone who knocked. Ten days later, he passed away in Scheveningen Prison; his burial was in an unmarked grave in Loosduinen Cemetery. Locked in her cell, Corrie endured beatings and mourned the death of her father. A shred of solace arrived with a letter; hidden under its stamp were the words, "All the watches in your cabinet are safe."

Corrie and Betsie entered the valley of the shadow of death: Ravensbrück, the only all women's concentration camp. Life was a treadmill of torture, with sadistic guards, a starvation diet, and lice-infested blankets. Numbers replaced names; Corrie's was 66730. The Ten Boom sisters conducted clandestine services in their barracks using a contraband Dutch Bible. Betsie succumbed to the terrible conditions in 1944. Corrie received a red card: Those over fifty years old were earmarked for extermination. But through an administrative error, Ravensbrück officials released Corrie.

Upon her return to the Beje, Corrie continued her humanitarian work. She established a center for concentration camp survivors and, in the spirit of Christian forgiveness, permitted the inclusion of collaborators. In 1946, the humanitarian Corrie began to organize a worldwide ministry that took her to sixty countries over the course of thirty-three years. Her platform included preaching in condemnation of the Vietnam War and the advocacy for the inmates of San Quentin prison. In a church in Munich, she encountered a man in a trench coat, a former guard from Ravensbrück concentration camp. She took his outstretched hand, and of the instant that she did so, she later recalled that she had never known God's love as intensely as she did at that moment. The motto of her ministry, "What I spent, I had; what I saved, I lost; what I gave, I have."

Although she never sought recognition, Corrie was the recipient of many honors: Queen Julianna of the Netherlands knighted her, Israel's Yad Vashem invited her to plant a tree in the Avenue of the Righteous Gentiles, and the Hopi Tribe adopted her as a sister. Her story was the triumph of the *kryds*, the cross, over the *hakenkruis*, the swastika.

In 1971, Corrie published her memoir, *The Hiding Place*; four years later, evangelist Billy Graham turned it into a movie. At age eighty-five, Corrie rented a house in Placentia, California, that she named *Shalom*, the Hebrew word for hello, goodbye, and peace. In her late eighties, she suffered a series of strokes that left her paralyzed and unable to speak. On April 15, the date of her ninety-first birthday, the clock of Corrie's life wound down. Her epitaph in Fairhaven Memorial Park in Santa Ana, California, bears the inscription, *"Jesus Is Victor."* She left behind her adopted son, Do Van Nguyen.

**Corrie ten Boomhuis:** The history of the house at Barteljorisstraat 19 originated in the sixteenth century at the directive of the bailiff of Haarlem. The structure originally consisted of two houses that merged into one, the reason for its warren of rooms. The exterior of the museum is easily identifiable due to its second-story oversized clock with a blue background; underneath it, in the same color, is a sign: "Ten Boom Museum." Visitors gather in the living room, with its red carpet and floor-to-ceiling red drapes.

At first glance, the Beje appears to be a well-appointed 1940s house. On the walls hang photographs of the ten Boom family: her father Casper working on his watches or standing in the doorway of his shop, the patriarch with his wife and children. There are religious relics such as Corrie's English Bible and the sheet music on the piano with lyrics for the song, "You are My Hiding Place." A tapestry of a gold crown with a royal blue background serves as a metaphor: One side has the completed picture, the other, a tangled web of threads. The symbolism is man only understands the chaotic side; God sees the perfect plan. A wooden plaque on a blue background holds the same message found at her resting place, "Jesus is victor." Another wooden plaque states: *Corrie ten Boom Prisoner of the Lord Jesus,* September 1977, San Quentin Prison.

The artifacts from the Nazi era are jarring: the wooden Alpina sign, a green contraband radio, a Ravensbrück-issued suitcase, decaying ration cards located by the cubbyhole in the stairs. Over a doorway, a map of Europe displays the concentration camps; the number of fatalities for each is marked in red. A wall bearing the words "Tramping for the Lord" depicts every country Corrie visited during her years in the ministry.

When a tour guide entered Corrie's former bedroom, she explains that hundreds of Jews survived the Dutch Occupation because of the Ten Boom family. Part of the tour permits willing—and supple—visitors an opportunity to squeeze into the linen closet and stand in the hiding place they called "the Angels' Den." In the claustrophobic space, visitors can imagine the terror of the four men and two women who hid during the Nazi raid. They stood in the darkness, without water or bathroom facilities, fearful of discovery, till the Resistance rescued them after forty-seven hours. Five of the six survived the Holocaust.

A quotation from the Talmud encapsulates the life of Corrie ten Boom, "He who saves a single life, saves the world entire."

**Seen from Her Window:** If Corrie could gaze once more from the window of the Beje, she would see street signs reading: "Noord-Hollands Archief," "Frans Hals Museum," "Corrie ten Boomhuis."

# CHAPTER 30

# *Mariposas*

*"When injustice becomes law,*
*rebellion becomes duty."*

**—MINERVA MIRABAL**

◇◇◇◇◇◇◇◇◇◇

## Casa Museo Hermanas Mirabal

opened 1994 | Tenares, the Dominican Republic

A Hans Christian Andersen story proved prescient in the lives of the remarkable Mirabal sisters who achieved international respect during their all too brief lives. In his fairy tale, a butterfly states, "Just living is not enough. One must have sunshine, freedom, and a little flower." The siblings' childhood home, the Casa Museo Hermanas Mirabal, resonates with their courage.

The family was from the village of Ojo de Agua, near the city of Salcedo in the Dominican Republic. The family members were father Enrique Mirabal Fernández, mother Mercedes, and daughters Patria Mercedes born in 1924, Bélgica Adela (called Dedé) born in 1925, Minerva Argentina born 1926, and Maria Teresa born 1936. They lived on a prosperous farm where Enrique operated a coffee mill and general store.

Tragically, their homeland had been rife with turmoil ever since Christopher Columbus had set foot in their Caribbean homeland. When the sisters were young, in 1930, the island nation came under the control of Generalissimo Rafael Leónidas Trujillo. Due to his control of his country, he was called "El Jefe" (The Boss); because of his voracious sexual appetite, he was also known as "El Chico," which translates to "The Goat." He gloried in his self-proclaimed formal title:

"Father of the New Fatherland." The megalomaniac rebuilt the capital, which he renamed Ciudad Trujillo, and christened the country's highest mountain Pico Trujillo. The consummate narcissist mandated every home display his photograph with the slogan, "In this home, Trujillo is boss," and churches had to hang a sign: "Dio en Cielo, Trujillo en Tierra" ("God in Heaven, Trujillo on Earth"). The government censored *El Cáribe*, the national newspaper. Enemies of the state received a visit from the Servicio de Inteligencia Militar (SIM), Trujillo's trigger-happy goon squad who arrived in black Volkswagen Beetles.

The Mirabals' path of activism ignited when Minerva attended college in Santo Domingo and heard from fellow students of the human rights abuses that plagued the country. The national horror took a personal turn when the beautiful Minerva caught the eye of the Goat. He attempted to exercise his *droit du seigneur*, (the right of the Lord), and ordered her to attend his 1949 gala in San Cristobal. As the dictator danced with Minerva, he suggested retiring to his hotel room for a romp, an offer she refused. Terrified at how the evening was unfolding, the Mirabals left the party. Their early departure further enraged Trujillo as protocol demanded that no one depart before el presidente.

Enrique's letter of apology failed to smooth the waters, and he spent the next two years in prison. Fifteen days after his release, he passed away from the jail's unsanitary conditions, as well as malnutrition and beatings. The family farm suffered financial loss as customers were fearful of reprisals. Despite Minerva graduating at the top of her law school, the university denied her a diploma.

Minerva, Patria, and Maria Teresa married democracy-seeking spouses who shared their vision of a free Dominican Republic. Dedé married Jaime Fernández, whom she described as "a violent and handsome man." Of their thirty-four-year long relationship, eighteen years proved happy. As Jaime insisted that his family take the stance of the three proverbial monkeys, Dedé never engaged in anti-government activities. In contrast, Minerva and her husband Manolo were organizers of el 14 de Junio, the Fourteenth of June, that was named after the date of a failed coup against the dictator by Dominican exiles living in Cuba. The

*Family home of the Mirabal Family* | *Wikimedia Commons, The Singularity*

siblings went by the code name "the Butterflies." Dedé, in her memoir, *Vivas en Su Jardín* (or *Alive in Their Garden*), wrote, "We lived in fear, and there is nothing worse than living in fear." News of the sisters' resistance reached Trujillo, leading to his pronouncement, "The only problem my government has are the Catholic Church and those Mirabal sisters." Paranoia fueled his violence, and human rights violations escalated. The police arrested Patria, Minerva, and Maria Teresa, as well as their husbands. In a move to curry favor with his people, Trujillo freed female political prisoners. Their husbands received sentences ranging from twenty to thirty years; the authorities interned them in different facilities to prevent the Underground from organizing their escape. Then, in a surprising move, the sisters' three husbands ended up in the same penitentiary in Puerta Plata. Just as inexplicably, their wives received permission to make a joint visit. Did the Goat have a heart after all?

In 1170, King Henry II had cried out, "Can no one rid me of this meddlesome priest?" The remark resulted in the murder of Thomas Becket, the Archbishop of Canterbury. A similar scenario took place in 1960 in the Dominican Republic. As the government had confiscated the sisters' cars, Rufino de la Cruz, a fellow fighter in 14 de Junio, offered to serve as their driver. On their return, as they drove along a desolate road, a black Volkswagen Beetle forced their Jeep into a sugarcane field on the outskirts of Puerto Plata. Members of the SIM strangled the sisters and Rufino. Afterwards, the thugs deposited the bodies back into the Jeep and sent it tumbling down La Cumbre Cliff. To commemorate the site of their murders, three bronze busts of the sisters mark the spot, each bearing a plaque giving their name, date of birth, and testimony as to how they died. Evil had removed the wings of the Butterflies, but their spirits lived on. When the caskets arrived at the funeral home, there was an official mandate demanding they remain sealed. Dedé defied the order, thereby confirming the deaths had been homicides.

When her friends and family had voiced concern over Minerva's activism, she had responded, "If they kill me, I'll reach out my arms out from the tomb and I'll be [even] stronger." Posthumously, David slayed Goliath. Trujillo's assassination of the sisters who had been devoted to their country, church, and families was the straw that broke the populace's back. Six months after the murders, at ten in the evening, as Trujillo's chauffeur-driven limousine made its way along a remote road heading toward San Cristobal for a rendezvous with his mistress, instead of a black Jeep, a Chevrolet emerged from the shadows carrying four armed men. They made manifest the biblical admonition, "He who lives by the sword shall perish by the sword." El Jefe's enemies pronounced his death an *ajusticiamiento:* a bringing to justice. The thirty-one-year reign of Trujillo's terror was at an end.

The Butterflies—as their country remembers them—became symbols of democratic and feminist resistance. The Dominican Republic made the date of Trujillo's assassination a national holiday. In 1999, the United Nations designated November 25, the anniversary of the sisters' murder, the International Day for the Elimination of Violence Against Women. The country honored their famous daughters by placing their images on a postage stamp and paper currency. In another tribute, the place of their birth changed from Provincia de Salcedo to Provincia Hermanas Mirabal. The dedication page of Dominican American novelist Julia Alvarez's 1994 novel, *In the Time of the Butterflies*, reads "For Dedé," as she survived to become the keeper of the flame of her siblings' legacy. In addition to her three children, Dedé raised her six nieces and nephews. Minerva's daughter, Minou Tavárez Mirabal, became a congressional representative and vice foreign minister. Dedé's son, Jaime David Fernández Mirabal, served as vice president of the Dominican Republic for four years.

**Casa Museo Hermanas Mirabal:** Dedé founded the Museo Hermanas Mirabal in Salcedo situated in the family's 1954 home; there she conducted tours that explained how her martyred sisters toppled a brutal regime. When asked why she did not suffer the same fate as her siblings, Dedé responded, "I stayed alive to tell their stories." She served as docent until her death at age eighty-eight.

On display are Patria's teacup collection, Maria Teresa's embroidery, and Minerva's law degree. The Fourteenth of June Movement flag hangs in Minerva's former bedroom, along with the sewing machine that stitched the original. Two mementoes of Minerva's incarceration in La Victoria prison are a sculpture of her daughter, Minou, and a three-leaf clover fashioned from the jail's stone. Teresa's former bedroom has a glass case that holds her glass-strewn braid alongside her photograph. On a table are the contents of the sisters' purses from the fateful night: a prayer card, a memento from Enrique's funeral, a hair roller. Next to the purse display is a kitchen towel stained with the sisters' blood. The garden houses the graves of the martyrs, as well as that of Minerva's husband Manolo, arranged in the shape of a cross with a fountain in the center. Three busts of Minerva, Maria Teresa, and Patria rest on stones. Across the street is the Plazoleta Hermanas Mirabal, that displays a monument with three butterflies. Another artifact is a remnant of their Jeep bearing damage from the assassination. The overriding symbol found not only on the walls and the gardens of the museum, but interspersed throughout the province, is the image of brightly colored butterflies, reminiscent of the Mirabal sisters' code name: *Las Mariposas*.

**Seen from Her Window:** The beauty of the land that Patria, Minerva, and Maria Teresa saw when they looked out the window of their family home must have inspired their courage to resist tyranny. Every year, the day their lives ended is commemorated by the UN's International Day for the Elimination of Violence Against Women, placed on November 25 in memory of "the Butterflies."

## PART VII

# The Eccentrics

# CHAPTER 31

# There's No Place

*"I am constantly having to make an upheaval
for some reason."*

**—SARAH WINCHESTER (IN A LETTER TO
HER SISTER-IN-LAW)**

◇◇◇◇◇◇◇◇◇◇

## Winchester Mystery House

opened in 1923 | San Jose, California

How the West was won—or lost, depending on one's perspective—was determined by who wielded the Winchester Repeating Rifle. The heiress to the firearms fortune, Sarah Pardee Winchester, lived a life bookmarked by guilt and guns.

A century ago, the region now known as Silicon Valley held only endless orchards. Now all that remains from yesteryear is a 160-room curiosity that sticks out amidst the suburban sprawl. Magician Harry Houdini sensed shades of the supernatural in the secluded mansion.

The chatelaine of the one-of-a-kind manor, née Sarah Lockwood Pardee (her parents chose her middle name after a family friend), was born in 1839, in New Haven, Connecticut, the youngest of six children. She was the third of her family to be called Sarah: it was also the name of her mother and a sister who had passed away at eighteen months. The surname of her paternal ancestor, George Pardee, derived from an old French oath, *par Dieu*, which translates to "by God." Sarah was also a descendant of Elizabeth Yale, a cousin of Elihu Yale, the university's namesake due to his gift of a significant fiscal endowment. Another

impressive connection was Sarah's father was a relative of Eli Goodyear, the patent holder for the vulcanization of rubber. Henry Bergh, the founder of the American Society for the Prevention of Cruelty to Animals (ASPCA), was a guest in the family home.

Her father, Leonard Pardee, was a carpenter, and Sarah enjoyed watching him and his workers craft products such as pedals for pianos and hitching posts for horses. Following in his footsteps was not an option; carpentry was then the sole domain of males. Leonard's business proved lucrative, and Sarah received private lessons in music and French. He purchased a large house in an affluent neighborhood whose next-door neighbors were the Winchesters. They were extremely wealthy because Oliver Winchester had invested in the Volcanic Repeating Arms Company, which manufactured the "Winchester repeater" that could fire multiple bullets in rapid succession. His competitors' weapon only fired one bullet at a time. Oliver sold his weapons to armies in Europe and Asia; however, they gained their most popularity in the United States, where settlers used them against Native Americans and ranchers used them for hunting.

At age twenty-three, Sarah married William Wirt Winchester, a match that set the course of her life on an unimaginable direction. William inherited the rifle company from his father, a gift that was to prove a two-edged sword. Buffalo Bill Cody claimed that for "Indian fighting," the Winchester was "boss;" Annie Oakley endorsed the product that made her a sharpshooter. President Theodore Roosevelt took several Winchester rifles on his hunting trips, and the Canadian Mounties adopted them as their official weapon. By 1876, the Philadelphia Centennial exposition showcased the iconic brand. To add to the joy of marrying the man she adored, her brother, who had fought in the First Battle of Bull Run in Manassas, Virginia, had returned home from the Civil War, as had her brother-in-law, Homer. In 1868, Oliver built a WW that he shared with William and Sarah.

Death shadowed Sarah; she lost her mother and sister in quick succession. Her daughter, Annie Pardee Winchester, passed away from marasmus (a

*Winchester Mystery House* | *Courtesy of Winchester Mystery House LLC*

condition that did not allow her to digest food), five and a half weeks after her birth. No further pregnancies followed. Thirteen years later, William succumbed to tuberculosis; Sarah buried her husband in Evergreen Cemetery next to their daughter. With New Haven heavy with the memories of her lost loved ones, Sarah decamped to California. Another factor in her decision was she had developed severe arthritis in her hands, and the Connecticut cold exacerbated her condition. In San Francisco, she befriended Leland and Jane Stanford, also consumed with grief over the untimely death of their child, Leland Stanford, Jr.

While the Stanfords became associated with the university that bore their doomed son's name, Sarah's claim to notoriety occurred due to the Guinness record worthy estate that she purchased in 1886. The fictional Miss Havisham had Satis House; the widowed Mrs. Winchester had Llanada Villa, Spanish for "the house on the plain." The wealthy women of the area thought the diminutive heiress (who stood only four-foot-ten inches tall), would join their inner circle, but they were mistaken. The initial reason they considered her odd was because rather than hiring an architect, foreman, and contractor, she assumed these positions herself, not a lady-like pursuit. Another trait that made her stand out was she dressed exclusively in black despite the broiling hot San Jose sun. However, her widow's weeds were something she shared with her contemporary, Queen Victoria, who also dressed in black after the death of her husband, Prince

Albert. Thus began the rumors that would dog Sarah all the days of her life... and beyond.

Sarah continued her renovations until her 1922 passing. The unfinished ballroom displays Victorian-era furniture. A window bears a spider web motif. A Louis Comfort Tiffany stained glass window showcases a quotation from Shakespeare's *Richard II*; confined to a cell, the king laments the lost world of what could have been, "These same thoughts people this little world." Sarah's bedroom holds a framed photo of herself along with a red rose. Even the owner herself did not know what lay behind all of the mansion's two thousand doors. A forerunner of Silicon Valley's association with technology, Sarah equipped her mansion with three elevators and high-tech devices that heated the house. As the overseer of the manor was fiercely private, gardeners planted a towering hedge that thwarted prying eyes. Sarah's wealth and estate made Llanada Villa a likely place for President McKinley to stay when he visited San Jose, but no invitation was forthcoming. The Winchester fortune had bequeathed the heiress $20.5 million—$530 million in today's currency—providing Sarah with ample means to construct a seven-story mansion at a cost of $5 million ($71 million today).

Although the Great San Francisco Earthquake of 1906 was of less than a minute in duration, it claimed three thousand lives. The City Hall was left with only its dome intact. The devastating shaking damaged Llanada Villa's seven-story tower and most of its fourth floor. Rather than rebuild, she ordered that the rubble be cleared away and a new roof built on top of the half-destroyed residence. Laissez-faire renovations followed: skylights that never saw the sky, doors that opened onto brick walls, and staircases leading only to ceilings. When a decorating idea dawned, Sarah would write it down on napkins, paper bags, or any available surface. The United States' largest private residence of the era held forty bedrooms, seventeen chimneys, forty-seven fireplaces, and a multitude of trap doors. The exterior was equally outlandish, with a mishmash of turrets, gables, and towers. Sarah occasionally held nighttime séances in a turret of the blue painted house, aptly known as "The Witch's Cap." After thirty-eight years, the banging of the hammers came to a standstill with Sarah's death. The lingering question behind the bizarre building: Why?

One explanation is a medium told Sarah the reason for the Winchester family deaths was revenge perpetrated by bullet-riddled spirits, the victims of their rifles. Feeling the guilt of a Lady Macbeth, this theory posits that Sarah believed the endless additions would prevent wraiths from hunting her down. As a further safety precaution, Sarah always slept in different rooms. She believed that to stop building would signify her end. Sarah stated, "The ghosts are clever. That's why I have to baffle them, so they won't find and hurt me. Every room, closet, staircase, and window must confuse the evil spirits. They must never be able to find their way through my house. Each year I will add new rooms so that the spirits will grow weary of trying to get to me." Ensconced in her mansion, Sarah spent her days seeking safety—or perhaps absolution.

Sarah Winchester was a real-life Norma Desmond, a woman entrapped in a self-spun spiderweb. Of all the artifacts in her mausoleum, perhaps the most telling were those found after her death: A concealed safe held two obituaries and two locks of hair, mementoes of William and Annie. Upon her death at age eighty-two, she joined her husband and daughter in Evergreen Cemetery. A granite monument bears their names and dates of death.

**Winchester Mystery House:** America's most infamous haunted house bills itself as "an extravagant maze of Victorian craftmanship—marvelous, baffling, and eerily eccentric." After Sarah's passing, John H. Brown and his wife Mayme Brown leased Llanada Villa with the intention of turning the grounds into an amusement park. The plan was to feature a "Backety-Back Railway"—an early version of a wooden roller coaster that he had designed and bult for an amusement park in Crystal Beach, Ontario, Canada. But due to the overwhelming fascination with Llanada Villa, Brown switched gears and opened the house to the public. Mayme had the distinction of serving as its first tour guide. Acclaimed escape artist Harry Houdini, who had started life in Budapest as Erich Weisz, turned the spotlight of public attention on the architectural oddity. At midnight on Halloween, 1924, Houdini visited the estate in a bid to debunk what he felt could be a false association with the paranormal. His verdict was ghosts might well be tenants in "the Mystery House"; the name stuck. In the 1960s, the house's street address changed from Santa-Clara Los Gatos Road to Winchester Boulevard. No doubt Sarah would have been amazed at the impact she left on her adopted city.

The house held five fully equipped kitchens and six concrete safes. Artisans from around the world were represented in the unique décor, which featured French paintings, Austrian glass, and German chandeliers. However, the mansion only held two mirrors, one in Sarah's bedroom and one in an adjoining bath. The estate is now practically devoid of its original furnishings. There is a room of balconies where one can step off one balcony through a window and find oneself on the same balcony. From another, one steps through a door that, once closed, cannot be opened again from the inside, forcing the visitor to find an alternative exit. Although it remains unknown if the labyrinth deterred ghosts, it did keep away robbers, who feared they would not be able to make an easy getaway. Their fears had merit: after Sarah's passing, the movers took six weeks to bring the furniture down stairways that often ended in walls.

In the Walk with Spirits Tour, guests learn about the paranormal. The event begins with a simulation of a Victorian wake in the front parlor to showcase the era's traditions regarding mourning. After consulting mediums in Boston and other places in New England famous for their séances, clairvoyants, and spiritualism, Sarah conducted her own. No doubt the session was an attempt to communicate with her husband. In his memory, she contributed two million dollars to create a hospital in New Haven, the William Wirt Winchester Hospital. One school of thought holds that during these otherworldly communications, sympathetic spirits advised Sarah on her renovations. In her séance room, visitors can partake of a reenactment. If Sarah did indeed feel conflicted about the family source of wealth, she would not have appreciated the house's shooting gallery. In addition to contemplation of possible hauntings, the Winchester house now offers hospitality at its café, dispensing delicacies such as "Sarah's Spook Juice" (a whipped orange drink with whipped cream topping).

Throughout the 160-room manor, the number thirteen held sway. The historical association of the number as a harbinger of evil likely began with the Last Supper, which included the thirteen apostles. After Judas' betrayal, thirteen received such a bad rap that it led to triskaidekaphobia (a phobia related to the number), a condition from which Napoleon Bonaparte and President Franklin D. Roosevelt suffered. The Winchester association: Windows have thirteen panels, and some of the stairways have thirteen steps; the ballroom floor has thirteen squares of wood, and the chandeliers hold thirteen globes. The gift shop sells an illustrated guidebook explaining the Winchester will has thirteen sections, which Sarah signed thirteen times.

In the front garden resides a classical statue of Hebe, the Greek goddess of youth. Under Sarah's tenure, the statue, along with a matching companion, flanked the mansion's entrance. But making the hands of time stand still—erasing never-ending heartache—was something even the inheritor of the Winchester Rifle fortune could not obtain.

Upon reaching the parking lot, some tourists feel they have viewed a monument to madness. They would agree with the Dorothy Parker observation, "If you want to know what God thinks of money, just look at the people he gave it to." An alternative view is Sarah was merely eccentric, for which she paid a price in the court of public opinion. Her relentless building, rather than outwitting malevolent spirits, was a coping mechanism to help her through her agony. Her tragedy was the same as the biblical Lot's wife; she could not stop herself from looking back. In the heiress' defense, one can summon Aristotle's ancient observation, "There is no great genius without a touch of madness." In either case, the greatest mystery of the mansion is the widow Winchester herself. However, what is certain is that the San Jose Sarah, like the Kansas Dorothy could have observed, "There's no place like home."

**Seen from Her Window:** In contrast to the interiors of Sarah's random rooms, her four-acre grounds were an island of aestheticism. Her Victorian gardens held hundreds of flowers in a profusion of colors, while her private park displayed dozens of statues, such as a Cupid, a Native American hunter, deer, and frogs. Another nod to Greek mythology was a statue of a hippocampus, a mythical creature with the upper body of a horse and the lower body of a fish.

# CHAPTER 32

# *Not a Dwelling*

*"From my window I overlooked a pond in which a former butler had drowned himself. As one gloomy day succeeded another, I began to feel a deep sympathy for him."*

**—CONSUELO VANDERBILT,
UPON MOVING INTO BLENHEIM PALACE**

◇◇◇◇◇◇◇◇◇

**Blenheim Palace**

opened 1950 | Woodstock, Oxfordshire, England

During the Gilded Age, the mating dance between American heiresses and the British aristocracy subsumed the importance of matters of the heart beneath matters of money. In this prosaic process, the daughters of the nouveaux riche received titles, while their cash-strapped aristocratic husbands received an infusion of funds. *Downton Abbey*'s character Cora Crawley was a husband-hunter whose quest was to transform to Lady Crawley; Cora's nonfictional counterpart was Consuelo Vanderbilt, the chatelaine of Blenheim Palace.

In front of Manhattan's Grand Central Station is America's counterpart to Egypt's Ozymandias: a twelve-foot, four-ton, bronze statue. The likeness is of "Commodore" Cornelius Vanderbilt, the son of an impoverished farmer, who constructed the original Grand Central Depot and the New York Central Railway. His son William Vanderbilt, Consuelo's father, wrote, "Inherited wealth is a real handicap." He had the handicap of inheriting $90 million. In contrast, his wife, Alva, considered money the Holy Grail.

*Pearls and Books* |
*Wikimedia Commons, Unknown*
*Photographer*

As soon as Alva heard the words, "It's a girl," she had marital aspirations for her only daughter. To keep Consuelo under her thumb, Alva used a riding crop on the child's legs whenever she showed a streak of independence. Another childhood torment was that Consuelo had to wear a steel orthopedic corset to ensure an erect posture. While her brothers, William Kissam Vanderbilt II and Harold Stirling Vanderbilt, attended school, three governesses tutored Consuelo in the Vanderbilts' palatial "Petit Chateau" at 660 Fifth Avenue, modeled after a sixteenth-century French estate. The pale limestone was in marked contrast to the neighboring brownstones. The front door was a replica of the Ghiberti bronze doors in Florence. An eighty-foot-long dining room held two colossal Renaissance fireplaces and a stained-glass window depicted Henry VIII and Francis I. Adorning the walls were Rembrandt's *Man in Oriental Costume* and Gainsborough's *Mrs. Elliot*. Displayed in Alva's boudoir (the room corresponding to where Madame Pompadour had displayed the canvas) was François Boucher's *The Toilet of Venus*. The Petit Chateau also showcased Marie Antoinette's "secretaire."

The five-foot-eight Consuelo (whose erect posture made her seem taller) turned heads with her classic features and cascade of dark hair. At her debut at the Paris residence of the Duc de Gramont, she was the sun around which suitors gravitated, one of whom was the future French president, Paul Deschanel. (The belle received five proposals of marriage.) The heiress spent summers at the Vanderbilt "cottage" in Newport, Rhode Island, where their neighbors bore the surnames Astor and Morgan. (The mansion-museum is open for tours). The design of Marble House—so named after the amount of the stone used in its construction—carried traces of the White House and Marie Antoinette's Petit Trianon at Versailles.

Alva's mantra to her daughter: "I do the thinking. You do as you are told." As the child of a mega-rich "momanager," the youthful Consuelo was a timid, introverted bookworm dwarfed by her mother's shadow. Consuelo's escape lay with the man she loved, Winthrop Rutherfurd. But when Alva learned of their romance, she sent Consuelo's swain packing. Winthrop (or "Winty") was no slouch in the eligible male pool; he was a direct descendant of Peter Stuyvesant, the colonial governor of New York, and John Winthrop, the first governor of Massachusetts. Notwithstanding, Alva aspired for more in a son-in-law. In rebellion, Consuelo threatened to elope, upon which Alva swore she would shoot the young man. If that was not enough to cool Consuelo's ardor, her mother feigned a heart attack. Consuelo caved.

Alva grabbed hold of the matrimonial reins and looked across the pond for a peer for her daughter. The concept was in vogue: one quarterly publication of the time listed all the eligible, titled, British bachelors–a nineteenth century eHarmony. Cash-for-class liaisons birthed Britain's Sir Winston Churchill; his father, Lord Randolph Churchill, had proposed to Jennie Jerome only forty-eight hours after meeting the Brooklyn-born beauty.

Alva knew if she could pull off the social coup of the century, she would earn a spot as one of the Four Hundred, the number of upper strata guests who could fit into Mrs. Astor's ballroom. Mrs. Astor had snubbed Alva on the basis that the Vanderbilts were nouveau riche. Alva's alliance was a match between the American royal house of Vanderbilt with Charles Spencer Churchill, the ninth Duke of Marlborough. The dour, diminutive, and depressive duke went by the nickname "Sunny" after his title as the Earl of Sunderland. The Lord was the owner of Blenheim Palace, the financial maintenance of which had been an albatross for every Duke of Marlborough. The mother knew the marital merger would leave Mrs. Astor in the dust. Who needed her ballroom anyhow if one could mingle with His Royal Highness, the Prince of Wales?

The Manhattan wedding on November 6, 1895, was the most heralded society gala of the time, an event that would have been comparable to if William, Prince of Wales, had married Paris Hilton. The forthcoming nuptials had regulated to the back pages news such as the popularity of bloomers as cycling dresses, New York elections, and Cuba's war of independence. Sixty members of the orchestra filled the air of St. Thomas Episcopal Church with the strains of Mendelssohn's *Overture to A Midsummer Night's Dream*. Three hundred policemen guarded the door, holding back thousands of onlookers. *Vogue* magazine devoted pages to Consuelo's wedding gown: it had a five-yard train, and its white brocade corset had gold clasps

*Consuelo and Winston Churchill at Blenheim  |*
*Wikipedia Blenheim Palace Photographer: DeFacto*

and diamonds. The wedding ceremony had everything—except the bride. She was at home weeping in her father's arms, imploring him not to make her go through with the wedding. Still intimidated by his ex-wife and dreading an international scandal (as even Queen Victoria had sent a message of congratulations), William delivered Consuelo to the church. Father and daughter arrived twenty minutes late.

When Consuelo walked down the aisle, she carried orchids that had originated in Blenheim's greenhouses, flowers that had survived an Atlantic ocean passage in a refrigerated chamber. The couple's presents were on display, one of which was a string of pearls that had once encircled the neck of Catherine the Great. The queue to view the booty stretched halfway along Fifth Avenue.

As American authors Edith Wharton and Henry James both explored in their novels, such transatlantic unions carried emotional price tags. The honeymoon on the Vanderbilt yacht was no midsummer night's dream. Consuelo confessed she was in love with Winthrop Rutherfurd; her new husband shared that his mistress was Muriel Wilson of Tranby Croft. Marlborough might have cared for Muriel, but his truest love was Blenheim.

The newly anointed Duchess of Marlborough lived in the 170-room palace, the only British palace that was not a royal residence. Consuelo was miserable; she hated the estate's formality, which entailed at least four changes of clothes per day. Over eight-course dinners in a magnificent dining room, an uncomfortable silence reigned between Charles and Consuelo. Despite their mutual antipathy, they fulfilled their duty and produced sons John Albert Edward and Ivor. Lore holds that Consuelo coined the phrase, "an heir and a spare." With the obligation of continuing the dynasty accomplished, the couple embarked on lord and lady adultery. Consuelo derived brotherly (platonic) comfort from Charles' cousin Winston Churchill, with whom she forged a lifelong bond.

Consuelo seamlessly blended into the fabric of British society. Sir James Barrie, the author of *Peter Pan*, reported, "I would stand all day in the street to see Consuelo Marlborough get into her carriage." Queen Victoria welcomed the duchess to Windsor Palace. The hostess entertained the Prince of Wales and the Kaiser. She became known as "the democratic duchess," as she deeply cared about the well-being of her forty servants and the poor who lived on the margins of the estate.

The Marlboroughs were sought after as guests in England and abroad; Tsar Nicholas II and Tsarina Alexandra invited them to a New Year's Ball at the Winter Palace, where Grand Duke Michael, the tsar's brother, invited Consuelo to dance a mazurka. In 1902, after departing Russia, Consuelo caught a severe cold that left her slightly deaf. His wife's affliction proved a source of irritation to her husband. Four years later, Consuelo embarked on an affair with the similarly married Viscount Castlereagh, the eldest son of the Marquess of Londonderry, and they planned an assignation in France. At a dinner party in Blenheim, Consuelo mentioned she was heading to Paris to buy her winter wardrobe. An infuriated duke shouted that she should stay there—thus sealing the doom of both their dinner party and marriage. To lessen the blow, Winston Churchill sent John and Ivor gifts.

Months after their 1921 divorce, Charles married Gladys Marie Deacon, a Boston heiress; Consuelo wed Lieutenant Colonel Louis Jacques Balsan, a Catholic French aviator. The couple built a villa at Eze on the French Riviera and entertained Winston Churchill, George Bernard Shaw, and Charlie Chaplin. Their next residence was a chateau near Paris that included a sanitorium for sick children. When the Germans invaded, the Balsans fled to the south, along with a fleet of vans to transport their ill charges. During the war, the couple settled in New York, where Jacques passed away at age eighty-eight. His widow died at the same age in 1964, one of the last survivors of America's gilded age—a term coined by author Mark Twain. During the service at St. Thomas Episcopalian Church, the sixty-voice choir sang the anthem, "How Lovely Is Thy Dwelling Place."

Consuelo chose interment in a churchyard near Blenheim Palace, close to Lord Ivor. Mourners included her son, the tenth Duke of Marlborough, her grandchildren, and Lady Clementine Churchill, who attended with her son Randolph. Sir Winston, at age ninety, was too infirm to attend.

**Blenheim Palace:** When King George visited Blenheim Palace in 1786, he remarked to Queen Charlotte, "We have nothing equal to this." Other royals who journeyed to Oxfordshire to see the historic home were the King of Denmark (1768), the Tsar of Russia (1814), Prince Albert (1841), and Edward VII (1859). The eighteenth-century poet Alexander Pope, overwhelmed by the estate's enormity, wrote, "Thanks, Sir, cry'd I, 'tis very fine / But where d'ye sleep and where d'ye dine?" The same question might be asked by those crossing the threshold of Blenheim into the inner sanctums of the British upper crust. In 1702, John Churchill became the first Duke of Marlborough when Queen Anne awarded him the title and the 2,000-acre estate for his victories against Louis XIV in the Battle of Blenheim. The Duke envisioned a palace that would rival that of Louis XIV's Versailles. When John passed away, his widow built the Triumphal Arch to serve as an entrance to the grounds, inscribed with the words, "This gate was built the year after the death of the most illustrious John, Duke of Marlborough, by order of Sarah, his most beloved wife." Three more years saw the completion of the 131-foot-tall Column of Victory, a Doric-styled limestone pillar topped by a statue of the first Duke of Marlborough, garbed in the attire of a Roman general.

The museum is an ode to Prime Minister Sir Winston Churchill. Visitors can enter his bedroom, which retains a red carpet, rose-print wallpaper, and a velvet-cushioned rocking chair. A shadowbox holds his curls from a haircut when he was five. Guests can stroll along in the rose garden where Winston proposed to his wife, Clementine. Adolf Hitler ordered his Luftwaffe not to bomb Blenheim as he planned to occupy the premises after he invaded England.

The Long Library, where Winston Churchill spent endless hours, is the repository of more than 10,000 books, many over a century old. Looking upon the room are busts of the first and third dukes of the Marlborough line. The ceiling in the Green Drawing Room—so named after the color of the furniture and wall panels—gleams with accents of gold. The Red Drawing Room has red wallpaper and furniture made by Thomas Chippendale.

Blenheim's nod to the American duchess is an ornate cradle that Alva gave her daughter, a replica of the one in the Doge's Palace in Venice. John Singer Sargent painted a portrait of their family and their two dogs; Charles' seated pose camouflages the fact that his wife towered over his five-foot two frame.

Consuelo harbored such an antipathy to Charles that she used a large silver vessel that bore the carving of the Battle of Blenheim as the centerpiece for their dining table. A portrait of Consuelo that once graced Marlborough House, one Alva had commissioned in Paris, hangs from the palace wall.

The current owner, the eleventh Duke of Marlborough, John George Vanderbilt Henry Spencer-Churchill, moved in Princess Margaret's circle, and there was a rumored romance. In addition to opening Blenheim as a home museum, the eleventh Duke of Marlborough has rented it out for events such as a Barry Manilow pop concert and Sylvester Stallone's wedding. In 1998, he built the 1.8-acre Marlborough hedge maze, the world's second largest, inspired by the Grinling Gibbons carvings etched on the colonnades. He also restored the castle's Rose Garden, created in the nineteenth century. A short walk from the palace on the other side of the Grand Bridge stands the Harry Potter Tree, a Cedar of Lebanon that served as the setting for the 2007 *Harry Potter and the Order of the Phoenix*. The site and the grounds have also appeared in other films: *Gulliver's Travels*, *Hamlet*, and *The Legend of Tarzan*.

In 2017, an antiques expert spied an unusual plant holder filled with tulips. Carvings adorning the "flowerpot" displayed a drunken Dionysius leaning on a satyr. The expert recognized the antique was part of a Roman sarcophagus dating from the second century AD; the duke moved the reliquary inside.

The stately met the profane in 2023 when thieves absconded with the palace's 18-karat gold loo, the theft of which caused a minor flood. The fully functioning toilet—estimated at $5.9 million—was an exhibit by the Italian artist Maurizio Cattelan, with the title, "America."

The last lines of the Alexander Pope poem, applied to the years Consuelo spent at Blenheim, "I find by all you have been telling / That 'tis a house, but not a dwelling."

**Seen from Her Window:** Looking from her palace's windows, Consuelo could have reminisced about the splendor of the palatial homes that bookmarked her life, alluded to in the title of her memoir, *The Glitter and the Gold.*

# CHAPTER 33

## *Eternal*

*"I am bound to the earth with sorrow."*
### —MARY TODD LINCOLN

◇◇◇◇◇◇◇◇◇◇

### Mary Todd Lincoln House
opened 1977 | Lexington, Kentucky

Stephen Foster's signature song, "My Old Kentucky Home," expresses an enslaved man's longing to be reunited with his family in his far away Bluegrass state. Trapped in the eye of the Civil War storm, Mary Todd Lincoln may also have pined for her old Kentucky home. To walk the same halls as Mary and President Lincoln, one can tour the Mary Todd Lincoln House.

British school children learn a rhyme to remember the wives of King Henry VIII, "Divorced, beheaded, died; Divorced, beheaded, survived." While the First Ladies of the United States never dealt with decapitation (at least not literally), their lives were often as dramatic as those of the consorts of the right royal rotter. The sixteenth First Lady's life proves inhabiting the East Wing is not for the fainthearted.

Mary Ann Todd was born in 1818, one of seven children, in Lexington, Kentucky, then known as "the Athens of the West." Her parents were Robert and Eliza Todd, the city's aristocrats. In theory, Robert was against possessing human chattel; nevertheless, he enslaved five people. A Todd family story relates how one of them, Mammy Sally, confided to Mary that their gate bore a mark signifying it was a place where runaways could seek help.

After bearing seven children, her mother Eliza passed away, a traumatic event for six-year-old Mary. Sixteen months later, Robert married Elizabeth Humphreys,

First Lady Mary Todd Lincoln |
*Wikimedia Commons, Matthew Brady*

with whom he went on to have nine children. Recalling a desolate childhood due to her stepmother, Mary retaliated with pranks such as putting salt in Mammy Sally's coffee. Stepmother Dearest pronounced Mary "a limb of Satan." Her father was unable to attend to his children as he was often away serving in Kentucky's House of Representatives.

By the time the Todds moved into an elegant fourteen-room house, Mary was enrolled in a school run by Charlotte Mentelle, who had fled her homeland during the French Revolution. A standout student, Mary understood she was highly intelligent but was also aware that the brass ring for a young woman of the time was hooking a husband. However, she determined to marry for love and vowed, "My hand will never be given where my heart is not."

At age twenty, Mary embarked on a prolonged visit to her married sister, Elizabeth Todd Edwards, in Springfield, Illinois. Her brother-in-law, Ninian Edwards, remarked of the beauty, "Mary could make a bishop forget his prayers." Through the Edwards, Mary met Abraham Lincoln, who later referred to himself as "a poor nobody then." He was a rough around the edges lawyer who'd been born in a Kentucky log cabin. At a cotillion, Lincoln told Mary, "I want to dance with you in the worst way." Physically, they were opposites: he was six feet four and rail thin, with dark hair; Mary was five foot two and plump with blue eyes. After a brief estrangement, during which period Abraham described himself as "the most miserable man living," the thirty-four-year-old tied the knot with his twenty-four-year-old bride. Although the Edwards agreed to hosting the ceremony in their home, they were against the match as Lincoln was not their social equal. A week after the wedding, Lincoln declared his marriage was "a matter of profound wonder." Mary told a friend, "He is to be President of the United States some day. If I had not thought so, I would never have married him, for you can see he is not pretty." As an observer noted, Lincoln was "a gloomy

**The Todd Family Home, now the Mary Todd Lincoln House** | *Wikimedia Commons, FloNight*

man—a sad man. His wife made him President." After his 1860 presidential victory, Lincoln strode along the streets of Springfield shouting, "Mary, Mary, we are elected!"

While her husband's legacy is arguably that of the country's greatest president, Mary was a magnet for malevolence. In a move that future First Ladies should have heeded (a hint Nancy Reagan should have taken), Mary went over budget redecorating the White House. Washington insiders viewed her as an American Nero who fiddled with wallpaper while the Republic burned. When Lincoln learned of the skyrocketing expenditures, it marked one of the few times his aides heard him berate her for splurging on "flub dubs" while his soldiers did without. Detractors pilloried Mary for her lavish clothing expenditures (an accusation also levied at Nancy Reagan). The First Lady loved the attire of Empress Eugénie, but the French styles did not love the middle-aged Mary back. She favored low-cut gowns that displayed what a senator called her "milking apparatus." Her husband critiqued a dress, which featured a long train and exposed shoulders and remarked she needed "a little less tail and little more neck."

Unlike Lincoln, who was "almost a monomaniac on the subject of honesty," she falsified bills and misappropriated funds. After accepting lavish gifts, she badgered her husband to award plum appointments to the donors. Her staff was disconcerted by her drastic mood swings and explosive temper; most likely, she was a victim of what is now understood as bipolar disorder. When the Lincolns had lived in Springfield, in the grip of rage, she threw hot beverages at her spouse and delivered a blow to his face that drew blood. Despite Mary's mercurial temper, she was forever supportive of her husband. In this she echoed the sentiment of future First Lady Mamie Eisenhower, "I had a career. His name was Ike." William Herndon, who had been Lincoln's law partner, denounced Mary as a "she-wolf." John Hay, Lincoln's social secretary during the Civil War, referred to her as "the Hellcat." Mary served as the whipping girl of the White House because Northerners distrusted her since her brother and three of her stepbrothers were fighting for the Confederacy; Southerners hated her because her husband was hell-bent on making the slavery-driven South a civilization gone with the wind.

In 1862, Mary grieved the death of her eleven-year-old son, Willie—probably from typhus—who had been preceded in death by his three-year-old brother, Eddie. In a way similar to First Lady Nancy Reagan, who relied on her astrologer, Mary arranged White House séances to communicate with her beloved boys. Yet there was something about Mary that made her husband remain devoted, saying, "My wife is as handsome as when she was a girl, and I...fell in love with her; and what is more, I have never fallen out." And there was much to admire as she visited wounded soldiers and donated to the Contraband Relief Association that provided food for its residents. After Mary asked for a pardon for a deserter, Lincoln complied "by request of the Lady President."

On April 14, 1865, the Lincolns, along with their guests, Major Henry Rathbone and Clara Harris, were at the Ford Theater watching a performance of *Our American Cousin*. Concerned about the appropriateness of holding her husband's hand, Mary inquired, "What will Miss Harris think of my hanging on to you so?" His response, in what were to be his last words, was, "She won't think anything about it." A few moments later, John Wilkes Booth fired his derringer. A hysterical Mary cried out, "Why didn't they shoot me!"

The widow, who wore black for the remainder of her days, remained in bed in the White House for forty days. Mary never recovered from the shock; six years later, she was subjected to another one at the loss of her third son, eighteen-year-old Tad. Her behavior became erratic; Robert, her only remaining child, initiated a trial that led to a jury declaring that Mary was indeed insane. The decision led to Mary's involuntary commitment at Bellevue Place, a women's insane asylum, where she remained for three months. Heartbroken, Mary lamented, "I wish I could forget myself."

**Mary Todd Lincoln House:** To prepare for her role as the First Lady in Steven Spielberg's *Lincoln*, Sally Field visited the Mary Todd Lincoln House, the first historic site dedicated to a First Lady. At the end of the film, Mary told her husband that if people wanted to understand him, they would have to understand her. Stepping over the threshold of the home museum, the pages of the calendar seem to turn in reverse. One can imagine the upper strata of Kentucky society, sipping their mint juleps, when they were guests at the Todd house: Henry Clay, the founder of the state's Republican party, John Breckinridge, a future vice president, and Cassius Clay, prominent abolitionist and founder of the Republican party. The halls rustle with the swish of silk and crinoline. The 1803 brick estate was originally an inn; when Robert purchased the property, he divided a room into twin parlors. The most famous guest, Abraham Lincoln, stayed for three weeks in 1847, during which time he indulged in the extensive library. Guests thrill to touch the cherry wood banister on which the Great Emancipator once placed his hands. In the front parlor is a painting of Mary at forty-five, her hair adorned with flowers. The desk in Mary's bedroom holds a miniature painting of Charlotte Mentelle; Meissen porcelain perfume jars remain on display. In the parents' bedroom, where Robert conceived many of his sixteen children, hang silhouettes of Mary and Abraham. The children's room has a display case with a silver cup a friend gifted Tadd Lincoln after the loss of his brother Willie.

Amid the treasures in a guest bedroom are prints of the assassination. The talisman transports viewers to the fateful Good Friday evening in the nineteenth century that destroyed those in the presidential box. Clara married Henry, and the couple had three children; however, in 1883, in the grip of madness, he murdered his wife and repeatedly stabbed himself. He survived and ended his days in an insane asylum. The slain president's remains underwent seventeen exhumations until arriving at his final resting place under ten feet of cement.

A recluse in her sister Elizabeth's home, nearing her end, Mary requested that she should lie "beside my dear husband & 'Taddies' on one side of me." Mary passed away in 1882; her coffin situated in the same spot where, forty years earlier, she had stood as a bride. On Mary's finger was the wedding ring on which Lincoln had inscribed, "Love is Eternal."

**Seen from Her Window:** In the back of the Todd house was a magnificent garden. Gazing upon the beauty of the flowers, a young Mary never could have fathomed what an incredible tapestry the Fates would weave out of her life.

# CHAPTER 34

# Lovers and Lovers

*"Please come down here soon. The house is full of pianists, painters, pederasts, prostitutes, and peasants...Great material."*

## —MABEL DODGE LUHAN IN A LETTER TO GERTRUDE STEIN

◇◇◇◇◇◇◇◇◇◇

## The Mabel Dodge Luhan House

opened in 1996 | Taos, New Mexico

D. H. Lawrence slept in Los Gallos ("the Roosters"), so named after its owner's decorative Mexican ceramic roosters that still perch on its roof, as did Georgia O'Keeffe, Carl Jung, Martha Graham, and other luminaries. Mabel Evans Dodge Sterne Luhan, the eccentric heiress, summoned many visitors to her adobe castle, nestled at the foot of the Sacred Mountain in Taos, New Mexico. If the walls of Los Gallos could talk, what tantalizing tales they would crow.

Mabel, the future *grande dame* of a unique salon, was born in Buffalo in 1879, the daughter of Charles and Dara Ganson. She described herself as "not much to look at," and though her childhood was financially privileged, she was emotionally deprived. She bobbed her hair before it was in style, much to her father's chagrin. When Karl Kellogg Evans, heir to the Anchor Line Steamboat Co., pursued her despite already having a fiancée, Mabel accepted his overtures after daddy dearest forbade her to see him again. In 1900, Karl and Mabel eloped; two years later, he died in a hunting accident, leaving behind a son of questionable paternity. During her marriage, she had engaged in an affair with

*Mabel Dodge Luhan |*
*Wikimedia Commons,*
*Carl Vaan Vechten*

Dr. Parmenter, her gynecologist, a fact that scandalized her mother, who Mabel alleged was also sleeping with him. Maternity bored Mabel; for distraction, she set sail for Europe.

Aboard ship she met her second husband, Boston architect Edwin Dodge. The couple moved to the magnificent Villa Caronia in Florence; the mansion was soon transformed to a mecca for the art crowd such as Gertrude Stein, Arthur Rubinstein, and Pen Browning (son of acclaimed poets Robert and Elizabeth Barrett Browning). Some of the glittering guests supplied Mabel with both culture and sex. The outsider in this salacious salon was Edwin; Mabel derided him for his "inferior sophistication," (including his contemporary lingo and "vanilla tastes") such as his demand that in his villa, "certain forms of nonsense stop." Jacques-Emile Blanche painted Mabel as a Renaissance principessa. The idylls of the principessa ended when weary of Europe, the Dodges returned to America.

In New York, Mabel exiled Edwin to the Brevoort Hotel as a preliminary to their divorce. She transformed her Greenwich Village apartment into a mecca for radicals such as Emma Goldman and Margaret Sanger, poet Edward Arlington Robinson, as well as sundry socialists and anarchists. Expressing her ongoing affinity for art, she hosted a show of post-Impressionist paintings that introduced the United States to European modernism. She became involved with Maurice Sterne, a Jewish sculptor, the next to escort her down the aisle.

When three husbands did not serve as the proverbial charm, Mabel turned to psychoanalysis; she described it as "a kind of tattle telling." On the advice of her therapist, to distance herself from Maurice, she sent him to the Southwest under the pretext she wanted him to scout out new landscapes for his canvases. Although she was not keen on a reunion, his letters piqued her interest, "Do you want an object in life? Save the Indians, their art, culture, reveal it to the world!" His words resonated as Mabel's clairvoyant medium had foretold that a Native

American would one day play a role in her life. Moreover, she had experienced a dream where Maurice's face had morphed into an indigenous visage.

Upon her arrival, Mabel became so excited by her first glimpse of the Southwest that she disembarked from her train and cried out, "Holy! Holy! Holy! Lord God Almighty! ...I am Here." To break with her old life, she cut her hair and donned a serape. Her first stop was at an adobe hut where a blanket-wearing Tony Luhan, from the local Tewa tribe, was beating on a drum and singing. Mabel was convinced his face was the one from her dream; Tony said he had also seen her in a vision. Over dinner, Tony claimed that he could make himself invisible, and that the fire in her grate was his good friend. Although he was married to a woman from his culture, he fell hard for Mabel and gave her peyote as a cure for dysentery. After attending a Corn Dance, Tony said, "I comin' here to this teepee tonight, when darkness here. That be right?" Who could blame Mabel for resisting such a proposal? The sexual shenanigan scenario proved the breaking point for husband Maurice, who slapped Mabel and took the next train east. The marriage of Mabel and Tony resulted in hostility from both the Native and white communities. Although she attributed her catching syphilis to Tony, she appreciated his ability to control her mood swings.

With her considerable wealth, Mabel set about building her dream home: a three-story, seventeen-room adobe estate. Initially, she christened her compound "Las Cruces," in reference to the two crosses at the nearby "Morada," the meeting house for the brotherhood of the Hispanic "penitenters." However, when her mail ended up in the town of Las Cruces, Mabel renamed it "Los Gallos" after the brightly colored Mexican ceramic roosters she placed on her roof. "Mabeltown" also held five guesthouses, barns, and stables. By 1922, the two-story Big House included living and dining rooms. The décor was eclectic, with French, Italian, and Oriental sofas and chairs. The accents included European paintings, Taos Indian blankets, and pottery, juxtaposed with Hispanic saints. Immune to the irony, Mabel praised the locals for their lack of materialism. In response, a local wrote to the Taos *Star* suggesting the heiress change places with him: "You drink muddy water which came down from the mountains, and my five children will drink nice clean water from your faucets."

During the 1920s and 1930s, Mabel was one of the first to fight for legislation to protect the rights of Native Americans. She also spearheaded a writer's colony where she hoped to entice creative types she referred to as "changers of the world." Deeply

**Taos Artist Colony** | *Julianna Spotted Corn Courtesy of Mabel Dodge Luhan House*

desirous of D. H. Lawrence's presence at Los Gallos, she used ESP, pleading letters, and an offering for his wife, Frieda, of a necklace seeped in indigenous magic. They agreed and left England for a scene where they were both participants in and had ringside seats as observers to a southwestern soap opera. Uma, the wife of guest Robinson Jeffers, a famed poet from Big Sur, California, was upset with her husband's affair with a younger woman—one Mabel had encouraged—and attempted to shoot herself in the heart in one of Los Gallos' bathrooms. D. H. Lawrence ended up painting the bathroom windows in colorful geometric and animal designs to deter prying eyes, an odd act considering his novel *Lady Chatterley's Lover* was the subject of an obscenity trial.

Other denizens of the desert hideaway included Aldous Huxley, Thornton Wilder, Ansel Adams, Greta Garbo, and Martha Graham. Art collector Leo Stein, Gertrude's brother, taking a break from Europe's modern art, left his calling card. Ansel Adams painted a portrait of Tony; Willa Cather reportedly used him as inspiration for the character of Eusabio in *Death Comes for the Archbishop*. Not everyone was a fan of the mountain retreat. Thomas Wolfe arrived late one evening, inebriated, and took off the next day. Relations eventually soured between the Luhans and the Lawrences, and Mabel provided them with a mountain ranch seventeen miles north of Taos. D. H. Lawrence died in Provence in 1930; five years later, Frieda Lawrence arranged for his ashes to return to Taos for interment on their ranch.

When death came for the heiress in 1962, actor Dennis Hopper purchased the estate from her granddaughter. Under his occupancy, Los Gallos remained a who's who of the counterculture, with guests such as Bob Dylan, Leonard Cohen, Jack Nicholson, and Joni Mitchell. Part of Dennis' interest was the home's association with D. H. Lawrence, whom he called "the first freak." He rechristened Los Gallos the Mud Palace and promptly married singer Michelle Phillips from the Mamas and the Papas in the solarium with the Sacred Mountain as witness; she left him a week later. Dennis managed to lower the bar of strangeness, and Mabel's old home became a den of free love and drugs. The bathroom, the site of the abortive suicide and Lawrence's artistry, appeared as the setting for a scene in *American Dreamer* that showed a nude Dennis in the bathtub with two Playboy bunnies. Mabel would have approved.

**The Mabel Dodge Luhan House:** Today, Los Gallos is a home museum, guesthouse, literary shrine, and retreat. In the *Taos News*, writer Teresa Dovalpage wrote, "Declared a National Historic Landmark in 1991, the Mabel Dodge Luhan House is more than a historical place; it is a living, breathing haven for all creative types. Inspiration is everywhere." After dinner, dancers and drummers from the pueblo provided entertainment. Teachers include "transcendental painters" and Tibetan monks. The place where Mabel penned her memoirs retains its wooden beams, painted to resemble a Native blanket. Her presence, which a friend likened to "an airplane laden with explosives," yet looms. In her book, *Winter in Taos*, Mabel wrote that her home "is a kind of treasure trove, but it is a treasure that needs a key, and I am the only one who has it."

Mabel transferred ownership of her secondary ranch to D. H. Lawrence, the only home he ever owned. In appreciation, he gave her the original manuscript of *Sons and Lovers*. The deal did not work out in the Lawrences' favor. The ranch was worth $1,000 at the time, whereas the original Lawrence manuscript could have brought in $50,000. But perhaps more priceless than even such a literary treasure was Mabel Dodge Luhan's effect as a catalyst to her community of creative genius. As historian Lois Palken Rudnick said of her, "She was an artist of life." Considering the free love that flourished, another name for Los Gallos could be Sons and Lovers and Lovers.

**Seen from Her Window:** Mabel was always taken with the scene that greeted her from the third-story solarium of Los Gallos, nestled in the Taos Mountains. From a second-floor room, she could see the D. H. Lawrence House and the desert environs that had seduced Mabel at first sight.

# PART VIII

# Madame Midas

# CHAPTER 35

## An Estate of Her Own

*"Why do I always marry stinkers?"*
## —MARJORIE MERRIWEATHER POST

◇◇◇◇◇◇◇◇◇◇

### Hillwood Estate: Museum & Gardens

opened 1977 | Washington, DC

It is difficult for modern readers to imagine how rapidly the breakfast cereal industry mushroomed up from religious and health-nut origins, but by the time cereal heiress Marjorie Merriweather Post's father Charles Post died in 1914, she could easily afford her own Xanadu: Hillwood Estate.

Marjorie, whose life was for the most part as sweet as the sugary concoctions behind her stratospheric wealth, was born in 1887 in Springfield, Illinois, to Christian Science father Charles William Post, the creator of cereal classics, and mother Ella Post, née Merriweather. Seeking a cure for his own physical and mental breakdown, Charles checked into Dr. Kellogg's sanatorium in Battle Creek, Michigan, where he relocated with his family. On the barn's two-burner stove, Charles concocted Elijah's Manna, later renamed Post Toasties, a product that launched the Postum Cereal Company.

Eight-year-old Marjorie joined him in a hayloft where she glued labels onto packages; sixty years later, she still recalled the taste of the glue. With the money rolling in, Charles kept his daughter grounded. When Marjorie wanted a moleskin coat for her doll, he made her set traps to catch the moles. Afterwards,

*Post Cereal Heiress* |
*Wikimedia Commons, C. M. Stieglitz*

she had to skin, tan, cure, and sew the fur. Two years later, Marjorie was accompanying her father to board meetings and visits to family factories.

Charles had gifted his only child shares of Postum that were worth three million dollars by the time she was sixteen. Despite her wealth, Charles was concerned over her extravagant clothing. In 1904, when Marjorie insisted on buying new furs, he wrote to his daughter, then a student at Washington, DC's elite Mount Vernon Seminary for Girls, "You have more than double the clothes, shoes, and stuff that any girl no matter how rich should have at 17. Now make some of the furs you have do and don't order more dresses or clothes before you return... Dad wants you *sensible,* so go slow." His daughter did not think her father was sensible when he divorced her mother Ella to marry his secretary, Leila Young, twenty years his junior.

With the heiresses' beauty, brains, and beaucoup bucks, the world was her oyster, one which she wanted to share with a man she loved. At age eighteen, Marjorie wed Edward Bennett Close, a New York lawyer from old Greenwich money, and they honeymooned—along with her father—in Egypt and Italy. Crack lines formed in the Closes' relationship due to Edward's love of the cocktail hour, something Marjorie's religion frowned upon. Further tension arose when Charles realized that his son-in-law had no interest in running the Postum Cereal Company.

Along with marital problems, in 1914, Marjorie suffered the greatest trauma of her life when her father ended his life with a shotgun blast in his mouth. Speculation flew that he had come to the end of his rope due to ill health and depression. Another contributing factor was Leila's affair with Lawrence Montgomery, whom she subsequently wed. His death left his only child with a twenty-million-dollar inheritance that she would parlay into a billion dollars in contemporary currency. At a time when women could not vote, the intrepid Marjorie ran Postum, a reversal of the times when the man made the money which the Missus spent. When asked the reason behind her business acumen, Marjorie responded, "My father."

With her fortune, Marjorie wore the tiara of an American royal. Her floating palace was her 316-foot yacht *Sea Cloud*; the world's largest privately owned vessel at the time, it could hold four hundred passengers. The Duke and Duchess of Windsor were among the ships' glitterati guests. Upon viewing the *Sea Cloud*'s Louis XVI master suite, Queen Maud of Norway remarked, "Why, you live like a queen, don't you?"

On the surface, Edward appeared to be a doting husband. However, Marjorie worried his wandering eye had wandered to her French maid. She ordered their valet to dust the floor of Edward's bedroom with talcum powder to check how many footprints appeared. The incriminating evidence was something hubby could not refute. After fourteen years and children Adelaide and Eleanor, the couple divorced. Edward's second marriage produced descendants who led to his granddaughter, actress Glenn Close.

In 1919, Marjorie married Manhattan stockbroker Edward F. Hutton, with whom she had her third daughter, actress Dina Merrill. At Edward's urging, Post became a public corporation with 200,000 shares on the New York Stock Exchange; it also merged with Maxwell House Coffee, Sanka, and Jell-O. However, a literal goose laid the golden egg for the Huttons. On their yacht, a waiter served them a goose for dinner that had previously been frozen. Intrigued, Marjorie visited Clarence Birdseye, who had discovered the freeze-drying process. She bought his plant for twenty million dollars and changed her company's name to General Foods Corporation. Six years later, Marjorie froze out her second spouse.

Her third trip down the aisle was with diplomat Joseph E. Davies. When President Roosevelt appointed Joseph ambassador to the Soviet Union, Marjorie used her yacht to transport twelve lockers of Birds Eye frozen foods, two thousand pints of pasteurized cream, and twenty-five refrigerators to avoid the austerity of Stalin's rule. In Moscow, the consummate connoisseur gobbled up priceless art. Her passion for collecting had begun as a child with silver teaspoons; as an adult, her penchant was for objects with imperial ties. The heiress owned pear-shaped diamond earrings that Marie Antoinette had sewn into her pocket before her arrest at Varennes, a diamond necklace Napoleon had gifted to the Empress Marie Louise, and Empress Alexandra's diamond wedding crown.

*Hillwood Estate  |  Wikimedia Commons, Jllm06*

Husband number four was Herbert A. Mays, a union that ended after Marjorie saw nude photographs of hubby cavorting with young men at their swimming pool. The damning pictures reminded her of a dinner in Montmartre where Herbert had "seemed unduly interested in the waiters." When Marjorie asked her attorney why all her relationships had snapped, crackled, and popped, he responded, "The reason is you try to make them all Mr. Post." After the fourth fiasco, Marjorie resumed her maiden name.

The heiress took to heart the biblical admonition "To whom much has been given much is expected," and during World War I she furnished the Red Cross hospital at Savenay, France, with two thousand beds. Half a century later, Marjorie gave receptions in Washington for veterans wounded in Vietnam. She personally oversaw a Salvation Army feeding station in New York that served a thousand meals per day. Her largesse included a $100,000 grant to the National Cultural Center in Washington, a venue that became the John F. Kennedy Center for the Performing Arts. The National Symphony received a donation of $1.5 million.

Wilhelm I of Prussia was visiting a castle in Ferrières, just outside Paris, when someone complimented him on his magnificent estate. The Prussian royal responded, "No king could afford to live here, only a Rothschild." The same statement could have applied to the Post palaces. One of Marjorie's real estate crown jewels was her vacation home, the current property of President Donald J. Trump, situated between a lagoon and the Atlantic Ocean, a location that inspired the name Mar-a-Lago, Spanish for Sea-to-Lake. Viennese architect Joseph Urban, who had designed the Metropolitan Opera House, was behind the blueprints for the 115-room Palm Beach pink palazzo. The living room had a thirty-four-foot ceiling, on whose walls Marjorie displayed silk needlework tapestries that had once graced a Venetian palace. A four-thousand-pound, ballroom-length marble table, inlaid with semiprecious stones, bore a likeness to one in Florence's Uffizi gallery. Her husband E. F. Hutton's quip to overawed guests was, "Marjorie said she was going to build a little mansion by the sea. Look what we got!"

**Hillwood Estate:** The home closest to the heiress' heart was Hillwood, whose catalogue states of its founder, "In her lifelong pursuit of beautiful and finely made objects, she shared a common taste with the royalty and nobility of eighteenth- and nineteenth-century Europe and Russia." Hillwood possesses the greatest collection of Russian imperial art outside the Soviet Union. The marbled entrance hall showcases a painting of Catherine the Great in royal regalia; the walls by the staircase feature portraits of various Romanovs, reunited in a foreign land. Plum Hillwood possessions include Catherine the Great's Fabergé Easter Eggs and a chandelier that once cast light from her palace's ceiling. Another royal artifact on display is a diamond-studded crown worn by Empress Alexandra at her wedding to Tsar Nicholas II. The Icon Room holds a large pink Fabergé egg, encased with gold, diamonds, emeralds, and pearls that Nicholas II gave to his mother in 1914. Other historic treasures are the nineteenth-century red Aubusson rug that Napoleon III bequeathed to the doomed Emperor Maximilian of Mexico. Lore holds that William Randolph Hearst, another American with a castle complex, had been the carpet's one-time possessor. Miscellaneous objects abound: a walking stick with a handle of gold, diamonds, and rubies, and a silver ashtray decorated with quartz that never held an ash. The home's maintenance was left to a staff of eighty.

In Hillwood's grounds, ten gardeners labored on its upkeep, enhancing the grandeur of the estate. Shogo Myaida, who designed the Brooklyn Botanical Garden and those in the 1939–40 World's Fair, was the master planner of its formal Japanese garden. The French garden holds Marjorie's remains in a three-foot pink stone pedestal topped by a ten-foot column. Her ashes are near a putting green with a sign: "This ivy is from Buckingham Palace, London, England."

The estate museum is a prestigious venue for events, one of which was the 2011 showing "Wedding Belles: Bridal Fashions from the Marjorie Merriweather

Post Family, 1874–1958." The bridesmaids for Marjorie and her three daughters must have made quite the commitment as the Post heiresses took several trips down the aisle each: Marjorie, four; Adelaide, three; Eleanor, six; and Nedenia, three. The exhibition incorporated all Marjorie's wedding dresses and one from each of her daughters.

**Seen from Her Window:** A third Hillwood garden holds four statues representing the seasons surrounded by a profusion of magnolia, cherry, and dogwood trees. In the center of the lawn is a black Italian marble plaque embossed with words from Tsarina Alexandra Feodorovna, the last empress of Russia, "Friendship outstays the hurrying flight of years and aye abides through laughter and through tears."

# CHAPTER 36

# *Iron Butterfly*

*"The people need a role model...*
*especially in the dark of night."*

## —IMELDA MARCOS

◇◇◇◇◇◇◇◇◇◇

## Santo Niño Shrine and Heritage Museum

### opened 1979 | The Philippines

As First Lady of the Philippines, Imelda would take materialism to entirely new and fantastical heights. To experience a dwelling of fairy-tale proportions, visit the Santo Niño Shrine and Heritage Museum.

When thinking of historical figures associated with the Philippines, most do not visualize the island nation's namesake, King Philip II of Spain. Most recall a presidential wife, alternately revered and reviled. The larger-than-life, rags-to-(ill-gotten)-riches tale began with Imelda Remedios Visitacion Romualdez's birth in 1929 in Tacloban. Her father, Vincente, was a forty-three-year-old widower, whose reluctant bride was the twenty-seven-year-old Remedious. Their union added six more children to Vincente's five from his deceased first wife. Miserable in her marriage, Remedious, along with her two sons and three daughters, moved into the garage. When Imelda was eight, her mother passed away from pneumonia. Upon losing his house to creditors, Vincente relocated from Manila to his hometown of Tacloban. Conditions further deteriorated with the coming of the Japanese invasion, and the thirteen-year-old Imelda, to the backdrop of planes raining down death, sewed her clothes from the material of downed parachutes. The only currency Imelda possessed was her exquisite

beauty. At age eighteen, she garnered the moniker "The Rose of Tacloban" in the Miss Philippines Contest.

Imelda's destiny would have been as a Real Housewife of Manila had she not stepped into a congressional building in 1954 to avoid the heat and mosquitoes. Fernando Marcos noticed her in the Visitors' Gallery and rushed over to meet the strikingly beautiful girl. He invited her out for ice cream, and over dessert declared his love. The smitten suitor sent Imelda a diamond for each of the next eleven days, until they became husband and wife. Referring to the daily delivery of diamonds, Imelda quipped, "I wish he could have courted me longer." Their church ceremony was a society gala; the bride's wedding band held eleven symbolic diamonds. The reception at the park opposite Malacañang Palace hosted three thousand guests. One who did not receive an invitation was Fernando's common-law-wife, Carmen Ortega; neither did their three children. With his newly minted legal spouse, Ferdinand fathered daughters Imee and Irene and son Fernando Jr., nicknamed Bongbong. Marriage did not, however, stop Ferdinand from engaging in serial adultery.

Upon Marcos' election as the country's tenth president, he credited his wife's campaign among the poor for his election, praising her as his "secret weapon." *Life* magazine pronounced Mrs. Marcos "the Jackie Kennedy of Asia." Rather than merely serving as arm-candy to her husband, the First Lady's pet project was erecting buildings dedicated to the arts. One of her architectural structures was a film center she touted would be "the Cannes of Asia," designed to host large-scale events such as Miss Universe contests and boxing matches between reigning champions Mohammad Ali and Joe Frazier.

As the daughter of a political dynasty and as the wife of the president, Imelda served as the governor of greater Manila. Reveling in the position, Imelda met Presidents Nixon, Reagan, and Johnson, as well as Donald Trump, Prince Charles, Princess Margaret, Andy Warhol, Gloria Vanderbilt, Saddam Hussein, Fidel Castro, and Mao Zedong. She also became a Philippine Lady Macbeth who used her wifely wiles to influence her husband to substitute dictatorship for democracy in her quest for power and wealth. One Filipino anecdote related how President Marcos and General Fabian Ver met in hell, where the former general inquired, "Boss, I've committed treacherous acts, but yours were far worse. So how come I'm covered in burning tar up to my neck, and you're only covered up to your knees?" The deposed president replied, "I'm standing on Imelda's shoulders."

Over the next two decades, the president and his First Lady presided over a regime that tortured, incarcerated, and killed tens of thousands of "enemies of state." They also amassed a ten-billion-dollar fortune that they hid in dozens of oversea accounts. A world-class shopper who would make the Kardashians appear miserly, Imelda embarked on multi-million-dollar shopping sprees in Manhattan, Rome, and Copenhagen. One real estate plum she turned down was the Empire State Building, which came with a $750 million price tag, as she felt it was "too ostentatious." Their art collection held Picassos, Michelangelos, and Botticellis; in the San Francisco airport, the First Lady bought two thousand dollars' worth of gum. She purchased perfume by the gallon and once emptied duty-free shops across the globe of her favorite so no one else would have her signature scent.

Amidst the laissez-faire spending and palatial residences, horror intruded. In 1972—the same year the president imposed martial law—while the First Lady presided over a televised award ceremony, Carlito Dimahilig stabbed her eleven times with a twelve-inch bolo knife. A security guard shot the assassin twice in the back. Imelda, who received seventy-five stiches, commented, "If somebody's going to kill me, why such an ugly instrument?" She took to wearing bulletproof bras. President Nixon called with his condolences.

With the economy in shambles due to the First Couple using the Philippines as their personal piggy bank, protests erupted from students, opposition leaders, and the poverty-stricken populace. Nevertheless, just as Nero fiddled while Rome burned, Imelda boogeyed in Manhattan's Studio 54. A megalomaniac till the end, Ferdinand clung to power. However, fearful of the mob demanding their heads, Ferdinand, Imelda, and their children escaped in a helicopter. Imelda said of their flight, "The slipper was lost. And everything turned into a pumpkin." When protesters stormed the Philippine Versailles, they found a treasure trove of art masterpieces, a multi-million-dollar collection of jewelry, and uneaten caviar on a dining room table. The reported three thousand pairs of shoes in Imelda's

*One of Imelda's palatial estates* | Santo Niño Shrine and Heritage Museum

closet captivated the world's attention; in reality, there were 1,060, including one battery-equipped pair that glowed in the dark. Of the brouhaha, Imelda remarked, "They went into my closets looking for skeletons, but thank God all they found were shoes, beautiful shoes." The media dubbed her "Marie Antoinette with shoes." The woman who had graced magazine covers now faced mugshots. Billionaire gal pal Doris Duke bailed her out for five million dollars.

Three years later, Ferdinand died in exile, and his widow was distraught when the Philippine government refused to allow burial in his homeland. The future president, Rodrigo Duterte, relented, and Imelda arranged for her husband's reburial in the Heroes' Cemetery in Manila. His tombstone read: "Filipino" beneath his name and the years of his birth and death. The yo-yo, invented in the Philippines, is an apt metaphor for Imelda, who refused to stay down. The former First Lady became a congresswoman for her hometown province of Leyte. Imee, who told her people "to move on" from the past, served as the governor for the province of Ilocos Norte. Perhaps due to historic amnesia, in 2022, Bongbong became the seventeenth Philippine president.

**Santo Niño Shrine and Heritage Museum:** Imelda Marcos told biographer Katherine Ellison, "All I ever dreamed of when I was a tiny girl was a little house with a little picket fence by the sea." As an adult, Imelda had no fewer than twenty-nine pleasure domes. One was a grandiose red mansion with dozens of white arches set amidst a huge plot of land. The 21,500 square foot seaside residence was a present from Marcos to his wife, built in her hometown, dedicated to its local saint. A chapel dominates the ground floor with an image of Santo Niño. Hallways display paintings of the Stations of the Cross, as well as a gargantuan mosaic of Jesus. Rather than a domicile (as Imelda is alleged to have stayed at her home for only one night), the estate is a shrine to Imelda. The Presidential Commission on Good Government turned her residence into a museum, where visitors marvel at the Olympic-sized backyard swimming pool, enormous state dining rooms, and ballroom, a replica of the one in Malacañang Palace. In the center of the grand room is a shell-encrusted fountain. All twenty-one bedrooms represent various Filipino regions, with the commonality that each displays a signed photograph of the president and his wife along with a diorama of Imelda. The largest suite, which belonged to Imelda, has more square footage than the average Filipino home. A floor to ceiling painting shows the lady of the manor rising from the sea holding a giant shell with miniature portraits of the Marcos family.

The mansion features ecclesiastic paintings from Italy, France, and Germany, along with secular treasures that include Ming dynasty vases, grand pianos, and ivory sculptures. An international treasure chest displays Czech Republic chandeliers, Argentine carpets, Chinese porcelain vases, Italian tiles, and Austrian mirrors. Departing the shrine, visitors are left wondering at the magic wand that transformed a Cinderella into the Iron Butterfly.

**Seen from Her Window:** Peering over from her heritage house-museum, Imelda might have envisioned an alternate road, one where she might perhaps have worshipped Santo Niño over Mammon, god of greed.

## CHAPTER 37

# *And No Friends*

*"A menace to happiness."*

*(Her pronouncement on money)*

**—HUGUETTE CLARK**

◇◇◇◇◇◇◇◇◇◇

### Bellosguardo Foundation

opened 2018 | Santa Barbara, California

In 1797, in the grip of an opium-induced dream, British poet Samuel Taylor Coleridge imagined a fantastic paradise that inspired his poem, "In Xanadu did Kubla Khan / A stately pleasure-dome decree / Where Alph, the sacred river ran / Through caverns measureless to man / Down to a sunless sea." The nonfictional Kubla Khan was Huguette Clark, whose pleasure dome offered panoramic Pacific Ocean views. To gaze upon a mansion whose halls echo an enigma, enter Bellosguardo.

This most storied of Xanadus belonged to an enigmatic heiress whose biography offers a peephole into the era when the Astors, Guggenheims, Rockefellers, and Vanderbilts ruled the social registry roost. Huguette Marcelle was the daughter of copper king William Andrews Clark, the Gilded Age robber baron who founded Las Vegas. Her mother, French-Canadian Anna Evangelina Clark, had undergone the transition from having been the fifteen-year-old ward of William to his lover to his wife. His children from his first marriage learned of the newest Mrs. Clark from a newspaper and were far from pleased with their stepmother, many years their junior. The Clarks' second child, Huguette, was born in Paris in 1906 to her sixty-seven-year-old father and twenty-eight-year-

old mother. A photograph of the toddler captures her impeccably dressed in white, surrounded by her doll collection. The main family home was a Fifth Avenue Victorian mansion, excessive even in an excessive age, built at a cost that surpassed that of the construction of Yankee Stadium. The mansion held 121 rooms, 31 bathrooms, four art galleries, a theater, and a swimming pool. The walls were bedecked with masterpieces by Degas, Monet, and Renoir. As a teen, Huguette took dancing lessons from Isadora Duncan.

Tragedy entered with the death of sixteen-year-old Andrée from meningitis, a loss that shattered her family. She had eluded death seven years earlier when the Clarks had failed to use their passenger tickets for the *Titanic*. Six years later, upon William's passing, his will divided his fortune amongst his four children from his first marriage and his only child from his second. The bequest left the nineteen-year-old Huguette with a half-a-billion-dollar inheritance. At twenty-two, America's most eligible woman fell for William MacDonald Gower, a Princeton grad of modest means. Anna spared no expense for her daughter's 1927 Bellosguardo wedding. Their union lasted nine months. She charged desertion. His take, however, was that they had never consummated their marriage. After their 1930 Reno divorce, the heiress went by the name Mrs. or Madam Huguette Clark. The end of her marriage marked the beginning of a retreat into gilded real estate shells. While Coleridge's dream envisioned a damsel with a dulcimer, Anna's Fifth Avenue sanctuary echoed with the strains of her harp and Huguette's violin. The music loving Huguette owned four Stradivari violins, including the 1709 instrument known as "The Virgin," a gift from her mother for her fiftieth birthday; another bore the engraving of Joan of Arc.

When Anna died in 1963, her passing left Huguette the only survivor of the Clark Camelot. The estate Anna bequeathed to her daughter included Cartier jewelry, museum-worthy canvases, and antique French furniture. Huguette also

*Bellosguardo that translates to beautiful lookout* | *Wikimedia Commons, Photographer Unknown*

became the sole possessor of a real estate treasure chest: the twenty-three-acre oceanfront Santa Barbara mansion Bellosguardo, its nearby Rancho Alegre, and three Fifth Avenue suites that comprised Anna's former home, Huguette's marital residence, and an apartment adjacent to her mother's. Another holding in her property portfolio was Le Beau Château, a twenty-two-room Connecticut mansion where she never spent a night.

The loss of her mother was gut-wrenching, and the fifty-seven-year-old heiress transformed into a *Great Expectations* Miss Havisham. Part of her reclusive nature, as was the case with fellow multimillionaire recluse Howard Hughes, was a fear of germs, a result of Andrée having contracted her fatal disease. In a sense, Huguette did not feel alone since she had the company of her French dolls. The modern-day Greta Garbo only ventured forth from her insulated splendor to attend Christian Dior fashion shows, where she ordered scale replicas for her porcelain-faced girls who sat in silk miniature armchairs. The heiress had arranged for one to be flown in from France, on an airplane where the doll occupied a first-class seat. An artisan from Bavaria created dollhouses; the heiress once contacted him explaining that one of the ceilings had to be raised because, she told him, "The little people are banging their heads!" A housekeeper ironed the dolls' couture dresses. Another interest was television; Huguette favored *The Dick Cavett Show, The Forsyte Saga*, and cartoons such as *The Flintstones*. While watching her shows, she ate her daily lunch of sardines and crackers.

The pages of the calendars turned with the regularity of a metronome until skin cancer ravaged the eighty-four-year-old Huguette. When Dr. Henry Singman paid a house call, he was the first person—other than her staff—she had seen in more than a decade. He discovered a home caught in a time warp: the rotary phones still identified the exchange number as "Butterfield 8." Amid the fallen splendor was the emaciated centenarian, dressed in a filthy robe, lips and eyelids disfigured by disease. Huguette insisted on going to the hospital on a stretcher to avoid the stares of the apartment's staff and residents. Suzanne Pierre, the wife of her former physician, hired Hadassah Peri, an immigrant from the Philippines, to work for madame. Hadassah and Huguette hit it off, and the nurse agreed to shifts of twelve hours a day, seven days a week. Suzanne delivered the dolls to Huguette's bedside.

After two months, with the skin lesions under control, the doctors pronounced their patient ready for discharge. Unbelievably, Huguette insisted on remaining in her hospital room with its view of an air-conditioning unit rather than gazing upon Bellosguardo's Pacific Ocean or through her Fifth Avenue window that looked upon the sailboat pond of Central Park. As always, Huguette had her way when she waved her checkbook. Fiercely private, her name as a patient was Harriet Chase. While the hospital-bound Huguette's habits did not change—she continued to order dolls and watch *The Flintstones*—Hadassah's life underwent a drastic transformation. She had gone from tenuous nursing assignments and her Israeli husband's job as a cabbie to a six-figure annual income. In addition, her boss gifted her a series of ever more pricey cars: a Lincoln Navigator, a Hummer, a $210,000 Bentley. Throughout the years, Hadassah received thirty million dollars, making her the highest paid nurse in history.

While Citizen Kane died in his Xanadu, the mansion that held Rosebud, his childhood sled, Huguette passed away in Beth Israel Medical Center in the company of her beloved dolls. Her interment was with her parents and sister in the Clark Woodlawn Cemetery mausoleum in the Bronx. Upon her death at age 104, the forgotten heiress became fodder for media inquiries that centered on the million-dollar question: Why would the possessor of palatial homes not have visited them in decades? Perhaps a hint lies in her favorite French fable, whose moral holds that it is better to live quietly as a cricket than flamboyantly as a butterfly. For the woman who hated to be in the limelight, she would have been aghast when her paternal relatives, whom she had cut out of her fabulous fortune, girded for battle, claiming

Tante Huguette, in the words of King Lear, was not "in her perfect mind." The best glimpse into the soul of Madam is found in her home museum.

**Bellosguardo:** The translation of the mansion's name is "beautiful lookout" in Italian, a phrase that does not begin to describe the breathtaking architectural jewel. Although the Clarks had last visited their summer home during the Truman administration, Huguette turned down Mohammad Reza Pahlavi, the Shah of Iran's offer of one hundred million dollars for the 1936 twenty-seven room property, twice the size of President Jefferson's Monticello. Her will left her summer home to the Bellosguardo Foundation "to foster and promote the arts." In keeping with the family's priority on privacy, the estate is perched on a bluff, with its only neighbor the Santa Barbara Cemetery. In the ground-floor music room—the estate's largest— are two large paintings of Andrée and Huguette, two Steinway pianos, and two of Anna's custom created gold harps, her instrument adorned with sculptures and paintings. The old house echoes the silence. Flourishes hint at the eccentricity of its former chatelaine: Her dressing room's covered chairs come in two sizes, one for the adults, the other for "the little people." The white 1904 carriage house holds a 1933 Chrysler Royal Eight convertible and a black 1933 Cadillac seven-passenger limousine, both bearing yellow and black license plates dated 1949. When Huguette's cousin, Paul Newell, asked why she never visited Bellosguardo, the heiress responded, "When I think of Santa Barbara, I always think of times there with my mother, and it makes me very sad."

Upon entering the once upon a time estate, visitors are overcome with its grandeur; upon their departure, they are left wondering how magical it would be to live in such Gatsbyesque splendor. However, upon learning about the woman who turned its key, the golden pleasure dome takes on a less magical aura. In a sense, all Huguette's homes were cells that imprisoned her with memories, with loneliness. Intermingled with awe at the magnificence is the realization that money cannot buy love, happiness, or a shield from pain. The poet Ezra Pound's words proved prescient: "Let us pity those who are better off than we are...The rich have butlers and no friends."

**Seen from Her Window:** Perhaps when Huguette gazed upon the hospital air-conditioning unit, memory took over and she was once again in Bellosguardo, with her mother and her progeny, the girls with the porcelain faces.

# PART IX

# *The Legendary Ladies*

# CHAPTER 38

# Old Glory's Maker

*"I am not certain if I can. At least I'll gladly try."*

**—BETSY ROSS**

◇◇◇◇◇◇◇◇◇◇

## The Betsy Ross House

opened 1937 | Philadelphia, Pennsylvania

Within the stripes of the American flag lies a treasure trove of history, mystery, and controversy. "Old Glory" appears in fifty states and on the moon; thousands have died fighting for or against it. The Marines raised the Stars and Stripes to commemorate the victory in the Pacific; the draft-dodgers burned it in protest of the military in Southeast Asia. As the Twin Towers crumbled, three New York City firefighters rigged a makeshift flagpole, a symbol of resilience. The Betsy Ross Home in Pennsylvania pays homage to the universal icon.

Beneath the legend is Elizabeth (Betsy) Griscom, born in 1752 in Gloucester City, New Jersey, one of seventeen children of Samuel and Rebecca Griscom. The family were members of the Society of Friends, known as Quakers (so called after members quaked in church due to the presence of the Lord). When Betsy was three, the family relocated to Philadelphia, where Samuel worked as a carpenter.

A person who left a lasting impact on Betsy was her paternal great-aunt Sarah, who operated a business that fashioned women's corsets. She taught Betsy how to sew and how a woman could be her own boss. When Betsy visited her sister, an employee at an upholstery shop, the eleven-year-old fixed an issue that a seasoned seamstress could not; proprietor John Webster offered her a six-day-a-week apprenticeship. Betsy's education ended, and her seventy-year vocation began.

Betsy remained in her position until she fell in love with a fellow employee, John Ross, whose uncle, Colonel George Ross, was a member of the Continental Congress. The thorn in the romance was that John was Anglican, and the Society of Friends forbade intermarriage. Putting love before all else, John and Betsy eloped. They crossed the Delaware River to nearby Gloucester, New Jersey, where they wed in Hugg's Tavern, a local inn. Betsy joined her husband in worshipping at Christ Church, where General Washington attended when he was in Philadelphia. The couple rented a second-floor room on Arch Street from landlady Hannah Lithgow and ran their upholstery business from the ground floor.

Although committed to one another, the couple was not immune to the cauldron bubbling outside their door. Weary of King George III viewing his overseas empire as a source to enhance his coffers, the colonists prepared for rebellion. The patriots—one of whom was John Ross—formed the minutemen. In defiance of the Quaker tenet of pacifism, Betsy sewed thousands of canvas cartridges that held gunpowder for muskets.

While guarding a stash of munitions, John suffered injuries from an explosion of gunpowder. His death left Betsy a twenty-four-year-old widow in the middle of the Revolutionary War, cut off from her family, friends, and faith. What helped her financially was the fighting proved profitable for business, as there was a huge demand for uniforms and blankets. However, it was another product that made Betsy Ross an integral thread in the tapestry of Americana.

In 1776, each unit of the revolutionary army flew its own flag, that mainly consisted of red, white, and blue, the colors of the British Union Jack. Colonists clamored for a standardized design to represent the fledgling country. The quest for a uniform flag provided Betsy's immortality.

*The birthplace of the American flag* | Wikimedia Commons, Beyond My Ken

Lore holds that General George Washington, Colonel George Ross, and Robert Morris, in Philadelphia to attend the First Continental Congress, visited the Arch Street upholstery shop to commission a new flag. The colonel had chosen Betsy for the task as she was the widow of his nephew; the general favored her as he was pleased with the bed hangings, pillows, and mattresses she had provided for his Mount Vernon estate. Their sketch showed a model with thirteen red and white stripes with a blue square in the upper left-hand corner bearing thirteen stars in a circle. Betsy suggested that the six-pointed stars be changed to five since that pattern was easier to make. The following year, on June 14, 1777, Congress passed a law that the United States had proclaimed the flag be "white on a blue field, representing a new constellation." Although no proof exists that Betsy was behind the historic enterprise, this does not negate the story's veracity. As colonial law held that producing any flag other than the Union Jack was treason, Betsy would have sewed hers in the utmost secrecy.

Although busy running her store, producing munitions for the army, and sewing slings for the wounded soldiers, Betsy found romance with sailor-soldier Joseph Ashburn, whom she wed at Philadelphia's Old Swedes' Church. The new wife sewed a flag for Joseph's ship, the *Hetty*. The Ashburns' baby, Aucilla, died before her first birthday; three years later, their second daughter, Eliza, was born. Once again, the war summoned Betsy's spouse, and Joseph set sail on the *Lion*, bound for Europe on a mission to destroy enemy ships. John ended up in the British Old Mill prison, where he succumbed to disease brought on by overcrowding and unsanitary conditions.

When the war ended, Betsy was once again a widow. John Claypoole, a man she had known when they were children, had also been a prisoner in the Old Mill. John headed to Arch Street to deliver the devastating news. In contrast to Cleopatra, who murdered the bearers of bad tidings, Betsy married John. The Claypooles became members of the Free Quakers, a branch of the religion whose views were less extreme than its traditional church. Eliza became the big sister to the Claypooles' four daughters. Their last baby, Harriet, died at ten months. Their upholstery business flourished, and the couple was able to afford a house, a horse, carriage, and private schools. John was also active in the abolitionist movement. The yellow fever bypassed the Claypoole family, although it claimed the lives of Betsy's parents and sister Deborah.

In 1800, John suffered from a stroke and remained bedridden for the rest of his life. The business faltered, and they depended on charity from the Free Quakers. John passed away seventeen years later; Elizabeth Griscom Ross Ashburn Claypoole, remembered as Betsy Ross, died at age eighty-four, one of the few females to feature in the saga of the Founding Fathers.

**The Betsy Ross House:** Eventually, the story of the first flag maker became so popular that Betsy's Arch Street residence, where she had been a tenant from 1773–1786, became a tourist mecca. By the nineteenth century, a German immigrant family called the Munds commandeered the house, operating a tailor shop, a cigar store, and a tavern on the premises. As a business ploy, they hung a sign out front that read, "First Flag of the US Made in This House." In 1898, Philadelphia formally established the building as the American Flag House, an appellation that eventually gave way to the Betsy Ross House. From a flagpole hangs the Stars and Stripes with a circular star pattern, and a plaque bears the inscription, "She produced flags for the government for over 50 years. As a skilled artisan, Ross represents the many women who supported their families during the Revolution and early Republic." More than 250,000 people annually visit the historic home situated a few blocks from Independence Hall and the Liberty Bell.

In 1971, twenty-five demonstrators barricaded themselves in the Betsy Ross House to protest the Vietnam War. The activists released fifteen tourists from the souvenir shop and then proceeded to hang the flag upside down. Three years later, the museum transferred the remains of Betsy and her third husband from the Mount Moriah Cemetery in Yeadon, Pennsylvania, to the garden located in the courtyard. On July 4, 1961, a thief made off with the flag that continuously flies over the legendary lady's grave. The museum immediately found a replacement.

A docent dressed as Betsy leads tours of the house, where visitors can experience an eighteenth-century upholstery shop and view six rooms furnished with period pieces and antiques. The guide points out the parlor where Betsy met with George Washington, her bedroom where she secretly sewed the rebel flag, and the basement where she produced contraband for the Continental Army. Personal effects on display include Betsy's walnut chest, Chippendale chair, eyeglasses, snuffbox, and Bible.

Even if Betsy's role in the creation of the first American flag is not historically substantiated, there is enough information to prove she was far more than a Paul Bunyan or a Johnny Appleseed. She was a remarkable eighteenth-century woman who withstood excommunication from her family and church and the loss of three husbands, and who lived in the epicenter of the American Revolution.

**Seen from Her Window:** The woman, memorialized on a three-cent stamp in 1952, witnessed famished Philadelphians trying to survive the British blockade and burning furniture to keep warm.

# CHAPTER 39

# *Of Them All*

*"The only way we can kill for a moment our pain
is by unselfishness."*

**—JULIETTE GORDON LOW**

◇◇◇◇◇◇◇◇◇

### Juliette Gordon Low Birthplace

opened 1956 | Savannah, Georgia

"The cookies are coming! The cookies are coming!" sounds the annual cry that leads to Thin Mints, Tagalongs, or Caramel deLites. Girl Scout cookies satisfy a sweet tooth while supporting a charitable cause. Troops around the world make pilgrimages to Georgia to visit the Juliette Gordon Low Birthplace to salute their founding mother.

In Savannah, the Girl Guides are more than a seasonal presence. The movement originated in the Wayne-Gordon House located on Oglethorpe Avenue. The street name is an allusion to James Oglethorpe, the British founder of Georgia. His creed for Savannah, "No Liquor! No Slaves! No Lawyers! No Catholics!"

The 1821 four-story mansion became the marital home of Eleanor (called Nellie) and William Washington Gordon II, scions of wealthy families. The second of their six children, Juliette Magill Kinzie Gordon, was born at home on October 31, 1860. Her given first name, Juliette, was in honor of her maternal grandmother; her nickname, Daisy (which came to supersede her birth name), originated with an uncle.

Six months after Daisy's birth, the Civil War erupted. As the owner of the Belmont Plantation, William served as a Confederate officer. Eleanor's three

*Mother of the Girl Scouts |*
*Wikimedia Commons,*
*Photographer: Unknown*

brothers fought for the North. Southern relatives took refuge in the Gordon home, and Eleanor was hard pressed to feed her children, extended family, and household slaves. In 1864, the Northern general, William Tecumseh Sherman, arrived at the Gordon home to hand deliver letters from his friend, Eleanor's mother. Juliette asked Oliver O. Howard, one of the wounded officers who had accompanied General Sherman, why he had a missing arm. After his explanation, "Got it shot off by a Rebel," Daisy responded, "I suppose my father did it. He shot lots of Yankees." The general warned Eleanor of the danger in remaining in Georgia, and she left for Chicago, where her family had erected its first residence. With the end of the fighting, the Gordons reunited in Savannah.

Due to her mischievous nature, young Juliette became known as Crazy Daisy. An animal lover, Daisy had a dog, Bow-wow, and a cat, Kittle. Tragedy struck with the scarlet fever death of her sister Alice.

Not far from the Wayne-Gordon House was the Andrew Low House (currently also a Savannah museum), owned by a Scottish immigrant who had made a fortune in cotton. Andrew moved his family to Britain, but on a visit to Savannah, his son, William Mackay Low, became reacquainted with Daisy. William was enamored of the belle's beauty. Edward Hughes captured her in a painting that portrayed her Scarlett O' Hara waist and auburn hair. Daisy and Billow, William's nickname, bonded over a love of animals, horseback riding, and travel. When letters failed to arrive after William returned to Oxford, Daisy embarked on a European tour. Unable to arrange a meeting, she sent him a telegram before her departure, "Goodbye, I sail on the *Gallia*." His return telegram read, "*Cum optimo amore*" ("With the best love").

When she returned home, Daisy suffered an agonizing earache; a doctor treated her condition with silver nitrate, resulting in hearing loss. What lifted her spirit was William's proposal. The Christ Church ceremony took place on December 21, the date of her parents' wedding anniversary. Her bridal bouquet held lilies of the valley, a nod to her sister Alice's favorite flower. The eight bridesmaids wore white dresses, each adorned with a brooch designed by the groom. The pin was of a daisy with heart-shaped silver petals encrusted with forty-four diamonds. The stem bore the year: 1886. As the newlyweds waved from their carriage, a grain of rice confetti landed in Daisy's good ear. The extraction left her hard of hearing in that ear.

Although saddened to leave Savannah, Daisy looked forward to moving to Europe with her husband. The couple's British home, Wellesbourne House in Warwickshire, encompassed fifty acres, with three wine cellars, stables for forty horses, and twenty bedrooms. In 1895, the Lows threw a party where the Prince of Wales engaged in only one dance, with Daisy. After a dinner at Rudyard Kipling's home in evening attire, she went fishing with the author.

In a nod to the saying "The bigger the house, the bigger the problems," Wellesbourne echoed with misery. As a strict Episcopalian, Daisy disapproved of William's excessive drinking, and he in turn looked down on his wife's charitable activities. After Daisy injured her back, William travelled to Albania, India, Africa, and Japan on his own. For company, Daisy turned to pets Polly Poons, her parrot, and Blue Bird, her South American macaw. Motherhood would have provided a balm, but gynecological problems precluded pregnancy.

During the outbreak of the Spanish-American War, Daisy returned to Savannah to organize a convalescent hospital. Within a few years, William suggested she live in one wing of Wellesbourne while he and his mistress, Anna Bridges Bateman, occupied another. During their divorce, William passed away. His will left everything to his mistress; Daisy fought for her share and came away with $500,000 as well as the Andrew Low home in Savannah.

The Girl Scout motto is, "Be Prepared," but those words did not describe the middle-aged Daisy, bereft at the way her "cookie" had crumbled. She was at an emotional low ebb until a 1911 luncheon where she sat next to Sir Robert Baden-Powell, the founder of the Boy Scouts, which had 40,000 members in France, Germany, and the United States. When 6,000 girls clamored for inclusion, Robert's sister, Agnes, initiated the Girl Guides. Their pledge: "I promise on my honor that I will do my best to do my duty to God and the King."

***Andrew Low Carriage House*** | *Wikipedia: Jefferson LH*

The evening Daisy arrived in Georgia, she called her cousin Nina Pape, principal of a girls' school, "Come right over. I've got something for the girls of Savannah, and all America, and all the world, and we're going to start it tonight!" The initial meeting took place on March 12, 1912. The first of the eighteen inductees was Daisy's niece, Margaret "Daisy Doots" Gordon. In a nod to the floral association of Daisy, the original troops were the White Rose Patrol and the Carnation Patrol. Uniforms were blue with dark stockings and huge hair ribbons. The members played basketball on outdoor courts surrounded by curtains so as to prevent men from seeing their bloomers. As the leader with the mostest, Daisy showed off a pair of shoes by standing on her head. The girls called their leader Miss Daisy. Organizational changes: Girl Guides—with its connotation of females as helpmeets—became the more adventurous sounding Scouts, the blue uniforms transformed to khaki, and the revised pledge was, "To do my duty to God and to my country."

In the role of British aristocrat, Daisy had dressed in French couture; as head of her organization, her new uniform was a belted khaki jacket, white shirt, and black tie, accessorized with a scout knife, whistle, and wide hat. People described Daisy as possessing the "force of a hurricane." She only took a break to recover from the death of her father. Expenses came from her own finances, and, when funds ran low, she sold a valuable pearl necklace that had been a gift from William.

When asking for donations, she claimed she could not hear when people refused to contribute. Daisy met with various First Ladies, King George V, and Queen Mary.

Although women had subservient societal roles, Daisy wanted her Girl Scouts to understand they could nevertheless make an impact. In 1917, a troop from Muskogee, Oklahoma, sold home-baked cookies in support of the soldiers fighting in Europe. Under the patronage of Lou Hoover, a future First Lady, sales skyrocketed. Girl Scout cookies have generated millions of dollars. In the same year, Girl Scouts marched in President Woodrow Wilson's inaugural parade, the first time females participated in the official procession.

The woman who had founded a fifty-million-member movement passed away in her home at age sixty-six from breast cancer. Her epitaph bore the biblical quotation, "Now abideth faith, hope, and love, but the greatest of these is love." An honor guard of her troops escorted her casket to Christ Church.

**Juliette Gordon Low Birthplace:** If Daisy could eavesdrop from her grave in the Laurel Grove Cemetery, she would be astounded at her posthumous glory. The United States Postal Service issued a stamp with her likeness; her portrait hangs in the Smithsonian National Gallery; President Barack Obama honored her with the Presidential Medal of Freedom. She would also be thrilled to know that the Girl Scouts of the USA turned her home into a museum to honor her and her organization.

Visitors can view original pieces such as an impressive staircase with a curved mahogany railing. There are numerous works of art, some created by Daisy; for example, the monogrammed front gate, a skill she acquired in England. Savannah's first home designated as a National Historic Landmark houses historic documents, Girl Scout artifacts, uniforms dating from the organization's inception, and photographs. Daisy's personal effects on hand include letters, books, and her diary. When First Lady Edith Wilson became the 1917 Honorary President, Daisy presented her with a diamond, emerald, and ruby gold Cartier pin, which is currently part of the museum's collection. Far more sentimental to the Girl Scouts was the note placed in the breast pocket of her uniform before Daisy's burial that bore the words, "You are not only the first Girl Scout, you are the best Girl Scout of them all."

**Seen from Her Window:** The Girl Scouts congregating on her lawn helped make right what was wrong with her life. The Scouts became Daisy's surrogate daughters.

# CHAPTER 40

# *Farewell to Thee*

*"Never cease to act because you fear you may fail."*
**—QUEEN LILIUOKALANI**

◇◇◇◇◇◇◇◇◇◇

## Iolani Palace

### opened 1978 | Honolulu, Hawaii

If one craves a national infusion of royalty, the place to visit—no offense to Graceland—is America's only royal residence, now a museum that conjures the memory of Hawaii's first and only queen. Iolani Palace is a Victorian snow globe in the heart of Honolulu, a nod to the era when the island nation's royal family held sway over their tropical Shangri-la.

In 1795, Kamehameha the Great defeated rival chiefs, and after killing as many people as necessary, he unified the Polynesian Islands under his royal rule. A perk of power was that he could afford his twenty-one wives. The first crack in his dynasty was the 1820 arrival of New England missionaries who supplanted pagan gods with their personal one. In a nod to the Rudyard Kipling phrase, "the white man's burden," the Reverend Hiram Bingham wrote of its indigenous population, "Can these be human beings?" Aghast at the attire of the native women, missionary wives introduced the muumuu; their husbands banned the sexually suggestive hula dance. Their descendants accumulated enormous wealth from pineapple and sugar plantations, leading to the local saying, "They came to do good—and did well."

The last of the royal line was Lili'u Loloku Walania Wewehi Kamaka'eha, born in 1838, in Honolulu. Her Christian name was Lydia; as queen, she became Liliuokalani. Her parents, Chief Caesar Kapa'akea and Chieftess Analea

Keaohokāhole, had ten children. In
accordance with hānai, adoption to
forge alliances among chiefs, High
Chief Abner Pākī and Laura Kōnia
assumed Liliuokalani's care. As a
member of Hawaiian nobility, at age
four, she attended the missionary-
run Chief's Children's School, an
experience that she enjoyed as much as Jane Eyre did Lowood. Escape came when
the institution shuttered due to the measles epidemic—brought to the island by
the New Englanders—that claimed the lives of approximately 10,000 people,
mostly from the indigenous population.

Although a fierce proponent of her culture, the twenty-four-year-old
Liliuokalani married American John Owen Dominis in an Anglican ceremony with
King Kamehameha IV in attendance. The newlyweds settled in the magnificent
Washington Place, the home of John's widowed mother, with whom the couple
lived. John's marriage delivered the perk of being governor of Oahu and Maui;
Liliuokalani's marriage delivered grief. Her mother-in-law felt that her son's
choice of an ethnic wife was an unworthy match despite her royal status.

A rendezvous with history began when Liliuokalani's brother, David La'amea
Kamananakapu Mahinulani Naloiaehuokalani Lumialani Kalākaua, assumed the
throne in 1874. His nickname was the Merrie Monarch due to his fondness for
parties, pomp, and pleasure. His out-of-control spending crippled his country
with debt, owed mainly to Claus Spreckels, an American.

While her brother embarked on a world tour, Liliuokalani acted as regent. Her
position coincided with a smallpox epidemic that had originated with immigrant
Chinese workers. To curtail the deadly disease, Liliuokalani closed the ports. Her
decision caused foreign interest groups to understand the king's sister was not
a marionette whose strings they could manipulate.

And yet there were perks of being a princess. As King Kalākaua battled
political problems, he sent his queen and sister overseas in his place. President

***America's Only Royal Palace, Lolani Palace*** | *Wikimedia Commons, Gage Skidmore*

Grover Cleveland hosted a state dinner in their honor, and they were guests at Victoria's Golden Jubilee. The queen granted a personal audience to the Hawaiian royal ladies in Buckingham Palace, and they joined other dignitaries at Westminster Abbey. Liliuokalani's signature diamond butterfly adorned her hair.

Distressing news necessitated their return home. The Americans, led by Sanford B. Dole, forced the king to sign the Constitution of the Kingdom of Hawaii, known as the Bayonet Constitution, since he signed it at gunpoint. The document transformed the king to a figurehead; voting became the prerogative of property-owning whites.

Upon Kalākaua's passing, the newly anointed queen moved to Iolani Palace. Despite their marital troubles, John, who had accompanied her on her overseas trip, joined her in the royal residence. She bestowed upon him the title of Prince Consort. He died several months into her reign, a loss she deeply mourned. As the new ruler, Liliuokalani would well understand the Shakespearean admonition from *Henry IV*, "Uneasy lies the head that wears a crown."

Her first order of business was to revoke the Bayonet Constitution to restore the might of monarchy and reinstate the vote for her subjects. William Randolph Hearst, in his *San Francisco Enquirer*, portrayed her as "a Black, pagan queen." In contrast, Robert Louis Stevenson was her guest, and they drank Château Lafite from crystal goblets imported from Bohemia.

In 1893, Queen Liliuokalani stood on the balcony of the Iolani Palace, in front of which 162 US Marines and sailors had gathered. To avoid bloodshed, Liliuokalani refrained from any resistance, though she refused to waive her royal rights. The provisional government hoisted the American flag above Iolani Palace and confiscated a million acres of crown lands, worth billions in contemporary currency. The following morning, as Liliuokalani awaited her daily bouquet of red lehua flowers, soldiers lounged in the Throne Room. In allegiance to their dethroned queen, three women offered themselves as sacrifices so the gods would restore her regime.

Two years later, royalists decided to stage a counterattack to reclaim their kingdom. The following week, the new lords of the land squashed the rebellion and incarcerated 355 insurgents. Under the charge that the queen had been complicit in the uprising, the government placed Liliuokalani under house arrest.

The interlopers treated Iolani Palace as an open treasure chest. A soldier pried the jewels off King Kalākaua's crown, using them as payment in a game of dice. He sent his sister one of its mammoth diamonds, unaware of its astronomical worth. Other stolen treasures: vases that had been gifts from Queen Victoria, royal staffs covered with albatross plumes, dresses adorned with peacock feathers, furniture, and miscellaneous royal objects.

The death knell sounded for the Kingdom of Hawaii in 1893 with the queen's formal abdication. Her shaky signature, signed as Liliuokalani Dominis, revealed extreme agitation. Fearing that the execution of the deposed royal would lead to martyrdom, a military tribunal spared her life. Sanford B. Dole became the first president of the Republic of Hawaii.

During the eight months of her confinement, Liliuokalani worked on a quilt she embroidered with her nation's flag, the Kalākaua coat of arms, and the words, "Imprisoned at Iolani Palace." She wrote that she was a prisoner "for the attempt of the Hawaiian people to regain what had been wrested from them by the children of the missionaries who first brought the Word of God."

In 1993, on the hundredth anniversary of Queen Liliuokalani's deposition, President Bill Clinton issued a formal apology for the annexation of her kingdom that made it the fiftieth state of the Union. In the same year, Governor John Waihee, the state's first governor of Hawaiian descent, in a similar acknowledgment, ordered the American flag removed from state buildings for five days. In the accompanying ceremony, more than a thousand people gathered at the foot of the Queen Liliuokalani Statue situated between Iolani Palace and the state's Capitol.

**Iolani Palace:** The Iolani Palace, built by King Kalakāua during his tempest-tossed reign to showcase his pride, power, and prestige, is proof of the glory of Polynesia's royal past. Fittingly, "Iolani" translates to "bird of heaven." The architectural style is American Florentine; the Boston firm that supplied furniture for the White House also furnished the palace. In the Blue Room hangs a life-sized 1892 William Cogswell portrait of the queen in which she stands by her throne. On her hair is her diamond butterfly clip, and on her dress are the accoutrements of the royal House of Kawaii. The William Cogswell portrait is encased in a heavy gilt frame. The impressive central stairway consists of native koa wood sourced in mountain forests. Visitors can view the gold and velvet Throne Room, the venue for Queen Liliuolakani's trial. On a canopied dais stands a seven-foot narwhal tusk. Staring down from the walls of the entry hall are portraits of past rulers, from King Kamehameha I to Queen Liliuokalani. Most poignant is the former bedroom/cell where the queen languished during her months of captivity. The shutters remain half closed so as not to allow full sun into a room that echoes her sorrow. A large glass case holds her handmade quilt, an embroidered diary of her anguish.

Similarly evocative of the regal yesteryear is a lyric the queen composed that made its way into the film *From Here to Eternity*, Elvis Presley's song, "Blue Hawaii," and Disney's movie, *Lilo and Stitch*. The words are a love letter to Liliuokalani's lost kingdom, "Aloha 'Oe," "Farewell to Thee."

**Seen from Her Window:** In front of the palace was an eight-foot-high coral block wall that encompassed her coat of arms. What would one day make Liliuokalani avert her eyes was the gate that once kept the unwelcome from entering had transformed into prison bars.

# EPILOGUE

# *"That Damn Museum"*

The colloquialism "bucket list" originated sixteen years ago, an expression derived from the sixteenth century expression "kick the bucket." The bucket is likely an allusion to the object kicked away at a hanging. The term first appeared in the *Oxford English Dictionary* due to the 2007 film *The Bucket List*, in which two terminally ill patients determine their "must-dos" before their abduction by the Grim Reaper. The book industry has capitalized on the concept, with titles like *1,000 Places to See Before You Die, 1,000 Books to Read Before You Die, 1,000 Films You Must See Before You Die*. Die-hard bucket-listers engage in skydiving, run with the bulls at Pamplona, or scale Mt. Everest. In a nod to the meeting of a bunny and a mouse, Playboy Bunny Crystal Harris, a Hugh Hefner wife, claimed her goal was to visit every Disney theme park on the planet. After writing *A Room of Their Own*, mine is to visit the profiled women's home museums. They represent my passion for history, women's studies, trivia, and travel.

If you are fortunate enough to partake of the charms of Paris, in addition to touring the Louvre, take a side trip to the Édith Piaf museum to hear the strains of "the Little Sparrow's" "La Vie en Rose," view her precious mementoes, and even sit on her couch. In London's British Museum, visitors can see treasures such as the Elgin Marbles that once graced the frieze of Athens' Parthenon. Another indelible memory would be a drive to Haworth's Brontë Parsonage to gaze upon the dining room table on which sisters Emily and Charlotte wrote *Wuthering Heights* and *Jane Eyre*. The Smithsonian is a compilation of the treasures of Americana; on display is the storied Hope Diamond, one of the world's most priceless gems. To discover another Washington, DC museum, head to Hillwood, the former home of the heiress who could have snapped up the legendary diamond. Hillwood holds the greatest collection of imperial Russian artifacts outside the Soviet Union.

My first entry into the world of a home museum was Canada's Camelot. Sir Henry Pellatt was the king of a castle, and his ego was as vast as his hundred-room, medieval-style Casa Loma, meaning "House on the Hill." He earmarked his $17 million fortune ($412 million in current currency) to erect his personal fiefdom. The gray stone structure in my Toronto hometown was straight out of the German Grimms' fairy tales. In a startling reversal of fortune, a bankrupt Sir Henry auctioned his possessions and sold his castle. He died with eighty-five dollars to his name in the Mimico home he shared with his former chauffeur. Lady Pellatt passed away at home in Toronto in 1924, the year she left Point Loma. I would have included a chapter on Mary Pellatt; however, there is little biographical information available other than the fact that she was the patron of the city's Girl Guides. What intrigued me upon touring the castle was not merely its over the top opulence, but the riches-to-rags story that echoed in its halls and the hubris underlying the finery.

I experienced another millionaire's folly when I toured Hearst Castle in San Simeon, California. George Bernard Shaw told the media mogul that his castle was "what heaven would be like if God had your money." In the 165-room mansion he referred to as his "little getaway," Hearst hung his fifty-million-dollar art collection (worth a quarter of a billion dollars in today's currency); its grounds included a Roman-style pool used in the film *Spartacus*. Behind the eye-popping splendor, Heart's castle was redolent of his affair with Marion Davies, who held the keys to his castle...and his heart. What resonated more than the priceless artifacts was the love story between the tycoon and the showgirl. Both Casa Loma and Heart's castle showed that home museums carry an emotional appeal that traditional museums can not rival.

If one were to pen the stories of Sir Henry Pellatt and William Randolph Hearst, the balancing act for a biographer would be how best to portray such lives. The two extremes of the genre are hagiography and harmatography. The former is an idealizing and idolizing account of the subject, where all faults are airbrushed. The latter, by contrast, plays up all flaws so that the profiled individual is pilloried for the ages. When Sir Richard Attenborough produced his epic film *Gandhi*, Prime Minister Jawaharlal Nehru told him, "Do not deify him, He was too great a man to be turned into a god." I have tried to portray the ladies of women's home museums as accurately as I could. However, for the best telling of their tales, visit their homes.

Over the span of years, I remember the thrill of touring the British Library and marveled at the Rosetta Stone, the key that unlocked the secret of hieroglyphics. But what proved more memorable was when I entered the building's domed Reading Room. The guide pointed out the chair Karl Marx sat upon when writing *Das Kapital*—a book that altered the history of the world. When I mentioned to the guard what a thrill it would be to sit on Marx's chair, he looked at me as if I were odd. However, as no one else was present, he motioned to the chair, thus tacitly permitting me to shimmy under the velvet rope. As I sat in Marx's chair, I was awash in a kaleidoscope of fragments of another era. In the swirl of the past was Empress Alexandra in her magnificent Winter Palace surrounded by her priceless possessions. The colors shifted, and the granddaughter of Queen Victoria was in the basement of a house in the Urals where the Bolsheviks assassinated Alexandra, her husband, and their five children. The reverie ended when the guard motioned once more; my moment with Marx was at an end. Of all the artifacts of the past, the one I interacted with remains the lasting memory. That afternoon at the British mausoleum, a repository of the world's sacred relics, illustrated how a museum's interactive experience overshadows passive observation. Although I did not purchase a particular button from the gift shop, I can well relate to its words, "*Veni Vidi Museum Britannicum*" (or "I've been to the British Museum").

When I was a student at West Prep Elementary School, I was thrilled when a yellow school bus pulled up to take us on a field trip to the Royal Ontario Museum. I still remember that special long afternoon, moreso than years spent in classes where the teachers abided by the maxim students should be seen and not heard.

After his expulsion from Pencey Prep, Holden Caulfield, the protagonist of *Catcher in the Rye,* spent a day in Manhattan. He headed to the Museum of Natural History, where he had spent happy times as a child. J. D. Salinger wrote, "Sometimes we looked at the animals, and sometimes we looked at the stuff the Indians had made in ancient times. It always smelled like it was raining outside, even if it wasn't, and you were in the only nice, dry, cosy place in the world. I loved that damn museum."

# Acknowledgments

There are many emotional milestones in birthing a book: firstly, the instant the idea dawns, a bolt of inspiration from an unseen source. When *A Room of Their Own* was only a twinkle in my eye, I believed there would be readers interested in learning about home museums, a fascinating niche. As a teenager, I visited William Shakespeare's birthplace museum in Stratford-upon-Avon, a magical moment. Author Jill G. Hall shared on social media regarding her experience when she took a road trip to the Mount—the Berkshires, Massachusetts, home museum of author Edith Wharton. At the end of the tour, guests could revisit any room. Jill made a beeline to Edith's bedroom, where she took a selfie on the writer's bed in what was certainly an up close and personal home museum moment. A post by another Facebook friend captured her visit to London's Charles Dickens Museum, located in his former residence at 48 Doughty Street, King's Cross. In her post, she mentioned a stuffed raven. I was perplexed; wasn't it the American Edgar Allan Poe who was associated with a raven? Charles Dickens, however, had a talking raven named Grip—whose favorite expression was, "Halloa old girl," and whom he included in his short story, "Barnaby Rudge." Grip met an untimely end after ingesting paint, and his grieving owner hired a taxidermist to stuff Grip and mount him in an impressive case of wood and glass. Shortly afterwards, in 1845, Poe wrote his famous poem, "The Raven," inspired by the British bird. The raven who served as muse for two famous writers now resides in the Free Library of Philadelphia's Rare Books Department. Based on the three home museums we all enjoyed, I felt a book would appeal to travelers, both the armchair and in-person variety.

After inspiration arrives, another milestone is convincing the powers that be that your idea is marketable. Fortunately, my literary agent, Roger Williams, and my editor, Brenda Knight, were on board. I'd like to give a shout-out to my husband, Joel, and my daughter, Jordanna, for bouncing off ideas. How true that the various stages of our lives can be measured by the topics by which we are consumed.

If there were a museum of friendship, Jamie Lovett would hold a place of prominence. Jamie, who went far above and far beyond the clarion call of friendship, was present at every stage. My book would be much less, my wrinkles would be much more, if it were not for Georgia's peach *sans* pit. I love words but am at a loss to come up with adequate ones to express my appreciation. In one of her Facebook posts, Joyce Maynard shared her philosophy, "Whenever possible, I say yes." I am so fortunate that Joyce said "yes" to writing the Foreword to *A Room of Their Own*. Her lovely words provides the gift bow on my book, and for that I will be forever grateful.

For those who love museums, appreciation must be extended to the tour guides, whose formal title is "docent," a word that derives from the Latin verb meaning "to teach." They are the ones who provide background knowledge, as well as interesting asides. Not only must they be well-versed in their subject matter, they also need to whet visitors' interest. In some instances, for example, in the Betsy Ross Museum, they do this by dressing in period attire. In Washington, DC, at the National Museum of Natural History's Orkin Insect Zoo, part of the docents' job description is to give demonstrations of tarantula feedings. The guides in George Washington's Mount Vernon estate, whom that institution calls "historic interpreters," take visitors to various stops from the mansion to the slave quarters.

Although a docent's position may seem like a dream job—and there are countless applicants for few positions—there are drawbacks, such as dealing with guests who think they know more than the experts and kids who have an overpowering urge to carve their initials on Greek antiquities. However, walking in hallowed halls makes the positions an enviable calling. A collective thanks goes out to each docent for enhancing museum visits.

On this page, I want to acknowledge the women whose contributions and fascinating lives merited their own museums. The Dominican Republic's Casa Museo Hermanas Mirabal (Mirabal Sisters Home Museum) provides the lesson of how David can defeat Goliath. Haworth's Brontë Parsonage demonstrates that genius can bloom despite societal roadblocks. Mexico's Museo Frida Kahlo is testimony to the healing power of art.

And lastly, from the bottom of my heart I want to thank my readers, whose encouragement continues to be the wind beneath my writer's wings.

# A Note to Readers

Dear Readers,

Thank you so much for accompanying me on my writer's journey—my once and future dream. One of the most wonderful aspects of publishing a book is interacting with readers. I have received emails from wonderful people whom I would never have otherwise met, including some who have become friends. In 2008, after I wrote my first book, *Once Again to Zelda: The Stories Behind Literature's Most Intriguing Dedications*, I received an email from Avis Weeks. She rued that instead of anyone dedicating a book to her, she just received grocery lists. When I spoke at Yale University Library, Avis let me stay at her lovely home, where she had written literary quotations on her kitchen wall. Fellow English teacher Jamie Lovett contacted me about the same book; ever since, she has been the sister I never had.

Please share memories and/or photos on my Facebook page regarding a museum you have visited from *A Room of Their Own*, or one I did not cover in these pages. Are any of the women's home museums on your bucket list?

As I researched the profiled women and their homes, the Internet led me down some circuitous alleys. And that is how I discovered some of the world's strangest museums.

Japan's Momofuku Ando Instant Ramen—the go-to meal of starving students—has a museum that honors Momofuku Ando, who created the inexpensive meal for his country's World War II survivors. The museum holds a colossal stone cup that features the instant meal, and visitors can make their own in its kitchen.

Hugh Hefner would be in his element in Manhattan's Museum of Sex, dedicated to human sexuality. In a spin on a childhood classic, there is a bouncy castle of breasts. The museum's permanent collection houses 15,000 artifacts.

In response to the Whitney Houston question, "Where do broken hearts go? / Can they find their way home?" there is Croatia's Museum of Broken Relationships. The emporium consists of stories of heartbreak, chronicled through notes alongside objects such as a wedding ring and an axe (that had been used on an ex's furniture). Would you have anything to contribute?

From the bottom of my heart, I want to thank you, for your encouragement, and for your solidarity. An author's world is chiefly one of solitude; you make it less so.

I would love to hear from you. Please contact me through:

*marlenewagmangeller.com*

*www.instagram.com/marlenewagmangeller*

*twitter.com/mwagmangeller*

*wagmangeller@hotmail.com*

*www.facebook.com/marlene.wagman.5*

and take a look at more of my writing on GoodReads:

*www.goodreads.com/author/show/2120381.Marlene_Wagman_Geller*

Please sign up for my email list to receive information about my upcoming news, blogs, and future releases:

*marlenewagmangeller.com/sign-up-for-email*

Happy reading trails,
**Marlene Wagman-Geller**
San Diego, California (2024)

# Dearest Docents

I would like to thank the following for their kindness as well as their invaluable assistance. You are the docents with the mostest.

### Foursquare Heritage Center—The Parsonage of Aimee Semple McPherson

*Steve Zeleny, Archives Manager*

If Steve Zeleny's resume ever lands on your desk, hire him on the spot! Steve returned each of my emails, often within moments. He always supplied the requisite information, and much more.

### Judy Garland Museum

*John Kelsch, Museum Curator (former Executive Director)*
*Janie Heitz, Executive Director*

John has encyclopedic knowledge of all things Judy, information he was kind enough to share with me in two Zoom meetings. His intelligence and kindness crossed the miles from Grand Rapids, Minnesota, to my home in San Diego, California.

Janie was so kind in facilitating the Zoom meetings and for other invaluable assistance.

### The Anne of Green Gables Museum

*George Campbell, Owner and Operator*

George was gracious enough to call me from his museum in Prince Edward Island, Canada, to provide additional information regarding author Lucy Maud Montgomery, who also was his cousin!

### Beatrice Wood Center for the Arts

*Kevin Wallace, Director*

The best way to describe my interaction with Kevin is "wonderful." Thank you for the anecdote, "Not *that* scarf…"

## Mary Todd Lincoln House

*Kate Hesseldenz, Assistant Director*

Kate provided wonderful feedback and insider insights.

## Corrie ten Boomhuis (Corrie ten Boom House)

*Frits Nieuwstraten, Director*

Before contacting Frits, I had never interacted with someone from the Netherlands. He was so kind, which reflects the spirit of Corrie ten Boom.

## Katherine Mansfield House & Garden

*Cherie Jacobson, Director*

After reading Cherie's informative notes, I truly had a sense of what it would be like to walk in the New Zealand home of Katherine Mansfield. The chapter could not have been as detailed had it not been for Cherie.

## Farleys House & Gallery

*Lori Inglis Hall, Lee Miller Archives*

The chapter on Lee Miller would not be as thorough had it not been for Lori, who went through every word and provided detailed and fabulous feedback.

## The National Shrine of Saint Elizabeth Ann Seton

*Lisa Donahue, Research and Exhibitions Coordinator*

Lisa did all she could to help a Canadian-Jewish author understand a Southern-Roman Catholic shrine.

## Monk's House

*Alli Prichard*

Thank you for your warm words about *A Room of Their Own*.

## Lyme Regis Museum

*Dr. Paul Davis, Geology Curator*

Paul was an invaluable resource, and I can't wait to visit there again.

## Sarah Orne Jewett House

*Susanna M. Crampton, Public , Relations officer Historic New England*

Susanna kindly provided a peephole into Sarah's heart and home.

### Ivy Green: Birthplace of Helen Keller

*Sue Pilkilton, Executive Director*
Sue was kind enough to share an insight into Helen's world.

### Anne Frank House

*Annemarie Bekker, Communications Anne Frank House, Amsterdam*
*Dr. Gertjan Broek, historian*
The insights shared were invaluable and enlightening.

### Jane Austen's House

*Lizzie Dunford, Director*

### The National Susan B. Anthony House

*Allison Hinman, Deputy Director*

### Juliette Gordon Low Birthplace

*Shannon Browning-Mullis, Executive Director*
*Elizabeth Srsic Manager, Education and Tours Administrative team*

DISCLAIMER: I sent each chapter to their respective museums. For those who responded, I incorporated all revisions and suggestions. For those who did not reply, I used due diligence to describe the museums as accurately as possible.

# About the Author

**M**arlene Wagman-Geller received her Bachelor of Arts from York University and her teaching credentials from the University of Toronto and San Diego State University. She recently retired after teaching high school English and history for thirty-one years. Reviews of her books have appeared in *The New York Times* and dozens of other newspapers such as *The Washington Post, The Chicago Tribune,* and *The Huffington Post.* When not researching or writing, she devotes her time to her guilty pleasures: a Starbuck's run (venti latte, nonfat milk, extra hot, extra foam) and reading.

# Bibliography

Mango Publishing, established in 2014, publishes an eclectic list of books by diverse authors—both new and established voices—on topics ranging from business, personal growth, women's empowerment, LGBTQ studies, health, and spirituality to history, popular culture, time management, decluttering, lifestyle, mental wellness, aging, and sustainable living. We were named 2019 *and* 2020's #1 fastest growing independent publisher by *Publishers Weekly.* Our success is driven by our main goal, which is to publish high-quality books that will entertain readers as well as make a positive difference in their lives.

Our readers are our most important resource; we value your input, suggestions, and ideas. We'd love to hear from you—after all, we are publishing books for you!

Please stay in touch with us and follow us at:

Facebook: Mango Publishing

Twitter: @MangoPublishing

Instagram: @MangoPublishing

LinkedIn: Mango Publishing

Pinterest: Mango Publishing

Newsletter: mangopublishinggroup.com/newsletter

Join us on Mango's journey to reinvent publishing, one book at a time.